American Aid and India's Economic Development

OTHER BOOKS BY

S. Chandrasekhar

Red China: An Asian View
Communist China Today
China's Population: Census and Vital Statistics
A Report on South Indian Reading Habits
Population and Planned Parenthood in India
Infant Mortality in India
Hungry People and Empty Lands
Demographic Disarmament for India
Census and Statistics in India
Indian Emigration to America
India's Population: Fact and Policy
India and the War

American Aid and India's Economic Development

S. Chandrasekhar

FREDERICK A. PRAEGER, *Publishers*
New York · Washington

PALL MALL PRESS
London

Published in the United States of America in 1965
by Frederick A. Praeger, Inc., Publishers
111 Fourth Avenue, New York 3, N.Y., U.S.A.

Published in Great Britain in 1965
by Pall Mall Press
77–79 Charlotte Street, London W.1, England

Library of Congress Catalog Card Number: 65-24722

Printed in the United States of America

To the Memory of

Gobindram J. Watumull

(1891–1959)

Who devoted a lifetime of quiet and
unostentatious work to promoting
Indo-American understanding in many spheres

And so we have to labour and to work and work hard, to make our dreams real. These dreams are for India, but they are also for the world, for all nations and peoples are too closely knit together today for any one of them to imagine that it can live apart. Peace has been said to be indivisible, so is freedom, so is prosperity now. . . .

—JAWAHARLAL NEHRU, *Discovery of India* (1946)

To those people in the huts and villages of half the globe struggling to break the bonds of mass misery, we pledge our best efforts to help them help themselves, for whatever period is required—not because the Communists may be doing it, not because we seek their votes, but because it is right. If a free society cannot help the many who are poor, it cannot save the few who are rich.

—JOHN F. KENNEDY, *Inaugural Address* (1961)

PREFACE

THREE YEARS AGO, while I was on my annual lecture tour of American universities, a student in one of my audiences asked me to recommend a book on American aid to India. With some surprise, I realized that there was no book on this important subject, only numerous articles on various aspects of the topic scattered in countless newspapers and periodicals. As a result, I embarked on this study.

On returning to India, I met C. Tyler Wood, Minister for Economic Affairs and Director of the U.S. Technical Cooperation (now the Agency for International Development) Mission to India, and told him of my project. He was kind enough to encourage me in the task and to arrange for me to meet Americans working in India and to visit many Indo-American projects across the country, as well as to spare me some of his valuable time answering my queries.

This book is addressed to the intelligent layman, and not particularly to fellow economists and other social scientists. Hence, I have kept the technical discussion on certain controversial aspects of the subject to a minimum. It is also designed to be used as a supplementary text in undergraduate and graduate courses on economic development, for India is an excellent example of an aid-receiving country.

I have attempted to organize the available data under certain arbitrary but convenient chapter headings. Each chapter provides, in summary form, information on the major American aid projects and the quantitative data in aid allocations. The data on the projects and the amounts allocated are scattered in numerous documents and often overlap. I have brought them together under one heading in as coherent a fashion as possible. The listing, however, is selective rather than exhaustive.

I realize that there is bound to be some difference of opinion in any evalution of the total impact of American aid—in money, technical personnel, equipment, and advice—on the Indian economy.

It is my belief that the impact has been one of considerable and unqualified benefit to India. If India today is economically stable and if the present picture marks a distinct improvement over that of 1950, which even the severest critics of the government of India cannot but concede, not a little of the credit is due to American aid. The facts and figures speak for themselves.

Those who have been helpful in my task are too numerous to thank individually here. Several officials in the American Embassy, the USAID, and USIS in New Delhi and Madras and many private individuals have also been helpful in answering queries and supplying information. My special thanks, however, are due to Sol Schindler, Roger Ernst, Dr. Kenneth Kauffman, Dr. William E. Schenk, Jim Miller, and Elizabeth Horan. I am particularly grateful to my wife for her encouragement and unfailing assistance in various ways to make this book possible. The responsibility for facts, figures, opinions, and such errors as may be in the study is, of course, mine.

S. CHANDRASEKHAR

University of California, Riverside

CONTENTS

American Aid and India's Economic Development

Explanatory Note

1 lakh	= 100,000
1 crore	= 100 lakhs or 10 million
1 rupee	= 100 paise or 21 cents or 1/6d.
$1	= 7/2d.
£1	= $2.80
1 crore of rupees	= $2 million or £750,000

INTRODUCTION

I HAVE ATTEMPTED to present in this book a simple, direct, and factual account of American aid to India from 1951 to 1964. This period covers what I call the first experimental phase of American economic (nonmilitary) aid to India, which began on June 15, 1951, when the U.S. Congress approved the India Emergency Food Aid Act to ward off hunger in India, and ended in October, 1962, when the Communist Chinese launched their massive, unprovoked, and undeclared attack on India's Himalayan frontiers.

The unhesitating readiness with which the United States Government rushed unconditional military aid to India to resist Chinese aggression ushered in the second phase of American (military) aid to India. (This military aid is given, of course, in addition to the continuing economic aid.) Such ready help from the United States at a time of distressing need revealed, as no act could have done during the fifteen peaceful years of India's political freedom, who India's real friends are. The beginning of American military aid to India in the interest of mutual security against external Communist aggression and the "assertion" of India's political freedom and national sovereignty mark the second significant phase of Indo-American aid and relations. This new relationship is bound to grow stronger, bringing the two large democracies closer together in view of the threatened change in the balance of power in Asia.

This book, however, is concerned with the first phase of American aid to India.

The subject of American aid to India and its contribution to free India's planned and rapid economic and social development has several aspects.

To begin with, what exactly is "American aid"? Today, the term is generally understood to mean U.S. Government help, in the form of money, equipment, technical personnel, and training, to various underdeveloped countries. This aid began shortly after Secretary of State George Marshall's Commencement Address to

Harvard University, on June 5, 1947, pleading for the rehabilitation of war-devastated Europe. President Truman's Point Four Program and President Kennedy's Alliance for Progress were both extensions of the concept.

Although this type of assistance is official and government-organized, American aid to underdeveloped and underprivileged countries is almost as old as the American Republic itself. In India, the number of schools and colleges, clinics and hospitals that American missionaries of various denominations have been running for a century and more is considerable; and the support for those admirable educational and medical institutions came and continues to come from the dimes and dollars of the average American churchgoer, whose conscience does not let him forget those less fortunate than himself.

Various American foundations have also sought to help many underdeveloped nations, long before they attained their political freedom, in matters of education and research, public health and hygiene. Despite this admirable and selfless record, American aid today is often equated primarily with an effort to stem the influence of Communism in the uncommitted nations. In fact, however, America was aiding India long before Mao Tse-tung was heard of.

This book deals primarily with government aid because it is official, organized, large, and extends over and beyond the period covering India's first two Five-Year Plans (1951–61) and a part of the Third Plan. A brief account of help given by certain American foundations, universities, private (individual and corporate) investors, and other miscellaneous organizations is presented in Chapter 10.

Chapter 1 examines the nature and dimensions of the central problem of the Indian economy. No matter how one looks at it, this problem is simply one of incredible poverty, low standards of living, and poor levels of consumption. And the problem is rendered more acute yearly with the annual addition of some 9 to 10 million people to the already large population of about 460 million. This not unfamiliar combination of poverty and population pressure complicated by certain obscurantist and uneconomic social attitudes and institutions constitutes the core of the challenge to the government of India, which is dedicated to the evolution of a welfare state through democratic planning. The government is determined to assure the people of India the basic, irreducible, minimum requisites of decent human existence. Hence India's Five-Year Plans and the need for external aid.

Chapter 2 explores the concept of foreign aid. The history of the economic development of most present-day advanced countries is strewn with the controversy of the pros and cons of accepting external assistance from richer countries. The controversy is by no means dead today. A country that has recently become independent is naturally extremely jealous of its political freedom. No country, no matter how poorly developed, is prepared to barter its hard-won political freedom for material help toward economic advancement. To some countries, the acceptance of foreign aid appears to be a compromise of their freedom of action and national sovereignty. And hence the apparent hesitation and unwillingness to accept it, to look for strings where there may be none, and sometimes even to attribute uncharitable motives to the generous giver. Yet, all the underdeveloped countries realize that political freedom without economic betterment and social progress is meaningless, and therefore the compelling necessity to accept foreign aid.

The United States, the Soviet Union, the United Kingdom, Germany, France, Japan, Canada, and other advanced countries have all accepted some kind of external economic assistance at some period of their industrial development from some country or other. India should have no qualms either about asking for or accepting foreign aid, for in the long run such aid has beneficent repercussions on both the giving and receiving countries and on the world economy in general. Economic aid is a two-way street.

Chapter 3 traces the origin and growth of American aid to India. The conflicting intricacies of American domestic policies have made the question of foreign aid a controversial and even an acrimonious one. From the debates on this question in the U.S. Congress, one can draw a picture, on the one hand, of the nation's extreme unwillingness to give aid to India and other so-called neutral nations, and, on the other, a ready willingness to extend all possible aid to India in her efforts to develop her resources through democratic planning. Despite some objections, the great majority of the American legislators and the Government itself have gone on record as being in favor of large-scale aid to India. Some of the relevant official record, which speaks for itself, has been reproduced in Chapter 3.

Chapters 4–8 give a brief account of American aid for the scientific development and modernization of Indian agriculture, planned industrialization, the promotion of better health in India, more purposeful educational opportunities at all levels, and increasing rapid and effective communications and transport facilities in India.

Chapter 9 discusses various miscellaneous Technical Cooperation Mission (TCM) projects that do not come under any of the five categories mentioned above. (This chapter is confined to aid offered by TCM alone, whereas in Chapters 4–8, besides the aid offered by TCM (now known as the Agency for International Development, or AID), the aid of several other American agencies is included.)

Chapter 10 outlines the role of private American aid to over-all Indian development. American private aid is not confined to Indian private enterprise or nonofficial projects. This private aid is offered by individual private investors, foundations, universities, and small, nonprofit, philanthropic organizations. Aid from this sector is extended to the projects of the government of India, schools, colleges and universities, scientific-research institutes, cultural organizations, and individual scholars, scientists, and writers.

Chapter 11 assesses the real magnitude of the aid given, and examines whether it has had any impact on the Indian economy. Although it is true that a dozen years constitute a very short period of time in the life of an ancient, large, and needy country like India, it is possible to highlight certain areas where American aid has bolstered a sagging sector of the economy, given a fillip to another depressed area, started an innovation in planning and organization, modernized certain procedures, introduced some labor-saving devices, eradicated malaria, promoted health and increased productivity, introduced new areas of research and study, and trained thousands of strategic personnel.

And although $5 billion spread over twelve years may seem like a drop in the bucket, the amount is a significant one constituting a large share of India's annual budget. In a word, American aid has given a much-needed shot in the arm to the Indian economy, boosted its morale, promoted its stability, and enhanced its productive capacity. What is more, without interfering with Indian thinking and planning, and scrupulously respecting India's priorities and prejudices, Americans, whenever invited, have offered Indians their constructive advice, counsel, and criticism.

The record of American aid to India is also the story of the labor of thousands of American "development diplomats," to use Eugene Black's picturesque phrase, and their personal impact on their Indian counterparts and the other Indians with whom they have come in contact. Their dedication, loyalty, and service to

India have been commendable. According to many of these Americans, India has given them something in return, something that cannot be defined in any material terms, but that has to do with an appreciation for a job well done, rich and lasting friendships, and an understanding of different but meaningful cultural values. Many Americans have confessed that initial feelings of frustration and impatience with the slow pace of India gradually changed until eventually something intangible about India has made them want to come back. And it is hoped that they do.

The Indo-American aid program is an excellent example today of the vast international development program that is going on in many parts of the world to raise levels of living and to promote hope, prosperity, good will, and understanding, and, through these, to lay the foundations for a lasting peace. Prosperity like peace, is one and indivisible. The "one world" of our dreams cannot be achieved if half the world is poverty-stricken.

1. *THE INDIAN ECONOMY*

UNDERDEVELOPMENT: THE CENTRAL PROBLEM

WHAT IS an underdeveloped country? An exact definition is impossible to give, for there are degrees as well as types of underdevelopment. Apart from the difficulty arising from the fact that "underdevelopment" is not a readily measurable phenomenon, there is the further complication that specific criteria of development may be applied by a particular observer at any specific point of time. And, there may be no consensus on the very criteria adopted, for these may vary between a native and a foreigner, between a rich man and a poor man, between an intellectual and a laborer, between an idealist and a realist, and between persons of conflicting economic and political ideologies. Further, every country in the world is, in a sense, underdeveloped—that is, no country or people has ever reached that ideal state in which full use is being made of all the possibilities that science and technology have provided to enable human beings to achieve the maximum limits of their potential. Cultural illiteracy and ignorance, discrimination and prejudice, superstition and obscurantism, apathy and inertia of various kinds continue to hinder, even in so-called advanced communities, the measure of economic and social progress for all groups that could be achieved. Thus a precise definition with quantitative criteria that will enable us to measure and grade the phenomenon of underdevelopment seems to be well-nigh impossible. There are, however, general areas of agreement on its definition: Jacob Viner defines an underdeveloped country as one that "has good potential prospects for using more capital or more labor or more available natural resources or all of these to support its present population on a higher level of living, or, if its per capita income level is already fairly high, to support a larger population on a not lower level of living."[1] To Eugene

[1] Jacob Viner, *International Trade and Economic Development* (Glencoe, Ill.: The Free Press, 1952), p. 125.

Staley, an underdeveloped country is one "characterized (1) by mass poverty which is chronic and not the result of some temporary misfortune, and (2) by obsolete methods of production and social organization, which means that poverty is not entirely due to poor natural resources and hence could presumably be lessened by methods already proved in other countries."[2]

According to Buchanan and Ellis, "an economically underdeveloped country is one which on the average affords its inhabitants an end product of consumption and material wellbeing appreciably inferior to that provided by the economies of the developed countries. Poor is a relative term. . . . To designate a country as underdeveloped also implies that its present economic performance—as evidenced by the average of consumption and material wellbeing—could be improved by means which are known and understood."[3]

According to P. T. Bauer, "over five-sixths of the population of the Commonwealth and three-quarters of the population of the world, live in underdeveloped countries, to accept the term which in spite of much valid criticism is still convenient to describe countries in which real income and capital per head are low compared to those in North America, Western Europe and Australasia; in which a large part of output is destined for the direct satisfaction of the wants of the producer and his family rather than for wider exchange or sale; and in which there is as yet no large-scale application of the fruits of technological advance to the arts of agriculture and industry."[4]

Paul G. Hoffman defines an underdeveloped country as "not simply a poverty-stricken version of a developed nation. It is a country lacking in factories of its own, without adequate supplies of power and light. It usually lacks roads and railroads, efficient government services, telephones and other communications. Even when large cities do have communications, outlying areas are terribly isolated. It has few hospitals and few institutions of higher learning. Most of its people cannot read or write. What wealth it has is concentrated in the hands of a few people who live in com-

[2] Eugene Staley, *The Future of Underdeveloped Countries: Political Implications of Economic Development* (rev. ed.; New York: Frederick A. Praeger, 1961), p. 13.

[3] Norman S. Buchanan and Howard S. Ellis, *Approaches to Economic Development* (New York: The Twentieth Century Fund, 1955), pp. 3–4.

[4] P. T. Bauer, *Economic Analysis and Policy in Underdeveloped Countries* (Durham, N.C.: Duke University Press, 1957), p. xii.

parative opulence surrounded by overwhelming poverty. Its banking system is embryonic; small loans have to be obtained through moneylenders who are often little better than extortionists. Not only are there few savings from which investments could be made, the people who have wealth usually refuse to invest it productively in their own countries. The underdeveloped nation's exports typically consist almost entirely of raw materials, ores, fruits or some other staple product with perhaps a small admixture of handicrafts or luxury goods. Often extraction or production of these export commodities is wholly or partly under foreign control, with little of the profit being reinvested in the country."[5]

Numerous indeed are the indicators of an underdeveloped economy: (1) lack of knowledge of physical resources; (2) illiteracy and low levels of education attained; (3) a high death rate and incidence of epidemics; (4) shortage of capital; (5) lack of trained people to bring the available physical and human resources into effective and purposeful use; (6) overpopulation in the sense of an adverse man-land and people-resources ratio; (7) low per capita real income; (8) lack of organized programs and development plans; (9) maldistribution of national income resulting in extreme (income) disparities between groups; (10) external indebtedness or inability to increase export earnings to pay for essential imports; (11) low productivity due to technological backwardness—that is, despite the low money wages paid for labor in an underdeveloped country, the cost of production per unit is much higher because of obsolete methods of production; (12) structural unemployment; (13) administrative incompetence and inefficiency; (14) social disorganization and cultural decay; (15) political instability, and (16) cultural, social, and religious attitudes, beliefs, and institutions that hinder economic development and social progress.

Although there are only a few countries in the world today that suffer from *all* of these denominators of underdevelopment, there are a number of countries that are characterized by many of them, and India is one. But fortunately, although India must definitely be classified as an underdeveloped country, she is also a rapidly developing one.

[5] Paul G. Hoffman, "Bread upon the Waters," *Britannica Book of the Year* (Chicago, Ill.: Encyclopaedia Britannica, 1962), p. 8.

The Social and Economic Landscape

Area and Population

India has an area of 1,269,640 square miles; she is slightly larger than one-third the size of the United States (including Alaska and Hawaii) or about two-thirds the size of Europe (excluding the Soviet Union). From North to South the country extends some 2,000 miles and from East to West some 1,850 miles. She has a land frontier 9,425 miles long and a coastline of about 3,535 miles.

India's total population according to the 1961 census was 439.235 million. Her 1964 population is about 460 million. This yields an average density of 373 people per square mile. If the world's total population is assumed to be 3 billion, India's population is 14.6 per cent of the world total. In other words, with 2.4 per cent of the total area of the world, India has to support approximately 15 per cent of the world's total population. Although India is the seventh largest country in the world (the Soviet Union, Canada, the United States, Communist China, Brazil, and Australia are larger), in population she is the world's second largest, after Communist China, whose population is estimated to be more than 700 million.

India's population increase has more or less followed the pattern of world population growth. According to some rough estimates, undivided India's population was about 100 million in 1600 A.D. This figure had increased to only about 150 million by 1850 as high birth rates were offset by high death rates. However, about two centuries ago, with the establishment of British rule in India, the subsequent restoration of a measure of internal peace, and the setting up of some health and medical services, the population began to grow. Between 1871, when the first and rather incomplete census was taken, and 1921, the population of the subcontinent increased from 206 to 318 million—a very small increase for half a century. But between 1921 and 1951 India's population burgeoned and the 1951 census—the first census after her independence and partition—recorded 357 million. The decennial rate of increase varied between 10 and 15 per cent. During the decade 1951–61, there was an increase of 78.1 million, or 21.5 per cent. Thus, the population has been steadily increasing through the decades of this century, and the largest rate of increase was registered during the last decade. The net decennial addition has exceeded the total population of any single country in Europe.

Apart from the massive size of the total population and the rather alarming rate of its growth, another significant feature is the heterogeneous increase of the population in the various states of the Indian Union. The percentage of increase in the states during the last decade covers a wide range, from 34.30 in Assam and 32.94 in West Bengal to 11.73 in Madras.

What about the future growth of India's population? Assuming more or less constant fertility (or rather a very small decline in fertility) and gradually declining mortality, particularly infant mortality, a projection of India's population may yield 525 million in 1971 and nearly 600 million in 1981. By 2000 A.D., less than 40 years from now, and in the lifetime of a majority of India's population alive today, the country's total numbers may reach more than 750 million.

Cultural, Ethnic, Linguistic, and Religious Diversity

India's history, which dates back to about 3500 B.C., is responsible for the diversity of the ethnic origins of her peoples, her languages and scripts, and her religions, customs, and traditions. Her ethnic diversity, her cultural heterogeneity, and the regional loyalties of her peoples are more easily understood when the antiquity of the Indian heritage—five millenniums—and the physical and populational immensity of the country are grasped.

India has been invaded many times in her long and rather checkered history and has absorbed many immigrant groups: Aryans, Persians, Scythians, Greeks, Huns, Mongols, and Tatars, Portuguese, Dutch, French, and British have poured into the country through the centuries. Each new incursion brought with it a new ethnic and cultural strain. A majority of these alien strains have been absorbed and blended, and the average Indian today is a composite of many types. India is as much if not more of a melting pot than contemporary America. Although the country's cultural pluralism presents a picturesque pattern, it has proved to be a barrier to the emotional integration of the country. It would be wrong, however, to deny the fundamental cultural unity and "Indianness" of India.

Students accustomed to Western and especially American traditions talk of India's racial problems. Although India has "races," she does not have racial problems. There is no simple dichotomy of the people into "white" and "colored." There may be color preferences but there are no color prejudices. There is no such thing as an "Indian race." Anthropologists point out that the people of

India are of Aryan, Dravidian, and Mongoloid origin. There are different groups in different parts of India but even here generalizations are apt to be misleading. All Bengalis are not Mongoloid any more than all South Indians are Dravidians.

India's linguistic diversity—the absence of a universally accepted and spoken tongue—poses a serious problem in fostering national unity. Apart from numerous dialects, a score of major languages and some fifteen scripts are in use in India. Of these the Indian Constitution recognizes fourteen languages for regional and national purposes. Linguistic loyalty is bound to be deep rooted anywhere, and it is particularly so in India, especially in view of the fact that the English language reigned supreme for more than a century, relegating the nation's languages to the inferior status of "local vernaculars."

Linguistic loyalties are so deep seated that in 1956 the country had to redraw the provincial boundaries on the basis of language. The sixteen states of the Indian Union (including Nagaland) have been demarcated largely on the basis of language in the hope that administration, communication, and instruction at the provincial level can be carried on through the regional language. There is no doubt that a people can express itself best in its mother tongue, but in the peculiar circumstances of the evolution of Indian administration and polity, the English language has served an extremely useful purpose and it would be a pity, indeed a tragedy, if it were discarded.

The Indian Government, despite serious opposition from the south and the east, is endeavoring to make Hindi the country's national language. Though the language as such is underdeveloped for modern purposes, the fact that some 150 million—a third of the total population—speak it is in its favor. English will, however, continue as an associate language until the non-Hindi-speaking people are able to master Hindi. It is more or less agreed that the future Indian citizen may have to learn three languages: the mother tongue, Hindi as the national language, and English as a necessary foreign language.

In the making of a nation, homogeneity and uniformity in culture and race, language and religion are desirable but not always indispensable. In a modern nation, the religious badge of a citizen should be a personal and subjective matter and of no concern to the state. But this is not true even of advanced countries in the West where anti-Semitism and anti-Catholicism are indulged in both by the citizen and the state. India, traditionally tolerant, claims adherents of all the major religions of the world. Her political strength would no doubt be enhanced if the entire population of the country professed a common religion, but the fact is otherwise. According to the 1961 census, 84 per cent of the total population are Hindus. Indian Muslims make up 10.2 per cent, and Christians and Sikhs 2.4 and 1.8 per cent, respectively, of the total population. Fortunately, however, India is a secular state and does not subscribe to any theocratic theory that assumes that every religious group must have a state of its own.

The cultural, ethnic, linguistic, and religious diversities have their impact on the nation's economic landscape. Indian political unity is federal in a very real sense and its strength lies in balancing and reconciling the conflicting demands of the federating units. Each state believes that its economic development is being neglected and that its citizens do not obtain a sufficient number of major administrative and political positions of all-India significance. The states quarrel with the center for more crumbs from the federal table, and they quarrel with each other over river waters, interstate commerce, and shares of national-tax revenue. As Nature has not distributed her favors equally over the entire country, the economic development of all the regions in an equitable manner becomes a difficult and an uneconomic proposition.

India's Agrarian-Rural Economy

That India lives in her villages is well known. According to the 1961 census, a great majority of Indians—some 82 per cent, or 5 out of every 6—live in rural areas. Farming is the major occupation of the bulk of the population. That is, roughly 4 out of every 5 persons living in rural India depend on agriculture for their meager livelihood. The average size of the agricultural per capita landholding is less than an acre. The average size of a farmstead is about 7.5 acres, but 2 out of every 5 holdings are less than an acre in area. There are some 50 million agricultural holdings in the country scattered throughout 564,718 villages.

Roughly three-fourths of the cultivated land is used for food crops. The major food crop is rice—India's staple product—which accounts for about 22 per cent of the total cropped area. Wheat is the second major food crop and accounts for about 10 per cent of the total cropped area. One-fourth of the cultivated land is devoted to such cash crops as oilseeds, cotton, sugar cane, and jute. Though three-fourths of the cultivated land is devoted to food crops and the rest to cash crops, the total money value of the food crops is just about equal to that of the cash crops.

A major problem of Indian agriculture is water. Too much rainfall means deluge and floods and crops are washed away, too little rainfall means drought and crop failure. The result in either case is famine and misery.

Only about 20 per cent of the cultivated land is irrigated, and of this irrigated land about 80 per cent is in food crops and the balance in cash crops. The water for the irrigation comes for the main part from canals, tanks, and wells. As the use of chemical fertilizer is not widespread—only about 5 pounds are used per acre of cropped area—agricultural yields in India are among the lowest in the world. On an average, an acre yields some 800 pounds of rice, 700 pounds of wheat, and 600 pounds of all other food grains taken together.

Industrialization

India is predominantly an agricultural country so it is not surprising that less than 10 per cent of the gainfully employed derive their living from industry. Until almost the end of the British rule the Indian economy was a typical colonial one. She tended to produce and export, in the main, raw materials and foodstuffs and to import textiles, iron and steel goods, machinery, and miscellaneous manufactures of a wide variety. However, with the adoption of protective tariffs in 1922, the country embarked on a policy of limited industrialization; steel, cement, paper, and sugar began to be produced. Industrialization, of course, has been stepped up during the years since independence, but India ranks only tenth among the world's industrial nations, so she still has far to go.

The prospects for the future are, however, bright, for India is rich in power and mineral resources. She has large deposits of iron ore and such mineral resources as bauxite, chromite, ilemenite, and gypsum. Despite these advantages, she has not been able to become a major industrialized country for want of technological know-how, skilled labor, and capital resources.

Occupational Composition

India's occupational composition reflects the depth of her economic underdevelopment. Whereas the 10 per cent of the American population gainfully employed in agriculture raises enough food and considerably more for 180 million people, the labor of

70 per cent of India's population does not provide sufficient food even at meager levels for India's 460 million.

India's Standard of Living

Per capita income. India is extremely poor and the disparities of income among her people are very wide. Her low standard of living in terms of the per capita "consumption" of such basic necessities and amenities as food, clothing, housing, education and health, and recreation and leisure stem from the very low per capita income. The low per capita income is both the cause and consequence of India's perennial poverty.

The per capita annual income in 1961 was about Rs.315 or less than a rupee a day. (In 1948–49 it was 246.9 rupees.) That is, the daily income of an average Indian is about 20 cents, or less than two shillings a day. However, there is a small group of some 10,000 people who earn more than Rs.50,000 per annum. According to the Ministry of Finance, "urban incomes in general are higher than rural incomes. According to an estimate the urban income per capita is a little over twice the rural income per capita. Thus for more than 80 per cent of the population living in the rural area the average income works out to less than 20 cents, or one rupee, per day."

About half of the nation's total income is derived from agriculture. Of the other half, a third is contributed by manufactures and mining, a third by banking, commerce, transportation, etc., and the remaining third by professions and services. Indian agriculture is a traditional way of life—not, like American agriculture, a successful business and commercial proposition. The government's dedication to the much misunderstood term "socialistic pattern of society" derives simply from its desire to promote equality of opportunity and a more equitable distribution of the nation's wealth.

Food. Food has been India's perennial problem. While the total production of rice and wheat has increased in recent years, the per capita caloric consumption of cereals continues to be low, and the country is not yet self-sufficient in the production of food grains. Thanks to the import of large quantities of wheat from the United States, India is not faced with anv acute shortage today, but per capita consumption is still about 2,000 calories per day. It is a strange irony indeed that India's most serious food shortage should be for milk and milk products because she has the largest cattle population in the world (about 180 million) and some millions of Indians are vegetarians. But oddly enough it is precisely because of this bovine overpopulation that the average Indian gets only a few ounces of milk per day.

The biological food requirements in tropical India are rather lower than in a temperate zone. Nutrition experts at the Food and Agriculture Organization have estimated the average daily per capita needs for India at 2,250 calories, as compared with about 2,650 calories for the United States.[6] The per capita calorie consumption in India today is about 2,000 as against 3,100 in the United States and 3,430 in New Zealand. Despite the relatively low requirement of 2,250 calories for India, her actual consumption is 250 calories below the estimated average need. The U.N. Conference on Food and Agriculture reported in 1943 that "malnutrition is responsible for widespread impairment of human efficiency and for an enormous amount of ill-health and disease; it reduces the resistance of the body to tuberculosis, and enhances the general incidence and severity of familiar diseases; mortality rates in infants, children and mothers are higher in ill-fed than in well-fed populations; food consumption at a level merely sufficient to prevent malnutrition is not enough to promote health and well-being."[7] Twenty years later, in 1963, President John F. Kennedy observed:

> The same central problem that troubled President Roosevelt when he called together the first World [Food] Congress in '43 is unfortunately still with us today. Half of humanity is still undernourished or hungry. In 70 developing nations, with over 2 billion people, malnutrition is widespread and persistent.
>
> So long as freedom from hunger is only half-achieved, so long as two-thirds of the nations have food deficits, no citizen, no nation, can afford to be satisfied. We have the ability, as members of the human race, we have the means, we have the capacity to eliminate hunger from the face of the earth in our lifetime. We need only the will. . . .
>
> The real goal, therefore, must be to produce more food in the nations that need it. Know-how is not the problem. For the first time in the history of the world we do know how to produce enough food, how to feed every man, woman and child in the world, enough to eliminate all hunger completely. Farm production has undergone a scientific revolution which is dwarfing the industrial revolution of

[6] *Second World Food Survey* (Rome: Food and Agriculture Organization, 1952), p. 22.

[7] *Report of the United Nations Conference on Food and Agriculture* (Hot Springs, Va., 1943), p. 5.

> 150 years ago, but this means that agricultural departments and ministries and governments and citizens must make a greater and more systematic effort to share this knowledge. For the first time to know how to conquer the problem and not conquer it would be a disgrace for this generation. We need to help transmit all that we know of farm technology to the ends of the earth, to overcome the barriers of ignorance and suspicion. The key to a permanent solution to world hunger is the transfer of technology which we now have to feed deficient nations, and that task is second to none in importance.[8]

Nutrition in a real sense is the key to India's productivity. Low wages and incomes lead to undernourishment and malnourishment, which in turn lead to poor health, poor work, and low productivity, and thus to low incomes. The vicious circle is complete.

As for clothing, the per capita consumption is less than 17 yards, far below minimum requirements, even for a tropical country, which may be estimated at about 50 yards. Less than 15 per cent of the population wear any shoes or sandals. This is a serious hazard to the people's health, for although there is no need to protect one's feet against cold throughout the year, there is a great need for protection against the blazing sun and, what is worse, dirty streets. But footwear is expensive.

Housing. Regarding housing, the situation is even more depressing. India's population has increased by 100 million in the years since independence, but fewer than 4 million new houses have been built during this period. The housing shortage in general, and the shortage of houses with elementary sanitary and hygienic facilities, which has been more or less chronic in India within living memory, has been rendered more acute since independence by the rapid growth in the country's population; the growth of cities; the constant influx of distress labor from the rural areas to towns and cities in search of seasonal and permanent employment; the postindependence influx of refugees from northeastern and northwestern areas seeking permanent employment and settlement (some 13,000,000 refugees had to be provided for); lack of repair and rebuilding of existing houses with the resulting loss of a certain percentage of them; and the fact that about 2 per cent of the total number of existing houses have to be written off

[8] President John F. Kennedy's opening address to the World Food Congress at Washington on June 4, 1963, *Public Papers of the Presidents: John F. Kennedy, 1963* (Washington, D.C.: Government Printing Office, 1964), pp. 435–36.

annually on the assumption that the average life span of a house in tropical India is about 50 years.

An illustration of the magnitude of the investment needed to provide housing for the existing and increasing population is provided by Eugene Black, former President of the International Bank for Reconstruction and Development. To illustrate the challenges involved, he cited statistics on the new housing that will be needed by 1986 if the present rate of population growth continues: Exclusive of rural areas or even of improvement of existing houses in such cities as Calcutta, the total investment required is estimated at approximately $25 billion. The Ministry of Information points out that:

> The problem of housing in India is a complex one requiring finances on a large scale and dependent for its solution on concerted efforts on the part of individuals, co-operatives, State and Union governments to be planned and executed over a number of years. There is acute shortage of housing in urban and rural areas and much of the available accommodation is of the qualitatively sub-standard variety. The shortage in urban areas has been largely due to considerable increase in population since 1921, the heavy shift of population from the rural to urban areas, the haphazard growth of towns due to lack of sufficient State or municipal control over building activity and comparative inability of private enterprise to keep pace with the growing demand.[9]

Education. According to the 1961 census, a person above the age of four was considered literate if he could read and write with understanding. The present literacy ratio is 240 per 1,000 persons, the male and female components being 344 and 129. A more refined literacy ratio can be obtained by excluding those in the 0–4 age groups but such figures are not available at present. The number of high-school "graduates" and the number of college graduates per 1,000 of total population are 19 and 1.8 respectively. In 1961 there were 1,712 colleges and 53 universities for a population of 440 million, an average of one college per 250,000 people and one university for about 9 million people.

Health. Poverty is an impediment to good health. The general poor health in India is a reflection of India's depressed standard of living. A few basic statistics tell their tale. During the five-year

[9] *India: 1962* (New Delhi: Ministry of Information and Broadcasting, 1962), p. 384.

period 1956–61, India's average birth and death rates were 40.7 and 21.6 per 1,000. In most advanced countries, the death rate is less than 10 per 1,000. The infant mortality rate (the deaths of infants under one year per 1,000 live births), perhaps the most sensitive index to the total cultural milieu of any country, during the same five-year period was 142.3 and 127.9 among male and female babies, respectively. The comparable figure in the United States and northwestern European countries is less than 25. The most vital index of the welfare of a country is the expectation of life at birth. The figures for India in 1961 were 41.68 for males and 42.06 for females, whereas comparable figures in the United States are 67.2 and 73.7 (whites) respectively. Though accurate figures are not available, what evidence we have points to the country's high rate of morbidity. Even as recently as 1963 cholera and smallpox raged in near-epidemic form in many urban and rural areas, and the incidence of filaria, tuberculosis, and leprosy is still high, despite efforts to fight these scourges on a national scale.

The reasons behind this substandard picture of the nation's health are simple enough. The public-health services in their preventive, diagnostic, and curative aspects are neither adequate nor modern. According to the Ministry of Health, "only 128 towns with a population of 50,000 and over, 60 towns with a population between 30,000 and 50,000 and 210 towns with smaller population had protected water supply. It was estimated that only 6.15 per cent of the total population was served by protected water supply and only 3 per cent enjoyed the amenity of a sewage system."[10]

In 1960 there were about 11,854 hospitals and dispensaries. These treated some 13 million patients. There were millions more —at least double that number—who needed but did not obtain any treatment. The number of hospital beds available in 1960 was 0.4 per 10,000 of population.

Table 1 shows the number of registered medical practitioners and other health personnel in 1960 in India and the United States.

The relative paucity of trained medical and other ancillary personnel in relation to the country's needs is explained by the fact that there are only 80,000 practitioners of modern medicine (that is, one doctor for 5,000 of population), 66 medical colleges (admitting nearly 7,000 students annually), 11 dental colleges, and 5 other institutions for training in the allopathic system of medicine.

[10] *Ibid.*, p. 109.

The quality of education and training in these colleges, of course, varies.

TABLE 1

HEALTH PERSONNEL IN INDIA AND THE U.S., 1959–60

Health and Medical Personnel	*India*	*Number per 10,000 Population*	*U.S.*	*Number per 10,000 Population*
Registered medical practitioners	88,389	2	236,618	13
Pharmacists	20,448	less than 1	n.a.	n.a.
Nurses	32,733	1	460,000	27
Midwives	38,528	1	n.a.	n.a.
Dentists	n.a.	n.a.	100,615	5

SOURCE: *Annual Report of the Directorate General of Health Services* (New Delhi: Ministry of Health, 1960).

n.a. not available

NONECONOMIC FACTORS IN INDIAN ECONOMIC DEVELOPMENT

In most discussions of economic development scant attention is paid to the role of cultural, social, and religious factors as either assets or liabilities to lasting and large-scale economic change. The attitudes, beliefs, customs, and habits of people in underdeveloped countries offer strong resistance to change, particularly when efforts are made by governments, even national governments, to foster developmental measures. This statement may contradict our earlier contention that the most significant phenomenon of our times is the revolution of rising expectation among the submerged millions of Asia and Africa. The truth is that the peoples of the underdeveloped countries do want the better things of life, but without too much effort or sacrifice; they do not particularly want to give up their anachronistic and juvenile attitudes and beliefs, their cherished but obscurantist social and religious institutions. India is an excellent example of the dilemma presented by traditional agrarian societies demanding change for the better but desiring to retain institutions inimical to progress.

This does not mean that these attitudes and institutions have not changed over a long period of time. Changes have set in, sometimes even within short periods, depending on the nature and magnitude of the particular incentive provided by the government, an alien but accepted agency, or an enlightened segment of the indigenous society itself.

We are confronted with the problem of assessing the significance and worth of these institutions, beliefs, and values and determining which should be preserved and which discarded. Certain religious rituals may be meaningless and uneconomic in the total context of human welfare, but these "useless" religious values, if harmless and inexpensive, might well be retained in the larger interest of maintaining the continuity and stability of a particular society. The desirability of retaining these ancient and worthwhile values while discarding those that hinder progress cannot be overemphasized. The objection might be raised that such a utilitarian and discriminatory evaluation of peoples' mores and values is not possible because of the fact that people live by a host of interdependent and intertwining values. And yet we know that various ancient values have been given up in the face of altered circumstances. The modern Hindu does today myriad acts he was forbidden to do a century ago: He eats with people of other castes in public restaurants; he travels abroad, crossing the black waters; his caste and occupation are often unrelated; his diet and dress no longer strictly conform to shastrik injunctions. In some cases where economic pressures have superannuated religious practices, compromises have been made, and with a few more radical and basic changes India can be propelled from the bullock-cart era into the atomic age.

Some of the current attitudes and institutions that impede India's economic progress are the inferior status of women, the caste system, the Hindu joint family, and the problem of her ubiquitous and useless cattle and other animals.

The Status of Women

That the status accorded to women in Indian, particularly Hindu, society has led to enormous economic waste, apart from other evils, is accepted by all thoughtful students. Here, as with most of the other cultural phenomena of India, a sharp cleavage exists between religion and the law. The Hindu shastras regarded men and women as well as all living beings as equal in God's eyes, but the ancient lawgivers reduced woman's status to that of chattel. The daughter lived under the direction of her father, the wife under the domination and dictatorship of her husband, and the widow under the sufferance of her son. Custom and tradition evolved to bolster this unequal and unhappy position, condoning family-arranged marriages (where individual partners have, by and large, no choice); early marriages, often below the age of consent; a social ban on widows' remarrying; laws prohibiting women to inherit; the difficulty in obtaining a divorce; social and even legal embargo on intercaste marriage; the purdah system—which, fortunately, is fast disappearing; unequal educational and employment opportunities; and the dowry system. (Of course, these are relatively minor evils when we remember that in earlier centuries Hindu society tolerated sati, or suttee—immolation of the widow on the husband's funeral pyre—and female infanticide.) British rule, contact with the West, and the small but influential minority of enlightened social reformers at home—all the way from Ram Mohun Roy to Sarvepalli Radhakrishnan—have fought these institutions with some success. The country has traveled a long way, and steady, if slow, progress has been made.

Legislation passed in 1856 established the legal validity of the marriages of Hindu widows, but such marriages are rare even now, rare enough to make a news item. Even the marriages of what are called "virgin widows" are not accepted by the society. In the 1951 census there were 2,225,600 widows, whose lot, despite all the efforts of the government, is not always a happy one. The relegation of millions of young women to permanent widowhood causes psychological damage to the women involved as well as considerable economic wastage to the nation, for widowed women are forced to rely for support on their families.

The Child Marriage Restraint Act (the Sarada Act) was passed in 1929 and made early marriage (males under eighteen and females under fourteen years of age) a punishable offense. But the legislation is so poorly framed that it is honored more in its breach than otherwise. According to the 1951 census, there were 2,833,000 married males and 6,118,000 married females, 66,000 widowers and 134,000 widows—all between the ages of five and fourteen.

Although child marriage has been outlawed, millions of girls, particularly in the countryside, continue to marry in their early teens. However, the situation is improving. What is needed are a further increase in the age of consent (twenty for males, say, and eighteen for females) and legislation that will punish the violators promptly.

The widow-remarriage problem and the child-marriage problem have both received the attention of the present government and a certain segment of the enlightened public. The recently enacted Hindu Law Code has dealt with some of the reactionary features of Hindu society as far as the status of women is concerned, although the code, a curious mixture of old and new attitudes, has not gone far enough. Perhaps it is too much to expect legislation to undo disabilities under which Hindu women have suffered for centuries.

However, there are two exceptions to the general picture. First, the women in the lower strata who, for reasons of economic pressure, could not conform to these social restrictions, have always been a part of the labor force and have been gainfully employed. Second, at the upper level, a thin strata of educated and emancipated women have emerged from these restrictions and have blazed a new trail of equal participation with men in all constructive and productive realms of human endeavor. But a vast majority of women who belong to neither end of the social scale continue to suffer. This nonparticipation of nearly half the total population in the life of the community and the nation is a source of colossal wastage. Today, the sole function of these women is to produce unwanted babies and suffer from improvident maternity, but once they are given the benefits of purposeful and rational education (and not the current formal education that leads to degrees without opening minds) an economic revolution can be set in motion. The women of India can then become intelligent homemakers and, when necessary, able breadwinners. They will refuse to be herded into the married state to become victims of the dowry system, and they will plan their families and take pride in healthy and happy children rather than in costly ceremonies and jewelry.

The Caste System

A country, whether it is India or South Africa or the United States, that permits or promotes the stratification of its society on the basis of prejudice and discrimination and on no more rational lines than those of the "in-group" and the "out-group" concept discovers, sooner or later, that it has indulged in an expensive luxury. Politically, of course, caste discrimination, color prejudice, and racialism are utterly incompatible with democracy. Of all of India's contemporary major social problems perhaps the most agonizing and intractable is the caste system.

It is unnecessary for our purpose to inquire into the genesis and growth of the caste system. Although Hindu philosophers and pandits still extol its former utility—at best dubious—no thoughtful Indian today can defend the system. No matter what its origin —racial, functional, or occupational—it is today an obscurantist anachronism par excellence.

That this system has been under a serious, if not sustained attack for nearly a century by those who have had the country's welfare at heart is well known. Nationalism, British rule, external ridicule, modern modes of travel, new educational opportunities, conscious reformism, and last but not least, natural decay have all contributed to the attack on caste. The sentiment against the system is so strong that the 1951 census—the first in free India—did not enumerate the thousands of castes on the supposition that thus labeling a citizen as belonging to a particular caste perpetuates the system. Those who contend that the system has almost disappeared, however, are living in a fool's paradise. Caste feeling, prejudice, and even discrimination are so entrenched in India that people even vote on the basis of caste. Indeed, caste has become the very basis of the parliamentary system. In fact, no individual or activity is judged today on his or its merits devoid of any connection with caste.

The economic consequences of caste are, first, that it tends to enforce uneconomic division of labor and militates against the healthy occupational distribution of a population on the basis of ability and aptitude. No profession or occupation should be debarred to any individual on the basis of birth, but this is exactly what happens in the caste system. It is true today that some Brahmans of the so-called high castes may trade in hides and skins, while a member of the so-called lower castes may be head of a professional college or even a member of a cabinet. But, on the whole, the Hindu population is stratified into one occupational pattern on the basis of the national caste system. "Success in professions cannot enable people to go up in the social ladder if they are born in a community which has been assigned traditionally a low place in the social hierarchy. This is inimical to economic progress, as business enterprise should provide opportunities of not only acquiring wealth but gaining social distinction."[11] The caste system also prevents vertical social mobility, a necessary prerequisite to economic growth. What is worse, such basic and simple occupations as street-sweeping, whitewashing walls, or cleaning drains have become the sole occupations of particular subcastes. The original four castes have proliferated into literally hundreds of subcastes, with the result that no one person can do more than one particular job. This fragmentation of society into

[11] R. Balakrishna, "Social Institutions Impeding Economic Progress," *Madras University Journal*, 1961. See also K. Wilheim Kapp, *Hindu Culture, Economic Development and Economic Planning* (Bombay: Asia Publishing House, 1963).

minute and often mutually hostile groups has led to the breaking up of all work into several hundred "occupations"—a kind of extended featherbedding. This has not led, paradoxically enough, to any intense specialization but rather to over-all ignorance in doing a decent job.

A few state governments have tried to legislate against the cruder manifestations of the caste system, but largely in vain. The only way to eradicate the caste system is to promote intercaste, and intersubcaste marriages on such a vast scale that the small minority of the so-called high castes can be physically assimilated into the great majority of the rest of the community.

If the problem of castes is uneconomic and wasteful to the country as a whole, the problems of the casteless are much worse. More than 50 million people are supposed to be, by virtue of their birth, beyond the pale of the fourfold caste system. These people, once known as the untouchables but called, in the kindly nomenclature of Mahatma Gandhi, Harijans, or children of God (and in the clumsy terminology of the government, the scheduled castes), are the real marginal men of the country's population. One can hardly imagine the cost to the nation of socially forcing millions of people to lead a degraded subhuman life. Although the situation is gradually changing under government efforts, the Harijans, in some rural areas, cannot send their children to the same schools as the other village children attend or even draw water from the communal well. In rural areas they are generally assigned to loathsome tasks considered too unclean for others: scavenging, tanning, cobbing, guarding cremation grounds, and so on.

The economics of discrimination is complicated. Segregation is financially burdensome to any community, as American experience in the southern states bears out. Underdeveloped India can hardly afford the luxury of untouchability, which deprives the nation of the useful economic activity, on the basis of aptitude, of a large segment of the country's population. India, however, is not an open society but a closed one; as far as the casteless are concerned, it is almost a frozen society.

The economic consequences of discrimination have, by and large, been ignored by economists. Sociologists, psychologists, and anthropologists have inquired into the *causes* of discrimination but seldom into its *consequences* to the economy as a whole. Whatever the criteria adopted it is obvious that a major obstacle in the path of economic progress is the discriminatory attitude existing in India toward people of so-called low castes or no castes.[12] Apart from economic costs, as Kenneth Boulding puts it, "Domination turns out to be almost as bad for the dominant as for the dominated, and we see from innumerable examples in history that societies based on the domination of one class, color, race or culture by another are essentially unstable. Domination corrupts the dominant and frequently purifies the dominated."[13]

The Hindu Joint Family

For several centuries in the Hindu family the basic unit was not the biological or nuclear family of husband, wife, and unmarried children but the extended family group. This joint family is the agnatic unit, which is at once corporate, economic, religious, and social. In the traditional joint family father, mother, sons, and grandsons, with their respective womenfolk, live together. The daughters on getting married become members of the joint families of their husbands. Thus, in a joint family, there is a greater generation depth—three or even more generations—than in a biological family. The members may be related collaterally or lineally and are bound together by common property, income, and certain mutual rights and obligations. However, provisions are made for division of property on the basis of one of three different systems, and one can leave the joint family and set up an independent household.

> The essence [of the joint family] is the common ownership of means of production and the common enjoyment of the fruits of labour. Both inherited and personally acquired belongings are regarded as common property; and the supreme authority is the family council, of which the head of the family, generally the eldest male, is the executive officer but not the dictator. The family may consist of dozens of persons, grandparents, uncles, sons and grandsons with their wives and children; and the ties of loyalty to which it gives rise are intense. Indeed to many Hindus the duty owed to other members of the joint

[12] See Gary S. Becker, *The Economics of Discrimination* (Chicago, Ill.: University of Chicago Press, 1957). "In most underdeveloped countries there is so much discrimination against women and persons of lowly origins [e.g., the "untouchables"] that this is uniformly agreed to be a major obstacle to rapid economic progress." Pp. 1–2.

[13] Kenneth E. Boulding, *Principles of Economic Policy* (Englewood Cliffs, N.J.: Prentice-Hall, 1958), p. 408.

family appears something far stronger than any duty owed to the State; what Westerners call nepotism is in India a positive virtue.[14]

The advantages of the joint family are well known. It provides a kind of social security in the event of illness and unemployment, and the old enjoy a secure and even an honored place. But we are concerned here with its economic limitations. First, the joint family tends to make the population immobile. It was an effective arrangement in ancient India when agriculture was the mainstay of the whole population, but today, when young men must go far afield in search of jobs, it is a force against occupational mobility.

Second, the joint family militates against any daring and risk-taking enterprise. One might expect the joint family to produce pioneers who can go far and wide seeking adventure, while those dependent on them remain at home, well looked after by the head of the family. But it does not. There is no doubt that the joint family definitely weakens initiative and undermines any spirit of adventure.

Third, though theoretically a joint family might have considerably larger resources at its command than a biological family, the head of the joint family cannot invest it for commercial or industrial undertakings, for the property is to be held in trust for transmission to posterity. The head of the joint family cannot invest the capital in any productive enterprise that would involve any risk. The only avenue of investment is agriculture—a fact that to some extent contributes to making the Hindus even more agricultural than they are, although it is a moot question whether the predominance of agriculture led to the joint family or vice versa. It is probable that rural and agricultural life made the collectivism of the joint family economically viable.

According to Hindu domestic law, the wealth acquired by any member of the family by his own personal efforts and knowledge may be held and enjoyed exclusively by him. But this saving benefit is negated by the injunction that, on his death, his property automatically accrues to the joint family. In other words, a member of the joint family has no right to bequeath his exclusive property to his children. The law of the joint family is governed by three systems of law and, according to one of them, the Mitakshara system, inheritance is by survivorship and not by succession. Therefore, the incentive to acquire wealth in the hope of bequeathing

[14] Rushbrook Williams, *What About India?* (London: Nelson & Sons, 1938), pp. 23–24.

it to one's immediate posterity is absent in a joint family. The joint family has thus been a disincentive force against innovation, experimentation, and capital accumulation.

Cows and Other Animals

The cow occupies a special position in the Indian cultural milieu. The cow is of crucial importance to a pastoral people and the ancient Hindus developed several taboos to protect it, particularly to prevent its slaughter in times of famine since the ancient Hindus were not vegetarians. But historical and useful traditions often degenerate, and today cow-worshiping Hindus abound in India. Although the Hindu is supposed to venerate the cow, no animal in any country is so badly treated as the cow is in India.

India, according to the latest livestock census (1956), has more than 180 million cattle. This is the largest cattle population of any country in the world and represents nearly a quarter of the world's total cattle. The Indian economy is burdened with "feeding" these millions of cattle, as though the burden of feeding and taking care of 450 million people were not enough. In almost all other countries cattle are an essential part of the total food resources and the investment in them, in pasture, and in fodder is returned in beef and dairy products. But in India cattle have to be maintained at the expense of food required by man.

First, India gets little or no protein for her meager diet from her cattle population because the average Hindu will not eat beef or veal, and indeed usually resents the killing of any cattle. Section 48 of the Indian Constitution directs the states to take steps for the prohibition of the slaughter of cows and calves and other milch or draft cattle. In recent years several states—notably Uttar Pradesh, Madhya Pradesh, Rajasthan, and Mysore—have enacted legislation prohibiting the slaughter of cows, and indeed of any cattle.

> The scope of these measures is exemplified by the Uttar Pradesh legislation (Uttar Pradesh Act, No. 1 of 1956). [This Act was amended in 1958 without affecting its substance.] This absolutely prohibits the slaughter, or the offer for slaughter, of any cow, and "cow includes a bull, bullock, heifer or calf." It also prohibits the sale, or transport of offer for same, of beef or beef products in any form. The legislation elsewhere is substantially similar, and in some instances covers buffaloes as well. This legislation was passed almost simultaneously with the official inception of the Second Five-Year Plan in April 1956.

Such measures might be thought to be redundant, as Hindus will in any case not kill a cow, and rarely countenance the killing of any kind of cattle. They nevertheless affect the position on at least two grounds. First, they reinforce the traditional attitudes and prevent their disintegration. Second, they prevent non-Hindus, especially Moslems, who are about ten per cent of the population, from slaughtering cattle. Before this legislation, and especially before Independence, Hindus ostensibly unaware of the fate of the animals, often sold cows to Moslems who then slaughtered them. Now, however, Moslems in many areas cannot get beef at all, and either have to go without meat or buy much more expensive mutton or goat meat.[15]

Second, though the importance of milk for the unbalanced Indian diet cannot be underestimated, India has so many cattle that she obtains very little milk, paradoxical as this may sound. In all biological species quality can be maintained only at the expense of quantity because of the available limited resources. The quality of India's cows is so poor that they yield the lowest amount of milk of any cattle in the world. Thus India's milch cattle amount to little in relation to the country's milk needs.

Third, Indian cattle are of some use as draught animals, but bullock power, though necessary in rural areas for drawing water from wells and pulling carts and ploughs, is an anomaly in the cities. The slow-moving bullock cart in a modern town or city is a nuisance and, with the ever-increasing use of buses and other motor transport, it should become a thing of the past. Even in rural areas, where electricity and electric pumps for irrigational purposes are a common sight today, bullock power may soon become obsolete.

Thus, the cattle are of no use to the Indian in providing him with meat or milk. Should he take to eating beef it would enrich his diet, but then the quality of the cattle must be improved. As for milk, his consumption must be increased fourfold and this means again reducing the number of cows and raising their milch qualities. As for muscle power, the bullock is gradually becoming an outmoded beast. Therefore, in a treble sense the Indian cattle population is a useless burden, a painful, sentimental, and expen-

[15] P. T. Bauer, *Indian Economic Policy and Development* (London: Allen & Unwin; New York: Frederick A. Praeger, 1961), pp. 23–24. While this book is unsympathetic to India, no one can deny certain grave defects in India's socio-economic structure and planning that the author points out. One would have expected the author to argue that just because of these difficulties and outmoded attitudes India needed external aid.

sive luxury. A drastic reduction in the number of cattle should be one of the major objectives of the country's economic policy.

> The Hindu notion of the sanctity of animals is no doubt admirable in theory but appalling in practice. One look at the pathetic state of the cattle roaming our streets is enough to prove this. Also, contrary to popular notions, less than 15 per cent of our population are real vegetarians. The rest consume some kind of meat or other.
>
> Therefore, there are only two ways out of the problem. We should either become meat eaters or destroy the unwanted cattle: The latter solution may shock only the Pharisees among us. They can save their sympathy for the useless cattle and divert it to the human destitutes —the hungry and destitute beggars! Political leaders and those who depend on votes for their position cannot speak the truth, whatever their inner convictions. And, therefore, some one must mention the unpleasant if only to start a discussion and ventilate unpopular views.[16]

There are also millions of monkeys; a rough estimate of their total population can only be guessed at. When monkeys become too much of a nuisance in any one community they are sometimes caught and carted away to a nearby jungle, but sooner or later they return to ravage orchards and raid food shops. The monkey has religious immunity because Hanuman, the legendary monkey god, helped Rama to regain Sita, as related in the epic, *Ramayana*. We Hindus are a grateful people! No estimate is available of the magnitude of the annual loss to the country through the depredation of her monkey population alone.

Religious Beliefs

That the religious beliefs of any community or country have a considerable impact on its economic advancement is indisputable. Religious beliefs and practices in all major religions range over a wide field of human activity from the prenatal to the post-mortem periods. These religious beliefs and practices are naturally complex and variegated in a country such as India that shelters all the great religions of mankind, and it is beyond the limits of this chapter to explore all those that are incompatible with economic growth. A few general observations will be sufficient for our purpose.

A careful examination of the histories of all religions reveals

[16] S. Chandrasekhar, "Population Growth and Food Supply in India," *Population Review* (Madras), January, 1959, pp. 83–84.

that, no matter how lofty their ethical codes, in practice they have all been at certain stages in their evolution a serious barrier to human progress. Religions tend to throw their weight behind the *status quo*, and even faiths founded by rebels forgot soon enough the reasons behind their revolts. A religion counseling a vegetarian diet, for instance, the Hindu religion, can foster all kinds of difficulties in an underdeveloped country. The opposition of Roman Catholicism to birth control can force its followers either to violate the Church's injunction or to be unhappy with numerous personal, economic, and social problems, as well as creating a demographic problem. Islam's objection to interest being paid on invested money, Hinduism's preaching against action and striving, idealizing poverty and promoting other-worldly attitudes, which, happily, are not always followed, and Buddhism's doctrine of karma all discourage economic progress. Such examples as these can be multiplied *ad nauseam*.

In any planned effort to promote such rapid economic development as India has embarked upon, the importance of these non-economic factors must be reckoned with. We must create the motivation for a better life and, when the present apathetic and indifferent attitude is changed, the powers that be will have no peace from the citizen who begins to demand that he be treated like a human being. Motivation is all-supreme: A purposeful, liberal, and rational education of the citizen is the way to create it.

As Sol Tax, the American anthropologist, points out:

> It is in creating this incentive and motivation and directing these attitudes on healthy lines that cultural factors play a tremendous role. We must bring about a change in culture, not from above but from within, not by coercion but by persuasion, which in turn will demand an economic change.
>
> The problem of democratically planned cultural change is to respect the general culture bias and the institutions and beliefs held dear by a community of people, at the same time that their level of living is raised and they are given both new wants and the means to attain them. The economically backward population is to get the benefits of our technology and science, our chemistry and bacteriology without important damage to their values and traditional way of life.[17]

In *Population and Planned Parenthood in India*, it is pointed out that:

[17] Sol Tax, "Selective Culture Change," *American Economic Review*, May, 1951, p. 315.

> Cultural integration must go hand in hand with economic change; economic change without a cultural response can only be alien and short-lived. Culture change must imply a consent to change. Education alone, in the broadest sense, can create this consent leading to an effective demand for a lasting change. And the creation of this demand is only the beginning in most underdeveloped countries.[18]

The facts that have been set forth reveal in outline India's economic and social landscape. It is obvious from the foregoing data that the level of living of the vast majority of the Indian people is below the poverty line. Indian poverty is so complex and pervasive that a solution to it has to be found in numerous directions and on many levels at once. And yet this picture of distressing poverty has a bright side too: India has a fairly large amount of natural resources as well as a talented population with a long and impressive cultural tradition. The Indian people could, under certain circumstances, use their resources to give themselves a fuller and more satisfying life. As someone aptly observed, India is like a "beggar sitting on a bench of gold."

This somber picture would pose a challenge to any government, but particularly to a nationalist and popularly elected government formed by the party that fought relentlessly for the nation's political freedom for nearly half a century. The simplest aim of any government under these circumstances would be to raise the entire level of living of the vast majority of the people and thus promote the general welfare of the nation. This means economic planning. For a country with limited resources, a socially desirable set of priorities and targets has to be set up and then achieved. In the concise words of the Planning Commission, the central objective of planning involves a "process of development which will raise living standards and open out to the people new opportunities for a richer and a more varied life." Economic planning is viewed as an integral part of a wider process aiming not merely at the development of resources in a narrow technical sense but at the development of human faculties and the building up of an institutional framework adequate to the needs and aspirations of the people. This, in a nutshell, means increasing over-all production and promoting fuller employment and thus promoting higher levels of consumption and reducing the present wide disparities in income.

[18] S. Chandrasekhar, *Population and Planned Parenthood in India* (London: Allen & Unwin, 1961), pp. 114–15.

India's assets

Now that we have discussed India's difficulties and deficiencies, highlighting the nature of her particular underdevelopment in the light of the above criteria, certain fundamental factors in her favor should be examined. To begin with, India has a stable government. Since 1947 the Indian Government has been carrying on the administration of a huge country without any major setback, except for the current difficulties in meeting Communist China's massive and unprovoked aggression and its aftermath. The relative peacefulness of the years since independence is all the more amazing when it is realized that India inherited, along with her political freedom, such harrowing problems as the rehabilitation of millions of refugees from Pakistan and the integration of some 500-odd Indian princely States into the Indian political structure.

The fact that India has gone through three general elections on the basis of a large adult franchise without any major or violent incidents speaks highly of the nation's response to democratic institutions. India's election process has received widespread commendation, particularly from the opposition parties in India. In fact, the strength and vitality of Indian democratic processes depend on the ever-alert vigilance of these parties. That an opposition party like the Swatantra party, for instance, can be so vocal in India is a tribute to the effectiveness of the parliamentary system in the country.

Second, India has been blessed with strong and dedicated leadership. Pandit Nehru and some of his colleagues have been passionately devoted to the country's welfare. The current leadership is not ideal at all levels; nor is it indispensable, but any alternative leadership to it cannot be especially superior.

Third, India can boast of an efficient and honest civil service; the Indian administrative organization is a valuable legacy from the British rule. While the fairly high traditions of the Indian Civil Service—the steel frame of the British bureaucracy—are being gradually whittled down, the standards of the present Indian Administrative Service can be favorably compared with their counterparts in other Asian or even European countries, though they are not as efficient as the administrative machinery in the United States.

Equally important, India knows that her problem is one of poverty, low level of productivity, and low levels of living. As an Indian proverb has it, "knowledge of the problem is half the solution." India is determined to transform her present economy of scarcity to one of self-sufficiency, if not abundance. She has a plan and a program dedicated to stepping up her agricultural production and industrializing the country within the framework of a mixed economy and a parliamentary democracy.

According to Professor Galbraith, the four crucial and minimum preconditions for development in the poor countries seeking external aid are: (1) a substantial measure of literacy and a substantial educational elite; (2) a substantial measure of social justice so that the benefits of foreign aid will percolate down to the really needy, instead of enriching the already prosperous; (3) a good administration and all that it involves; and (4) a clear and purposeful view of what economic development involves, namely, a long-term plan of priorities and targets. Professor Galbraith goes on to add that all these requirements are present in India: "She has a highly educated and trained elite and growing literacy; a first rate administration; she has a substantial measure of social justice, a good judicial system; and she has a clear-cut program of economic development. Thus nearly all the domestic ingredients necessary for advance are there excepting external capital, and foreign aid should fill this gap."[19]

And hence the need for external aid.

[19] John Kenneth Galbraith, "A Positive Approach to Economic Aid," *Foreign Affairs,* April, 1961, p. 446.

2. *THE CONCEPT OF EXTERNAL AID*

Economic Development: The Contemporary Revolution

If I were asked to name the most revolutionary phenomenon of our times, I would cite neither the release of atomic energy nor the exploration of outer space nor the population explosion. To me, the most significant event in contemporary world politics is a twofold awakening in the minds of men: the awakening of the masses in the underprivileged nations of Asia, Africa, and Latin America to the realization that poverty and miserable levels of living are not some inexplicable burdens to be borne fatalistically, but economic and historical crimes to be fought against with all the resources at the world's command; and the comparable awakening of the affluent and privileged nations of the world to the realization that their fortunate position is not a result of their innate superiority, but to a large extent an historical and political-*cum*-economic accident that carries with it the responsibility to share their capital and skills with the less-privileged nations of the world. Although international tensions and conflicts may make momentary headlines, the large-scale, near-global cooperation between nations to wage war on hunger, disease, and ignorance has already begun to produce a lasting impact on the current course of world history. The credit for this welcome trend belongs to the advanced and affluent West as much as to the dispossessed nations that have begun to forget the unhappy past and cooperate to create a new and a better world.

Although this growing awareness of both possibilities and responsibilities is new, the concept of aid—economic, military, or technical—from an advanced country to an underdeveloped one is not. The concern with the problems of underdeveloped countries is an ancient one, dating at least from Grecian and Roman times and running through to the present day as Professor Joseph J. Spengler has pointed out.[1]

[1] See his Introduction to Bauer, *Economic Analysis and Policy in Underdeveloped Countries,* pp. v–vi.

Discussions of the merits of accepting aid, particularly American aid, in government circles in New Delhi and later in the Indian press revealed a lack of knowledge of the fact that those advanced countries that today offer aid to underdeveloped countries were at one time, not many decades ago, themselves recipients of aid from the then advanced countries. In fact, since the advent of the Industrial Revolution in Britain, no country has registered great economic growth without considerable foreign aid. Not a single country has succeeded simply by pulling itself up by its own bootstraps.

Soviet Union's Development

For instance, the Soviet Union, which is now offering economic, technical, and military aid to countries within and without the Soviet bloc, was herself an underdeveloped country only two or three decades ago. "Only two decades earlier," writes Joseph S. Berliner, "the USSR itself had been a large-scale importer of capital goods and technical assistance. A considerable number of Soviet industrial enterprises owe their existence to the equipment and technical services extended by such United States corporations as Ford, Du Pont, General Electric, RCA and a host of others. World War II found the USSR once more a heavy recipient of economic as well as military aid under Lend Lease, followed by postwar credits that extended Lend Lease deliveries, and by the UNRRA programme, under which USSR was a recipient of aid contributed by the United States and other Western countries."[2] Russian economic growth owes a debt of gratitude not only to American but to German and French capital as well.

What about the development of the United States and of the United Kingdom herself, the pioneer of industrial revolution? What has been the role of foreign capital in the economic development of these nations? (We use the term "foreign capital" instead of "foreign aid," for the latter term came into use only after World War II when such aid was rendered for emergency relief measures. As already observed, many of today's advanced nations owed their early development primarily to foreign capital, enterprise, and even personnel.)

[2] Joseph S. Berliner, *Soviet Economic Aid* (London: The Bodley Head, 1960), p. 12.

Britain's Industrial Revolution

Great Britain became the industrial pioneer for several reasons, the availability of the resources of her far-flung colonial empire and the inventive brilliance of Britons at the time of the Industrial Revolution being perhaps the most important of them. Britain "invented" the Industrial Revolution, acquired her empire in Sir John Seeley's phrase, "in a fit of absence of mind," imported at cheap and preferential rates some of the world's most precious raw materials to feed her hungry machines and factories, and dumped her manufactured goods on the empire market where no other countries could compete. Her excess population could easily emigrate to her colonial empire, either as permanent immigrants or as preferred servants of the Crown, and the colonies acted or were forced to act as industrial outposts to the mother country. Britain imported much of her foodstuffs from the United States, much raw cotton from India, and other raw materials from Australia and Canada. In fact, the economic history of Great Britain for well-nigh two centuries demonstrates the potentialities of foreign capital and other resources.

England's industrialization and rise to economic advancement were thus due to "aid" and forced assistance from her daughter communities scattered throughout the world. It is inconceivable that she would have become the great industrial power that she was in the nineteenth century but for the money and material she received from her far-flung colonial empire.

Foreign capital played no insignificant part in the development of the United States. Millions of Europeans who emigrated to America brought with them not only their hands and brains but also their savings. A considerable amount of British investment was responsible for the development of American railroads, canals, and numerous other enterprises. (Some of this investment turned out to be unplanned economic assistance since a few of the states and railways defaulted on their bonds.) Perhaps the most important foreign contribution to American economic development was made by the hundreds of thousands of immigrants whose education and early training had been paid for by the countries from which they came. What is more, these immigrants settled in the United States—a source of what may be called permanent technical assistance.

Japan's Economic Growth

Perhaps Japan is an even better example of the role of foreign capital in a country's economic development. Foreign capital, however, was neither the prime mover nor the principal source of support for Japan, for dependence upon outside assistance was minimized by strenuous domestic effort, aided by certain favorable circumstances in the world economy. A long period of rather modest progress after the revolution of 1868 led up to an acceleration at the end of the nineteenth century when the growing emphasis on industrialization and armament caused the Japanese to seek substantial external aid. The subsequent inflow of foreign capital was appropriate in type and timing, and its absorption into the economy was efficient, although the goal of full self-support was not attained for more than thirty years.[3]

Japan's evolution is an extreme example of how much can be achieved in a poor country receiving a relatively moderate amount of foreign assistance. To the extent that underdeveloped countries today cannot or will not match the domestic performance of Japan, let alone surpass it, they face the prospect of either a low rate of development, or a heavier dependence on external assistance, or both, as in the case of India. Neither foreign capital nor imported ideas, personnel, and goods provided the driving force in Japan's evolution: the force was indigenous. Japan had a peculiarly positive and constructive reaction to both internal needs and external influences. Western contacts served as a stimulus and a guide only because the indigenous society provided a creative response. When Japan was opened to foreign intercourse in the middle of the nineteenth century, the impact of the West galvanized many of the earlier Japanese ideas and habits. The Japanese welcomed foreign ideas and were receptive to foreign methods and enthusiastic about foreign personnel and experts, but they never allowed foreigners to be their masters. Foreigners were respected, and to a great extent they were copied, but they were never allowed to hold sway over the native inhabitants. And though foreign personnel were recruited and foreign merchants were allowed to compete in the Japanese market, direct foreign investment was scrupulously discouraged.

[3] For a detailed exposition, see Edwin Rueben's "Foreign Capital and Domestic Development in Japan," in Simon Kuznets *et al.* (eds.), *Economic Growth: Brazil, India and Japan* (Durham, N.C.: Duke University Press, 1955).

Capital Resources

An underdeveloped society does not necessarily imply a poverty-stricken and stagnant economy. It may possess natural resources as well as a labor force, but its economic development may have been arrested by foreign rule or domination. The key word "underdeveloped" suggests that the country has some unutilized resources and that there is scope for development. But such factors as predominant illiteracy, unskilled labor, rapid population growth, and lack of capital resources may be serious obstacles in the path of the nation's rapid economic development. In this sense, Jacob Viner's definition of an underdeveloped country as one that "has good potential prospects for using more capital or more labor or more available natural resources or all of these to support its present population on a higher level of living, or, if its per capita income level is already fairly high, to support a larger population on a not lower level of living" has particular meaning with reference to India.

Of all the factors thwarting economic development the major one is lack of capital. This is true of India as well as of many other underdeveloped countries in Asia, Africa, and Latin America. All the erstwhile colonial countries that fought against foreign domination and regained their political freedom realize that, although political freedom is the most desirable of freedoms, it alone cannot guarantee other freedoms, particularly economic freedom. Political freedom is at best the key with which the nation's latent resources can be unlocked and developed. The underdeveloped countries, starting from incredible levels of poverty, find it extremely difficult to educate and train personnel, accumulate capital, and install machinery and other facilities on a scale that will bring marked improvement in living conditions.

The answer to this difficulty lies in obtaining large external aid. In the absence of such external aid the only way to accumulate capital is to increase production (although to increase production capital is needed to begin with), cut down consumption, and contribute the surplus as savings toward capital formation. To push consumption down in a country where the people are already near the subsistence level means considerable hardship. Despite the hardship, however, certain countries have not hesitated to resort to it as a means of forcing economic development. The rapid industrial development of Russia in less than half a century was achieved more or less in this manner and it is the method that

Communist China is using today. But it is always easier to cut down the production of consumer goods and to restrict over-all consumption till it hurts in an authoritarian society like the Soviet Union or Communist China than in a democratic society like India. Though this approach may appear to be better and quicker, ultimately it is self-defeating, for it destroys the incentive of the individual. What is more, such forced development leads to a paradoxical situation in which the nation becomes richer and more industrialized, but in which the people, from the point of view of daily consumption, remain as poor as before.

Objectives of Underdeveloped Countries

What are the primary national objectives of the newly emancipated but underdeveloped countries? More than anything, the countries that have recently emerged as free and sovereign nations prize their political freedom and national sovereignty as ends in themselves. Nationalism is their religion. For long years their leaders fought the powerful empires of the West—the British, the French, the Dutch, and the Spanish—against countless odds, suffering imprisonment and numerous privations, to regain their lost political freedom. They cannot, therefore, look upon their former masters with any particular sympathy or understanding. They are wary of any friendly approaches from those Western countries with imperialist pasts. Thus the first consideration of India and of all other newly independent countries is to maintain their independence at any cost.

Second, they realize only too well that while political freedom is the *sine qua non* of dignified and respectable national existence, political independence without economic betterment and an increase in the levels of living of the people is meaningless. Their new enemy is poverty and they can no longer blame it on their past rulers. They have, therefore, to embark on plans of economic development involving the rapid industrialization of their countries. They need raw materials, capital resources, technological know-how, managerial enterprise, skilled labor, an expanding market, and so forth.

Third, and in a sense this is even more important than their first two objectives, the underdeveloped countries earnestly desire a world at peace, for without peace there cannot be any prospects of economic progress. They understand the African proverb that "when the bull elephants fight the grass is trampled down." They are careful not to identify themselves with either of the bull elephants, whatever their individual merits, and they urge coexistence. Their general policy is one of nonalignment.

Objectives of Donor Nations: The U.S.A.

What are the objectives of the advanced donor nations in providing economic aid to the underdeveloped countries? And, more specifically, what are the aims and interests of the United States in the economic development of India and other underdeveloped and developing countries? These aims can be conveniently examined under three different headings: political, economic, and humanitarian.

Political Objectives

The main political objective of economic aid to the underdeveloped countries has never been put more succinctly than by President Eisenhower in his message to Congress on the Mutual Security Program for fiscal year 1958:

> This part of the (Mutual Security) program helps less-developed countries make the social and political progress needed to preserve their independence. Unless these peoples can hope for reasonable economic advance, the danger will be acute that their governments will be subverted by Communism.
>
> To millions of people close to the Soviet and Chinese Communist borders, political freedom is still new. To many it must still prove its worth. To survive it must show the way to . . . freedom from the poverty and hopelessness in which these peoples have lived for centuries. With their new freedom, their desire . . . to develop their economies [is] intense. They are fixed upon raising their standards of living. Yet they lack sufficient resources. Their need for help is desperate—both for technical know-how and capital.
>
> Lacking outside help, these new nations cannot advance economically as they must to maintain their independence. Their moderate leaders must be able to obtain sufficient help from the free world to offer convincing hope of progress. Otherwise their people will surely turn elsewhere. Extremist elements would then seize power, whip up national hatreds, and incite civil dissension and strife. The danger would be grave that these free governments would disappear. Instability and threats to peace would result. . . .
>
> The help toward economic development that we provide these countries is a means to forestall such crisis. Our assistance is thus insurance against rising tensions and increased dangers of war. . . .[4]

[4] *The Mutual Security Program, Fiscal Year 1958* (Washington, D.C.: Department of State, Department of Defense, International Cooperation Administration, 1957), p. 4.

President Lyndon B. Johnson in his State of the Union message to Congress in 1964 pointed out that "We must strengthen the ability of free nations everywhere to develop their independence and raise their standards of living and thereby frustrate those who prey on poverty and chaos. To do this the rich must help the poor and we must do our part."[5]

The political objectives of aid can be defined as those that bring about certain desirable relationships between the government and the people of a recipient country and those of the donor country, as well as between the recipient country and other countries whose friendship is valued by the aid-giving country. The United States naturally wants to promote good and friendly relations between her government and the government of India. What is more, she also wants to promote cordial relations between India and India's neighbors, particularly Pakistan, since the United States would in the long run derive benefit from peace in the subcontinent. No one need read any sinister design in the U.S. desire to promote peace and good neighborliness between India and Pakistan; obviously, such an aim is conducive to world peace and prosperity.

Second, the United States is interested in the long-range welfare of India, just as she was interested in seeing India gain her political freedom all through the years of India's nationalist struggle with Britain. There is no reason why her attitude toward India should now change, for India's political stability and lasting freedom contribute to international peace.

Third, America, despite (perhaps because of) her dominant position in the world today, is seeking sincere, strong, and willing allies. Which country, no matter how powerful, does not want to win and influence friends? If such friendships can promote the security interests of the United States, all the better.

Fourth, the United States, despite certain limitations arising from accidents of history, is dedicated to the freedom of all peoples, democratic processes of government, free enterprise, and peaceful world conditions in which to promote these objectives. Any political systems or economic institutions that deny these basic beliefs and practices of the American way of life are not welcome, to say the least, by the United States in the international arena. The United States considers it her legitimate duty to oppose the emergence of such ideologies that diverge from her own and

[5] *The New York Times,* January 9, 1964.

to their spread. The political and economic philosophy of Communism is diametrically opposed to the American way of life. If American aid to India and other uncommitted, underdeveloped nations can help them on the free and non-Communist path of economic progress, a major objective of the U.S. government will have been achieved. And those underdeveloped countries that prize their political freedom and economic independence and that are unwilling to embrace the Communist way of life for the sake of aid from the Soviet Union cannot but be happy that they have an alternative in accepting American aid and thus pursuing an unfettered path of economic progress.

But much as the United States would like to prevent the new and emergent nations from falling victim to Communist subversion, it would be misleading to infer that the *sole* objective of U.S. aid to India is to lure her away from the Soviet bloc. On the contrary, the United States Government has repeatedly assured the government of India that her aid does not imply any opposition to India's foreign policy of nonalignment.

However, U.S. aid to certain other underdeveloped and uncommitted nations (which do not suffer from the difficulties of India's particular *geographical* location with two large Communist countries as northern neighbors) may well have as its major objective the countering of Communism. The underlying thesis is simple enough. The newly free underdeveloped countries are anxious to develop their economies as rapidly as possible to give their citizens a rising level of living. This involves accepting a certain amount of economic and technical aid from the richer countries. If America is not willing to offer such aid, the emergent countries may accept it from the Soviet Union. They are so eager to become developed that they do not always care where the aid is coming from and whether in accepting such aid they may barter away their freedom to Communist dictatorship in the long run. Hence, to prevent the spread of Communism to these uncommitted countries America has to be the first with aid.

This thesis may not be completely true. Some neutral nations see the danger of Communism and its authoritarianism only too well, but they flirt with the Soviet Union and even accept some aid, play up their neutrality, and thus enhance their bargaining power with both the Soviet Union and the West. These countries may feel that the initial aim of Soviet aid is not so much to persuade them to embrace Communism as to make them effectively neutral in the war between the two ideologies. As Joseph Berliner points out, the "Soviet aid program increases the attractiveness of neutralism for the uncommitted countries. The availability of Soviet aid increases the independence of countries and strengthens their bargaining power with the West."[6]

Nevertheless, many American politicians are convinced of the efficacy of economic aid in preventing uncommitted nations from going Communist. Thus, for instance, the Special Committee of the Senate that in 1957 investigated the question of foreign assistance observed that "successful economic development contingent upon American aid, of a substantial number of underdeveloped countries, chiefly in Asia, is likely to lead to a decrease in political tension in the world at large, by substantially reducing the chance of Soviet political successes in that area."[7]

It can be argued, however, that Communist encroachment on any free country is not a peaceful phenomenon but a disruptive, subversive, and violent process. No country that has gone Communist during the last half-century, from the Soviet Union itself to North Korea, has done so without bloodshed, fighting, and revolution. The very basis of the Communist approach is struggle and revolution—the negation of the concept of peaceful change. Therefore, any effort directed against the spread of Communism is an effort dedicated to the promotion of peace and order, and every installment of economic aid to a poor country is a definite investment in establishing and fostering international peace. In this, American aid to the underdeveloped countries has been a much-needed ballast to ensure the smooth sailing of the new nations.

Apart from lessening the chances for the spread of Communism, economic aid promotes closer friendship and lessens friction between nations, particularly between the haves and the have-nots. There is no doubt that poverty—not absolute poverty, but informed poverty that is aware of possibilities for affluence—is a threat to peace, since it invites internal disturbance and attracts unwanted external attention. A nation that is better off economically is less likely to embark on aggression and less likely to attract the attentions of an external aggressor.

There is no doubt that economic aid of the right kind to the right country at the right moment promotes both prosperity and security not only to the donor and recipient nations but to an entire region. If even a modicum of prosperity is diffused and a cer-

[6] Berliner, *op. cit.*, p. 20.

[7] *The Role of Foreign Aid in Economic Development* (Washington, D.C.: Government Printing Office, 1957).

tain measure of mutual understanding is established among the underdeveloped nations through economic aid, these countries may be able to cut their defense expenditure and apply the savings to other, constructive purposes.

Cutting defense expenditures can have beneficent repercussions affecting both the rich and powerful donor and the needy and worried recipient. The tragedy of such small nations as Afghanistan, Burma, Ceylon, and Cambodia spending a tidy part of their budgets on national defense can be averted. India and Pakistan, for instance, feel obliged, because of Pakistan's aggression and the consequent mutual mistrust engendered, to spend a large proportion of their relatively meager national resources for defense against each other—resources desperately needed for economic development. Should ever a spirit of mutual security and tolerance permeate the world, what a staggering amount of money and effort could be saved for the economic and social betterment of the submerged millions. Paul G. Hoffman rightly observes that "spending on aid is an investment in peace. If the 30 to 40 billion dollars suggested as the U.S. share of the total investment should help us move toward peace to the point where U.S. defense expenses could be reduced by even 20 per cent, it would have paid for itself twice over."[8]

One would like to believe that economic aid to an underdeveloped country ensures its progress toward lasting democratic institutions, but our experience since the end of World War II does not bear out this contention. There appears to be no simple correlation between economic aid to an underdeveloped country and its political stability. Political stability and the firm adherence to democratic values depend upon numerous factors largely independent of economic aid. These factors are the country's political and economic history, cultural evolution, the degree of literacy and education, the political awareness of the populace, the nature of economic institutions and geographical factors, and so on.

According to C. Tyler Wood, American diplomat and an administrator of the Agency for International Development, the argument of political stability is one of the most popular of the false beliefs regarding American aid:

> The first of these is that economic development and rising standards of living produce political stability and guarantee rapid progress to-

[8] Paul G. Hoffman, "The Challenge of Economic Development," *The Hyphen* (Bombay), March-April, 1960, p. 16.

ward democratic institutions. This proposition is generally discredited among thoughtful and experienced people, but it is amazing how often the concept recurs in discussions and speeches. Those who have studied the question or have had experience in some of the lesser developed countries know that the effect of economic development is often, and in fact is more likely at the outset to be, precisely the opposite of that claimed. One of the reasons why this belief is so harmful is that great numbers of people upon whose understanding and support the continuation of the foreign-aid program depends reach the conclusion that the program is a failure because in some countries where it is operating there are serious and violent political disturbances and in others generals and armies are taking over and suspending constitutions and cancelling out the holding of planned elections.[9]

However, all that can be said is that underdeveloped countries that have no experience in running a political democracy and whose cultural and religious institutions are authoritarian in character are not likely to suddenly develop a love for parliamentary democracy just because some affluent and benevolent foreign country decides to give it substantial economic aid. The leaders of Indonesia and Pakistan have confessed in public, for example, that democracy in the accepted Western sense is not suited to the genius of their peoples and what is needed is either "guided democracy" or "basic democracy"—that is, anything but democracy as we understand the term. Nevertheless, "it can properly be held that the ultimate achievement of responsible, stable, dynamic societies, based on widespread understanding and consent of those societies, is impossible without economic development and rising living standards, whatever the immediate consequences of starting the process of such development may be."[10]

There are those who feel that whether aid promotes political stability or not, it certainly ought to influence to some extent the political events in the recipient country in favor of the donor country. The donor country would like to see a political party favorable to it come to power in the recipient country. At one extreme, to put it bluntly, there are some in the donor countries who would want to go to the extent of recommending candidates in the receiving country for elective offices and political power. This is the argument usually leveled against the United States by cer-

[9] C. Tyler Wood, "Role and Character of Foreign Aid," *American Economic Review*, May, 1959, p. 207.
[10] *Ibid.*

tain Latin American republics. Though there may have been some truth in this contention in the past, it is definitely no longer valid today.

It must be conceded that a country, like an individual, naturally prefers to have friendly neighbors. No nation likes the idea of being surrounded by countries with alien and unsympathetic, even hostile, ideologies. Roosevelt propounded the Good Neighbor Policy to cement U.S. relations with Latin America. A major grievance of the Soviet Union before World War II was that she was encircled by capitalist powers. This very natural desire for and expectation of friendship and neighborliness must be taken into consideration when we examine the relationship between the aid-giving and the aid-receiving nations. It is only natural for a donor country like the United States, say, to expect that large-scale aid will create friendly attitudes and influence the course of events in the recipient country. Charles Wolf points out that:

> Another political objective of economic aid can be variously described as the acquisition (or maintenance) of "friendship," influence, goodwill, and cooperation. Whereas the objective of political stability implied an *internal* relationship between the recipient government and its domestic constituency, promoting cooperation or friendship implies an external relationship between donor and recipient, or between donor and particular groups or individuals in the recipient country. . . . Promoting friendship toward the United States has been an aid objective in the direct sense that it has affected the allocation of aid. If the allocation of a resource is affected by a given preference then the preference is likely to reflect an objective, that is, a "value" which the resource is trying to "produce." If, for example, additional aid is intentionally allocated to recipients whose relationship to the United States is friendly and cooperative, it is reasonable to infer that encouraging or perpetuating this relationship is one of the aims of aid.[11]

This is certainly understandable, but the available, though limited, evidence shows that such expectations on the part of the donor country are not always realized. India and Pakistan are friendly to the United States, individually, for different reasons, and are indebted to her for considerable economic and military aid, but both countries at some time or other have taken what amounted to an anti-American stand in their foreign policy, not because they wished to be anti-American but because a pro-American stand on

[11] Charles Wolf, Jr., *Foreign Aid: Theory and Practice in Southern Asia* (Princeton, N.J.: Princeton University Press, 1960), pp. 264–65.

certain issues of foreign policy did not suit their particular interests. Both countries, more than once, have voted against the United States in the United Nations. Therefore, any amount of economic or military aid does not necessarily buy the unflagging allegiance of the recipient country.

American military aid to Pakistan was intended to be used to help her defend herself against aggression from either the Soviet Union or Communist China or both. The U.S. Government did not dream at the time that Pakistan would enter into a disadvantageous border treaty with Communist China, and one ceding to Communist China territory belonging to India! There seems to have been miscalculation all around: India cultivated and trusted Communist China despite U.S. warnings, and the U.S. aided Pakistan in order that she might stand up to any Communist intrusion, but China stabbed India in the back and Pakistan fraternizes with Communist China. Americans and others concerned can be forgiven if they are completely bewildered by this turn of events.

An American observer's comments in this connection are revealing:

> There are several preliminary questions concerning the purpose of foreign aid to get out of the way. "Perhaps the most naïve idea is that if you give a man money, he will love you; and there is the notion that if a country gets better off, it will become less likely to start an aggression. Both notions forget the role of ideology. *If the man aided by you believes that you are merely giving up a small part of what you have already robbed from him* (and that is precisely the Socialistic and Communistic outlook), will he love you? No! He will take your money and sharpen his knife.[12]

Chester Bowles voices nearly the same opinion when he says:

> Contrary to the assumptions of some diplomatic and military strategists, foreign aid will not enable us to purchase allies and friends. We can no more buy the loyalty of a free people than we can buy the loyalty of a free individual. . . . Nor will foreign aid even assure us the gratitude of a destitute people, in Asia, Africa or South America. Gratitude like loyalty is not for sale. If we petulantly seek gratitude we shall assuredly be disappointed.[13]

[12] McCord Wright, "True Growth Must Come Through Freedom," *Fortune*, December, 1959.

[13] Chester Bowles, *New Dimensions of Peace* (New York: Harper & Bros., 1955), p. 295.

Frederick Benham echoes the sentiment when he points out:

> It is very human to resent having to accept assistance even when it is badly needed; and we should not expect to buy friendship with money. In order to gain the goodwill and cooperation of the underdeveloped countries with whom we share this every shrinking world we must genuinely put their needs and interests first in the amount and type of aid which we provide, and in the manner in which we provide it, we must . . . avoid any semblance of patronage, superiority and racial discrimination. As time goes on, aid provided in this spirit will, we hope, gradually dispel bitterness and hostility where they exist.[14]

Economic Objectives

America's economic objectives in giving aid to India and other underdeveloped countries appear to be both rational and capable of realization. That America and the advanced West have a serious economic stake in the economic growth and stability of India and other underdeveloped countries is undeniable.

It is well known that the West imports from the underdeveloped countries such important industrial raw materials as tin, rubber, oil, and uranium ore, all of which are indispensable to Western prosperity. Second, the West is a major consumer of such cash crops of the underdeveloped countries as coffee, tea, cocoa, bananas, cashew nuts, and a variety of tropical fruits. Third, the underdeveloped countries import from the West a wide variety of manufactured goods that provide gainful employment to the workers and profits to the owners of the large manufacturing industries in the West. Fourth, the West profits from direct investments in the underdeveloped countries. These general economic interests have been expressed by President Eisenhower as follows: "We . . . have an economic interest in promoting the development of the free world. In the years to come, the increased economic strength of less-developed countries should prove mutually beneficial in providing growing markets for exports, added opportunities for investment, and more of the basic materials we need from abroad."[15]

These interests of America and the West generally can be examined more conveniently under three conventional categories:

[14] Frederic Benham, *Economic Aid to Underdeveloped Countries* (New York: Oxford University Press, 1961), p. 96.

[15] The President's Message to Congress on the Mutual Security Program for 1959, *The New York Times*, February 20, 1958.

(1) gains from trade; (2) gains from strategic raw materials; and (3) gains from investment income.[16]

Gains from trade. While some have argued that what underdeveloped countries need most is trade and not aid, a more realistic appraisal of what they need would be a combination of trade *and* aid. Aid promotes trade. The reasoning is simple and obvious. International trade takes place because the relative cost of producing the same commodities in different countries varies. The major reason for this is that different countries have different indigenous factors of production. Thus a country imports a commodity for which its costs of production are relatively high and exports a commodity in which its production costs are relatively low. A country's total gains through international trade depend both on the terms of trade and the volume of trade.

It is possible that with the increased growth of the underdeveloped countries, the terms of trade of the developed countries may decline, but this would be more than offset by the volume of trade between the developed and underdeveloped countries. Aid promotes development and development leads to higher incomes and greater demand. Despite the accelerated development of the underdeveloped countries, the growing demand for manufactured goods cannot be met by the internal market. Hence the greater demand for the products of the developed countries. "Experience shows that, where trade channels are not unreasonably blocked, the very countries which produce the most manufactured goods for themselves are the best customers for the manufactured goods of other countries."[17] In other words, "the economically advanced countries are each other's customers."[18] There appears to be, in the long run, a direct correlation between increased economic development and higher output incomes of a country and the value and volume of its international trade. As Eugene Staley points out, "There is another reason why America is in a peculiarly good position to benefit from the new trade opportunities created by successful economic development abroad with only a minimum of disturbance from the new competition. A high proportion of the goods which United States producers offer on the world market

[16] For details of these familiar objectives, see Wolf, *op. cit.*, pp. 270–81.

[17] See Folke Hilgerdt, *Industrialization and Foreign Trade* (Princeton, N.J.: League of Nations, 1945), p. 120.

[18] See Rognar Nukse, *International Trade and Development Policy* (Rio de Janeiro, 1957), p. 8.

are of kinds for which the demand is especially stimulated by economic growth. They are goods needed in development, like trucks and electrical equipment, or goods which are purchased in much larger volume by people, goods like refrigerators, radios, vacuum cleaners, and passenger automobiles."[19]

Gains from strategic materials. The strategic-materials objective of economic aid to underdeveloped countries poses several questions. America in relation to her area and population consumes a disproportionately large amount of the world's total output of raw materials.[20] In 1961, it was estimated that the United States, with only 7 per cent of the world's population and 7 per cent of its area, accounts for roughly half of the whole world's industrial output. But it produces only about a third of the world's annual output of the fifteen basic minerals. This means that the United States has to depend on foreign sources, mostly underdeveloped areas, for her supplies of valuable raw materials. While certain domestic synthetic substitutes can be evolved for a few of them, the need for importing these raw materials, is, if anything, likely to increase in the decades to come. Second, if aid can assure the all-around, balanced economic development of a country, the steady and increased flow of the exportable surplus of these raw materials into the United States can be assured. The importance of this situation can be realized when the raw materials happen to be "strategic" and "critical" ones indispensable to the defense needs of the importing advanced country.

From the point of view of the underdeveloped countries the advantages are that the increased production and export of surplus raw materials can provide them with much-needed foreign exchange. Further, an expanded exploitation of raw materials would necessitate the provision of such facilities as roads, railroads, canals, ports, trucks, wagons, and so forth. The creation of these facilities alone would give the necessary fillip to the economy, which need no longer be confined to the mere supply of raw materials, a condition which in turn can lead to certain beneficent reactions such as increased employment, better wages, and higher consumption.

Gains from investment income. It may be recalled that, before World War I, European capital investment accelerated the eco-

[19] Staley, *op. cit.*, p. 45.

[20] The President's Materials Policy Commission, *Foundation for Growth and Security: Reasons for Freedom* (Washington, D.C., 1957).

nomic development of the United States. Then the investment consisted of direct investment in private enterprise. No one ever accused the European investors of using their investment as a step toward the eventual imperialistic domination of America. There is no reason *today* why American investment, particularly private investment, in the free but underdeveloped countries should lead to any economic or political domination of the country. Second, as Wolf points out, "Economic aid can be used to raise the yield on private (U.S.) capital in underdeveloped countries by creating a variety of external economies, from a more literate labor force to the more familiar 'social overhead' facilities. To the extent that aid has this effect, that is, that such external economies predominate our tendency toward diminishing returns, it will raise income from U.S. private investment abroad and hence U.S. real national product."[21]

Humanitarian Objectives

Most Americans are hesitant to cite humanitarianism as a serious objective in providing aid to the underdeveloped world: They prefer to appear as hardheaded businessmen and not as "do-gooders." Modesty may be at the bottom of this wish to maintain a public image of the United States as a serious, practical, business-minded nation and not a sentimental people with give-away notions, but the people in the recipient countries may be better judges. That American aid—be it grants, loans, or technical assistance—has a genuine humanitarian character about it cannot be denied. Philanthropy is an innate part of the American national character. Americans, individually or collectively, privately or through official agencies, extended help to those in distress long before the "development of underdeveloped countries" became a major problem. In a word, America has always exhibited a serious "concern," in the Quaker sense of the term, with the problems of poor countries.

Foreign aid is an economic problem; it may well be a political problem; but it is ultimately a moral problem. It may aid the fight for freedom against tyranny; it may take sides in the fight between freedom and Communism; but in the long run it is a positive factor in the struggle of millions of human beings against the age-old enemies of hunger, poverty, disease, and ignorance.

It is not, of course, maintained here that humanitarianism alone

[21] Wolf, *op. cit.*, p. 280.

is the motive behind American aid, but it is contended that humanitarianism and the good-neighbor policy does, perhaps silently, permeate all American aid programs. This is perhaps an unconscious virtue of an affluent society. Chester Bowles points out that, "Help for a neighbor is as old in American history as the frontier communities where everyone turned out to lend a hand in rebuilding a burned-out barn. Assistance was offered not as a charity nor to instill a sense of gratitude or obligation. It was given because it was the decent thing to do, and because in an exposed and struggling settlement the fact of each man's dependence upon the strength and success of his neighbor was too plain to mistake."[22]

President Eisenhower observed in 1958 that "If any one wants to judge the entire program only on a what's-in-it-for-me basis, he can find all the justification he needs. But beyond this, if others want to add another element, do unto others as you would have them do unto you, I see no reason to apologize . . . for this kind of motive. I can see no great evidence of intelligence in sneering at 'do-gooders' if their 'do-gooding' helps America at the same time it helps our friends."[23]

President Lyndon B. Johnson, speaking in 1964 on the moral aspects of American aid to the underdeveloped countries, pointed out that: "Friendly cynics and fierce enemies alike often underestimate or ignore the strong thread of moral purpose which runs through the fabric of American history. Of course, our security and welfare shape our policies. But much of the energy of our efforts has come from moral purposes. It is right that the strong should help the weak defend their freedom. It is right that the wealthy should help the poor emerge from their hunger."[24]

[22] Chester Bowles, *Ambassador's Report* (New York: Harper & Bros., 1954), p. 322.

[23] *The New York Times*, February 26, 1958.

[24] "America's Efforts Toward World Order," *U.S. Department of State Bulletin* (Washington, D.C.), August 31, 1964, pp. 298–301.

3. *THE GENESIS AND GROWTH OF AMERICAN AID TO INDIA*

AID: THE MOTIVES AND THE METHODS

IF THE HONORS of the nineteenth century belong to the United Kingdom as the pioneer of the Industrial Revolution and as the nation that propagated the values of the liberal West, the honors of the twentieth century, in a far truer sense, belong to the United States. With her large area, vast resources, dynamic energy, incredible strides in science and technology, great wealth, and, last but not least, her moral idealism, America has been propelled into a position of unrivaled world leadership.

World War II wrought radical changes in the balance of power in Europe and throughout the world, and the United States was forced to give up her policy of isolation and nonintervention and reorient her foreign policy to meet new demands and pressures, particularly in Southeast Asia. In a sense, America's foreign policy today, fortunately for the less-privileged nations, is an extension of her domestic policy of encouraging and furthering the cause of freedom. It is her aim to liquidate colonialism, old and new, throughout the world.

If the major political objective of American foreign policy is to help other nations to withstand totalitarian subversion, the major economic aim of that policy is to promote economic stability and growth in all countries, particularly in the less-developed countries that may be threatened by Communist expansion. Newly won political freedom without substantial economic betterment might tempt these countries to try the Communist experiment. Thus, aid in the widest sense of the word has become the cornerstone of America's postwar foreign policy.

When did this official policy of foreign aid begin? It is convenient to date it from World War II. But dates can only be arbitrary, for, as observed earlier, serious American interest in the development of the less-privileged nations is not a seedling of recent planting. The genesis of American aid to and interest in the underdeveloped world is impossible to date. As Wolf rightly points out:

> In the study of foreign policy, no less than biology, origins tend to be elusive and, if found, are likely to be arbitrary. For foreign policies like biological species, usually evolve gradually and continuously. Whether we view foreign policy as a set of national objectives, or as programs or instrumentalities designed to achieve these objectives, or as a combination of the two, once we look behind the apparent origin of a policy we generally find precedents and prior circumstances that figured prominently in the policy's formulation. In short, origins have a way of receding as we approach them.[1]

But, despite this difficulty of assigning any definitive date or period to the origins of American aid, the history of American assistance during the last quarter of a century falls into five distinct periods: the period of Lend Lease before and after Pearl Harbor (1939–45); the period marked by the termination of Lend Lease and the wide allocation of aid for war-torn Europe and parts of Asia (1945–48); the period of the European Recovery Program—the Marshall Plan—(1948–51); the period characterized by the programs of the Mutual Security Act of 1951 (1951–continuing); and the present period, characterized by economic aid to underdeveloped countries in Asia, Africa, and Latin America. This last phase was introduced by the India Emergency Food Aid Act of 1951, which gives support to countries that are by and large neutral, that have not entered into military alliances with the United States.[2]

Although these may appear to be clear-cut phases with separate and independent programs, actually the programs and policies have been, to a considerable extent, interdependent and overlapping. For example, India, as an allied nation fighting the Axis powers in World War II, received some Lend-Lease aid during the period when most of the aid was going toward European recovery. China, Japan, and the Philippines also received considerable over-all aid. Mutual-security assistance involving primarily military aid can never be totally divested from economic aid. At the present time, economic aid to India includes a substantial

[1] Wolf, *op. cit.*, p. 11.

[2] W. A. Brown and R. Opie, *American Foreign Assistance* (Washington, D.C.: The Brookings Institution, 1953).

amount of military hardware to resist Communist Chinese aggression.

In a sense, it is difficult to decide where military assistance ends and where economic help begins. In the long run, there is no significant difference between giving economic aid and offering military assistance. For instance, the United States has given Pakistan considerable military aid—that is, with the aid Pakistan has received from the United States she has armed herself with the latest American military equipment. But, at the same time, the United States has been giving India economic aid through the sale of commodities and the services of expert personnel (P.L. 480), enabling her to divert her own resources to purchase arms from the United States and elsewhere and thus to keep pace with Pakistan's military strength. In such a situation as this, there is very little difference between military and nonmilitary economic aid, as far as the recipient countries are concerned.

American aid is like a huge umbrella under which all nations in need of economic aid, military support, or technical assistance can seek shelter. The countries that ask for and receive aid change periodically as the conditions and pattern of economic development alter, but the number grows each year. All the countries of the world, with the exception of Communist China, the Soviet Union and certain Soviet bloc countries, Andorra, Bhutan, Kuwait, Liechtenstein, Monaco, Masqat-Oman, Switzerland, and the Vatican City, receive some kind of aid from the United States. (The Soviet Union and China received considerable aid during the war years.)

As the balance of power shifts in Asia and Europe, the nations receiving military assistance may change allegiance, aligning with the U.S. when they were previously nonaligned, or shedding their pretensions of friendship and becoming aggressive and belligerent. Whatever might be the turns and twists in historical circumstances, political fortunes, and economic vicissitudes, America has, as the record will show, stood by nations in need, so long as they are dedicated to the pursuit of freedom in the widest sense of the term, democratic political institutions, free and unfettered economic enterprise, and social progress. These objectives America has tried to pursue not because she wishes to pose as a super Santa Claus but because she realizes that her own affluence, freedom, and security have content and meaning only in relation to the larger freedom and security of the rest of the world.

Lend-Lease Assistance

Before Pearl Harbor, American feeling toward the war was dominated by two conflicting but understandable factors—a desire to remain out of it and a conviction that an Axis victory would be inimical to American interests. World War II broke out on September 3, 1939. President Roosevelt invoked the Neutrality Act of 1937, putting an embargo on the delivery of war materials to Britain and France. On March 11, 1941, to help Britain and her allies resist Hitler's aggression, the United States passed the Lend-Lease Act to give Britain the necessary dollars to buy war materials.

Lend-Lease aid, which began before Pearl Harbor and increased in volume when the United States became a belligerent nation, lasted till the cessation of hostilities in Europe and the Far East. "Altogether Lend-Lease assistance was given to 38 countries, but the $49.1 billion of gross assistance was heavily concentrated on Great Britain ($29.0 billion) and the Soviet Union ($10.8 billion), the major active participants with the United States in the war. France received $2.6 billion, China $1.3 billion, Australia, $900 million, India $700 million and the American Republics as a whole $700 million, leaving about $3 billion for all the other countries combined."[3] After Pearl Harbor, America's interests and those of the Allied nations fighting the Axis powers became identical: The primary objective was to defeat the enemy and ensure a just peace. During the war, American aid began to flow in ever larger quantities to all the countries resisting aggression. Certain principles regarding mutual aid in the prosecution of the war against aggression were enunciated. With the termination of hostilities in 1945, American assistance to all foreign countries engaged in the prosecution of the war was estimated at some $41 billion.

The effects of Lend-Lease were twofold. Whereas the aid saved Europe from German domination, a substantial recipient, Soviet Russia, used part of the assistance to build up a totalitarian empire. Despite the unexpected and distressing development of the extension of Russian Communist hegemony over parts of Europe, Lend-Lease aid more than fulfilled its major objective of saving Britain and other European countries from Nazi tyranny.

The second phase of the American aid program lasted from the cessation of hostilities in Europe in mid-1945 to the beginning of 1948 when the United States embarked upon the European Re-

[3] *Ibid.*, p. 544.

covery Program. The United States had hoped earlier to close down the wartime program in a way that would smooth the transition from war to peace. It was hoped that the responsibility for the reconstruction of the war-weary economies and the expansion of trade could be transferred to the new United Nations specialized agencies and to private enterprise. But this was not to be and the United States had to devise a series of *ad hoc* arrangements "partly to deal with the unexpectedly devastating economic consequences of the war, and partly to deal with the situations created by the deteriorating relations between the Soviet Union and the Western powers."[4] During this period, a large part of the aid was directed to Great Britain and Europe in general, but special attention was given to the Greek-Turkish programs as well as to the rehabilitation of the Chinese and Philippine republics.

The third phase of U.S. foreign aid was ushered in when the United States was compelled to realize that, although military Fascism in Germany, Italy, and Japan was defeated, the world had to face the new threat of Communism. It was in this connection that the Truman Doctrine was formulated in 1949. The major concern of the United States was still the recovery and stabilization of Europe, but those nations threatened by Communist aggression also had to be helped. There was also a third consideration: the welfare of the underdeveloped countries that had recently gained their independence. The United States wanted to assure these nations of her desire to help raise their standards of living, both for their own sakes and also as a bulwark against their becoming easy victims of Communist infiltration.

It is against this background that President Truman made, in his inaugural adress on January 20, 1949, the now famous Point Four:

> Fourth, we must embark on a bold new program for making the benefits of our scientific advances and industrial progress available for the improvement and growth of underdeveloped areas.
>
> More than half the people of the world are living in conditions approaching misery. Their food is inadequate. They are victims of disease. Their economic life is primitive and stagnant. Their poverty is a handicap and threat both to them and to more prosperous areas.
>
> For the first time in history, humanity possesses the knowledge and the skill to relieve the suffering of these people.
>
> The United States is pre-eminent among nations in the development of industrial and scientific techniques. The material resources

[4] *Ibid.*, p. 545.

which we can afford to use for the assistance of other peoples are limited. But our imponderable resources in technical knowledge are constantly growing and are inexhaustible.

I believe that we should make available to peace-loving peoples the benefits of our store of technical knowledge in order to help them realize their aspirations for a better life. And in cooperation with other nations, we should foster capital investment in areas needing development.

Our aim should be to help the free peoples of the world through their own efforts, to produce more food, more clothing, more materials for housing, and more mechanical power to lighten their burdens.[5]

The philosophy behind Point Four and its subsequent interpretation as a program of technical assistance were widely welcomed both in America and abroad, particularly in the underdeveloped countries. The Act for International Development (Title Four of the Foreign Economic Assistance Act of 1950) embodied the central idea that the economic advancement of the underdeveloped countries was to be regarded as an abiding objective of American foreign policy. For the first time it was explicitly "declared to be the policy of the United States to aid the efforts of the peoples of economically underdeveloped areas to develop their resources and to improve their working and living conditions. . . ."[6]

The fourth phase emphasized rearmament and the significance of defense. The importance of world economic recovery receded to the background and the importance of American national security as an integral part of the security of the Free World became paramount. The result was the Mutual Security Act of 1951. With the passing of the Mutual Security Act of 1952, the preponderant share of foreign aid became military assistance. Aid for recovery became assistance for defense. But, economic strength cannot be separated from military preparedness, and in Asia the three major recipients were Pakistan, Thailand, and the Philippines, all members of SEATO. India was the major recipient of *economic* aid under the Mutual Security Program. "Thus, the Mutual Security Program in its first year brought a substantial increase in both the absolute amount and the proportion of economic aid allocated to the countries of Southern Asia. Most of this increase was due to the start of economic and technical aid programs in India and

[5] *The New York Times,* January 21, 1949.
[6] Wolf, *op. cit.,* p. 178.

Pakistan."[7] When the Mutual Security Program entered its fifth year in 1956, political disturbances and the "lure of Communism" had become rampant in Asia. Consequently, the United States Government was compelled to allocate greater amounts to Asian countries to avert the political dangers likely to arise out of their near-stagnant economies.

The fifth and current phase of American aid thus became a combination of economic, military, and technical assistance. India began to figure prominently as a recipient country. Aid now includes not only government grants and loans and sale of surplus agricultural commodities, but also U.S. private capital investment. Besides direct aid from the government and from the government-supported specialized agencies of the United Nations, substantial help has been forthcoming from various U.S. Government-sponsored lending agencies.

Prior to World War I, government aid was more the exception than the rule, and international capital movements were largely private investments. Foreign economic aid as a government policy developed after World War II when the war-devastated European countries suffered an incredible economic collapse. Today, the bulk of economic assistance provided by the advanced nations is government-sanctioned, but the United States is the only country by whom formidable amounts of aid are contributed by private agencies as well as by the government. Besides such government agencies as the Export-Import Bank, the Development Loan Fund, and the U.S. Agency for International Development, many private foundations have given aid to India.

U.S.–India Aid Relations

Relations between India and the United States have had their ups and downs since 1947, when India gained independence. Although every American administration since 1947 has gone on record as being in favor of large-scale aid to India, misunderstandings had arisen as to India's political objectives and policies. America's misgivings about Indian foreign policy, particularly in relation to Communist countries, have affected the magnitude of and the conditions under which aid has been granted.

American aid policy toward India has passed through several stages and has been influenced by such factors as India's attitude to the Soviet Union and her satellite empire in Europe, her re-

[7] *Ibid.*, pp. 179–80.

peated pleas for the admission of Communist China into the United Nations, her attitude toward North Korea's invasion of South Korea and toward the Soviet Union's suppression of Hungary's revolt, her voting record in the United Nations, her domestic economic policy of a mixed economy—i.e., her desire to evolve a "socialist pattern of society," and, last but not least, her foreign policy of neutrality and nonalignment.

It is not necessary to examine all of these issues, but it should be mentioned that at no time has sympathy for India been lacking in the United States, either in the government or among the people at large. Aid to India and other underdeveloped nations has been national policy in the United States, not party policy. Although the American Aid Bill has become an annual hurdles race in Congress—a matter of unavoidable constitutional process—the question is not whether America should offer aid to the underdeveloped and needy countries, but to whom, how much, for what purpose, and under what conditions.

Of all the American criticisms leveled against India, perhaps the major one is that she is neutral in her foreign policy. To an American, no nation can be strictly neutral in the modern world. (As one American wit has asked of India, "Whose neutral is she?") Every issue, the American contends, has two sides, but one side happens to be right and the other wrong. If India is dedicated to freedom and democracy, as India maintains she is, then there should be no doubt on which side India stands. India cannot be an uncommitted nation, for she is committed to freedom and democracy: She fought for her independence and she has an effective parliamentary system. Further, she has gone on record as being opposed to Communism as a political philosophy and economic ideology for her internal needs. Why then does India waver between the East and the West?

India maintains, first, that as a sovereign republic her foreign policy is an independent one. If her policy appears to be aggressively independent, it is only a measure of the degree of her political freedom. And since a nation's foreign policy is based on nothing more than enlightened self-interest, India's attitude, which may appear to be anti-West, is in reality simply pro-Indian.

Second, India, like all emergent countries, is anxious to devote all her energies and resources to her internal economic and social development and reconstruction; she has no real interest in taking sides, no matter what the relative merits, on any international question. In fact, she would like to follow a policy of isolation so long as such a policy does not threaten her own immediate interests and well-being. (To this the Americans reply that they would have no quarrel with India if India were consistently isolationalist. But, they point out, India takes an active part in the United Nations on all major issues, and her pronouncements, not always neutral, are sometimes unfavorable to the West.)

Third, India passionately desires peace, for without peace she cannot progress and catch up with the advanced countries in providing a more civilized standard of living for her people. Since Communism cannot be "wished away," the only answer appears to be, according to India, a policy of coexistence.

The fourth factor is one of geography. The importance of the geographical foundations of a nation's foreign policy is obvious and cannot be overestimated. Facts of geography determine not only a nation's climate and culture, politics and philosophy, but also its neighbors. Unfortunately, a nation, unlike an individual, cannot choose her neighbors. India, like any other nation, wants to pursue a good-neighbor policy and hopes that such a policy will be reciprocated. The fact that she has on the north two large and powerful neighbors of an alien economic and political ideology conditions much of her thinking, particularly when one neighbor insists on following the law of the jungle. India's tolerant attitude toward external Communism might be very different if she were bordered by, say, Canada and the United States. By the same token, the foreign policy of the United States might be very different if Russia were where Canada is. These factors explain to a large extent India's nonalignment policy. An understanding of India's difficult geographical situation can only lead to an appreciation of her neutrality. In fact, the West ought to be surprised that India tries so hard to be neutral, for it might be easier for her to take a partisan attitude.

The United States, naturally enough, expects a kind word from India on occasion, but she seldom gets one. Indian political leaders, with a few exceptions, all praise the Soviet Union and Communist China, but seldom feel it necessary to refer kindly to the United States. No defense of this is possible: It is an old Indian attitude to take one's friends for granted and to go out of the way to be kind to those who are not one's friends. Perhaps India may be forced to realize some day that it is never wise to take one's friends for granted because friendship, like a plant, requires care and cultivation to bear fruit.

During the early years of the aid debate (1951–52), U.S. legislators complained that India showed neither sympathy for nor understanding of America's international problems and urged that aid to her be terminated. The following sentiments were expressed in the United States Congress during the 1952 debate on aid to India:

Congressman Davis of Georgia: [This] is not a technical-assistance program. [It] carries $50 million for steel . . . $10 million for fertilizer . . . 2,000 deep wells in the Ganges Delta. It is full of items like that. They jumped from $5 million [for India] in 1951 to $77 million in this bill.
Congressman Smith of Virginia: They talk about the fact that this is to make friends, this is to help keep our friends. If there is anybody in the House who has ever seen or heard that Nehru has ever made a statement favorable to the United States, I would like him to say so now.
Congressman Fulton of Pennsylvania: I will say it: yes.
Congressman Smith: I deny the statement. I do not believe he ever did. I never did see it.[8]

Congressmen Kennedy, Javits, and Fulton, all sympathetic to India, contested the views of Congressmen Davis and Smith, but the Davis amendment proposing the cut was adopted and the aid to India was reduced.

India's "Socialist Pattern of Society"

The second major American objection to large-scale aid to India arises from India's dedication to the evolution of a "socialist pattern of society." India has begun to move toward this goal by constantly enlarging the state-owned public sector and, according to some, stifling the private sector.

What is this "socialist pattern of society" that India wants? To begin with, let us get over some semantic hurdles. To some, all shades of socialism portend nothing less than totalitarian Communism. Britain, Sweden, India, Ceylon, Burma, Algeria, Ghana, and a host of other countries call, or would like to call, themselves socialistic, but none of these countries is considered socialistic by Russia and her satellites, who practice what they regard as the "true revealed socialism." To Communist China, however, Russia is no more socialistic than India or Japan is! On the other hand, the United States, which thinks of herself as an example of capi-

[8] *Congressional Record,* June 28, 1952, pp. 8551–52.

talism par excellence and a pillar of free enterprise, has a greater percentage of her economic activities under the public sector (20 per cent) than India (about 10 per cent), which boasts of pursuing a "socialist pattern of society."

To most of the world, the term "capitalism" is a pejorative one because of its nineteenth-century connotations, but the popular conception of capitalism has no relevance whatever to capitalism as practiced in the United States today. Similarly, the word "socialism" connotes something enlightened and progressive. The socialists claim that they alone are civilized and beg not to be confused with the totalitarian Communists. The Communists damn everyone else and contend that real socialism is their monopoly. Therefore, the present terminology is not only incorrect but extremely misleading. We need a new nomenclature. Even a careful definition of every term does not help because of the popular interpretations of the basic terms "capitalism," "democracy," "socialism," and so forth. It is obvious that there are different roads to socialism and there is a whole spectrum of Communist faiths.

It is unnecessary here to discuss the various leftist economic ideologies and philosophies. To India, the questions that matter are: Can we promote the welfare of every segment of our society? How can a welfare state be achieved within the framework of a parliamentary democracy? And what is the minimum price in terms of liberty and freedom of the individual that we are prepared to pay to achieve such a welfare state?

A categorical definition of the concept of the "socialist pattern of society" is nowhere to be found in Indian official political literature, although there are countless references to it in the reports of the three Five-Year Plans and in speeches of the Prime Minister and his colleagues. That there is no official definition is deliberate and intentional, for no one, from the Prime Minister to the official economists, desires to be dogmatic and doctrinaire about it. Indian socialism implies a progressive reduction in the tremendous economic inequality between the small minority of relatively rich people and the overwhelming majority of the poor. Second, it is to be achieved within the framework of a democratic and parliamentary system. And third, it is to be realized through legislation and not through revolution, through enlightened persuasion and not through violent compulsion.

The First Five-Year Plan, which was published in 1952, made the following observations on democratic planning and the role of the state:

The question of the techniques to be adopted for planning is linked up with the basic approach that a community decides to adopt for the realisation of its objectives. It is possible to have a plan based on regimentation and on immediate measures for levelling down in the hope ultimately of being able to level up. It is possible to take the view that mass enthusiasm cannot be created except on the basis of reprisals against those classes which have come to be associated in the public mind with the inequities and deficiencies of the old order. But the basic premise of democratic planning is that society can develop as an integral whole and that the position which particular classes occupy at any given time—a product of various historical forces for which no individual or class as such can be held responsible—can be altered without reliance on class hatreds or the use of violence. The need is to secure that the change is effected quickly and it is the positive duty of the State to promote this through all the measures at its command. The success of such planning no doubt depends on the classes in position of power and privilege respecting the democratic system and appreciating the rapid changes it calls for. It is clear that in the transformation of the economy that is called for the State will have to play the crucial role. Whether one thinks of the problem of capital formation or of the introduction of new techniques or of the extension of social services or of the overall realignment of the productive forces and class relationships within society one comes inevitably to the conclusion that a rapid expansion of the economic and social responsibilities of the State will alone be capable of satisfying the legitimate expectations of the people. *This need not involve complete nationalisation of the means of production or the elimination of private agencies in agriculture or business and industry.* It does mean, however, a progressive widening of the public sector and a reorientation of the private sector to the needs of a planned economy.[9]

The Indian National Congress at its Avadi (near Madras) session in 1955 resolved that "Planning should take place with a view to the establishment of a socialistic pattern of society where the principal means of production are under social ownership or control."[10]

A year later, this objective was reiterated in the Government of India's Industrial Policy Resolution:

The state will progressively assume a predominant and direct responsibility for setting up new industrial undertakings and for developing

[9] *The First Five-Year Plan* (New Delhi: Planning Commission, 1952), pp. 31–32.

[10] *The Hindu* (Madras), August 15, 1956.

> transport facilities. It will also undertake state trading on an increasing scale. . . . The adoption of the socialist pattern of society as the national objective, as well as the need for planned and rapid development, require that all industries of basic and strategic importance, or in the nature of public utility services, should be in the public sector.[11]

The Second Five-Year Plan returned to the same theme:

> The State has therefore to assume direct responsibility for the future development of industries over a wider area. Nevertheless, there are limiting factors which make it necessary at this stage for the State to define the field in which it will undertake sole responsibility for further development and to make a selection of industries in the development of which it will play a dominant role.[12]

While it is admitted that the foregoing statements on the "socialist pattern of society" are somewhat nebulous and vague, they are official and as such can be taken to be considered pronouncements. One of India's basic objectives is to develop a mixed economy in which private and public sectors will continue to coexist to promote the welfare of all sections of the Indian population. If *this* is the "socialist pattern of society," it is difficult to understand how it can be misunderstood, for it is similar to the mixed economies found in several advanced Western nations, though it may be called by a different name. To say the least, it is a far cry from Communism.

To understand India's mixed economy, certain historical factors in Indian economic development should be recalled. During the British raj, Indian capital was supposed to be "shy" and, by and large, was not forthcoming for investment in nonagricultural enterprises, including public utilities. In view of the lack of private funds and private enterprise, the British Government in India had to establish railroads, telegraph, telephones, road transport, electricity, and so forth, as government enterprises. Indians who are accustomed to this traditional public sector are surprised to find that, in the United States, railroads, telephones, and telegraphs are in the private sector.

Second, it should be remembered that the Indian belief in state control and public ownership of certain key and strategic industries is more functional than ideological. Let it not be forgotten

[11] Government of India, Press Release, November 22, 1956.

[12] *The Second Five-Year Plan* (New Delhi: Planning Commission, 1956), p. 45.

that even the public sector is very much under the scrutiny of parliament and the auditor general. Thus, India's socialism is rather unique in the sense that it operates in a parliamentary democracy with a written constitution, fundamental rights, a free and vocal press owned by the private sector, and a free judiciary.

Despite all this, some Americans (and the number is fortunately decreasing) feel that to aid India is to subsidize Indian socialism. The U.S. philosophy of free enterprise and minimum state intervention seems in direct opposition to India's economic philosophy. As knowledge of the nature of India's socialism spreads, however, and as Americans become more aware of the importance of the public sector in their own economy, this criticism against Indian planning has been heard less frequently.

There are other objections in the West to aiding Indian economic development, but these objections are based more on personal opinions than on technical or theoretical arguments. Professor Bauer, for instance, contends that the role of the state in India's economic development is largely, if not entirely, misconceived.[13] He points out that India, instead of expending its energies and resources on such valuable and immediate dividend-yielding sectors as agriculture and education, has gone in for state-owned heavy industries in a big way. Since these state-owned industries can make only theoretical profits (by the government buying its own products irrespective of price and demand), such industrialization, Professor Bauer concludes, is bound to be wasteful in the long run.

> The Plan [the Second Five-Year Plan] however, largely neglects agriculture, roads and education, subsidizes high-cost cottage industry, and throttles private investment in those branches of secondary industry where in the absence of restrictions there would be an extension of capacity. In these ways the Plan obstructs further the growth of the market for the capacity in heavy industries which it establishes.[14]

Professor Milton Friedman's objections are more or less of a similar nature. In a memorandum writen at the end of 1955, he observed that:

> The form of investment is no less important than its kind. The chief problem in the Indian program that impresses me here is the tendency to concentrate investment in heavy industry at the one ex-

[13] Bauer, *Indian Economic Policy and Development.*
[14] *Ibid.*, p. 58.

> treme and handicrafts at the other at the expense of small and moderate size industry. This policy threatens an inefficient use of capital at the one extreme by combining it with too little labor, and an inefficient use of labor at the other extreme by combining it with too little capital.[15]

Professor Friedman examines elsewhere certain basic questions concerning the means and objectives of U.S. foreign economic aid and reaches the negative conclusion that the objectives are misconceived and the means inappropriate. His disturbing conclusion is:

> Though foreign economic aid may win us some temporary allies, in the long run it will almost surely retard economic development and promote the triumph of Communism. It is playing into our enemies' hands and should be abolished. Instead we should concentrate on promoting world-wide economic development through means that are consonant with the American tradition itself—strengthening of free-market domestic economies in the less-developed nations, the removal of obstacles to private international trade, and the fostering of a climate favorable to international investment.[16]

Friedman raises all the familiar objections to foreign economic aid to such neutral, socialist-oriented, underdeveloped countries as India. American aid, he says, has primarily consisted of grants to the governments of the less-developed countries. "It has thereby tended to strengthen the role of the government sector in general economic activity relative to the private sector. Yet democracy and freedom have never been either attained or maintained except in communities in which the bulk of economic activity is organized through private enterprise.[17]

Perhaps his major objection against providing capital to the underdeveloped countries is based on what might be called the "pyramid-building habits" of the poor countries. Without even granting that the key to economic development is the availability of capital, which the less-developed countries are short of, or that centralized economic planning is necessary in less-developed countries simply because resources and technical know-how are limited and private enterprise and initiative wanting, Friedman

[15] Quoted in *ibid.*, p. 59.

[16] Milton Friedman, "Foreign Economic Aid: Means and Objectives," *The Yale Review*, Summer, 1958, p. 501.

[17] *Ibid.*, pp. 503–4.

objects to the way the capital provided by the United States is used by these countries:

> The Pharaohs raised enormous sums of capital to build the Pyramids; this was capital formation on a grand scale; it certainly did not promote economic development in the fundamental sense of contributing to a self-sustaining growth in the standard of life of the Egyptian masses. Modern Egypt has under government auspices built a steel mill; this involves capital formation; but it is a drain on the economic resources of Egypt, not a contribution to economic strength, since the cost of making steel in Egypt is very much greater than the cost of buying it elsewhere; it is simply a modern equivalent of the Pyramids except that maintenance expenses are higher.[18]

Although this is more or less true, in the current international economic and political climate nothing much can be done about it. If Friedman's contentions are that nationalism leaves much to be desired and the economic behavior of most underdeveloped nations is rather irrational, no one can dispute with him. Economic autarchy is incompatible with the philosophy behind international trade. Economic nationalism, no matter how costly and inefficient, cannot easily be given up, any more than a citizen's patriotic instincts can be changed. A steel plant has become a status symbol aspired for by many underdeveloped countries. No economic theory can persuade these countries to give up such aspirations. Once these nations get over the status-symbol stage, however, constructive economic development can get going. State-owned steel plants and international airlines are merely the signs of the times, deemed fashionable because they are "socialistic," dear to the hearts of the leaders who learned in colonial jails to hate the bad old word "capitalism." They represent a reaction to colonialism and capitalism, to political domination and economic exploitation. The underdeveloped countries are bound to have state-owned airlines and hotels, even if they are losing propositions—such is the strength of ideology. Ideological concepts, perpetuated by unenlightened semantics and intellectual orthodoxy, persist long after the economic basis for their existence disappears.

While Friedman's strictures are true of most less-developed countries, they are not true of India, for she has fairly large reserves of iron ore and matching reserves of coking coal. Besides, India has nearly a century of experience in making steel. With

[18] *Ibid.*, p. 631.

her available raw material, cheap but trained labor, and competent entrepreneurial ability, India is able to make relatively cheap steel and is in a position to export and compete in the world market. Friedman's objection, apparently, is that the steel mills are operated in the public sector.

One is not even sure that this is socialism. As Professor W. Arthur Lewis points out:

> This large role of government in financing capital formation is not entirely due to modern socialistic trends; it is due to a greater extent to the burden of initiative which falls upon governments in underdeveloped countries where entrepreneurs are scarce and risks large. Everyone looks to the government to pioneer, and to mobilize finance from somewhere. So it is not appropriate to compare the role of government in Africa or Asia with the role of government in the United States or Canada.[19]

The United States should give aid for aid's own sake. As a rich country, she should feel morally obliged to help in the development of the poor countries of the world.

Five Stages in American Aid to India

American aid to India during the fourteen years 1951–64 progressed from a substantial grant of food grains as an emergency measure in 1951 to the prompt supply of military equipment to resist the Communist Chinese at the end of 1962. A brief historical review of Indo-American aid relations during this period shows how the mutual suspicions of the two countries were gradually transformed into mutual respect for common interests and common differences.

The First Phase

In 1950, a year after the Communists had captured power in China, America had not quite got over the tragic and unhappy failure of her massive aid to Chiang Kai-shek and the Kuomintang. The political events and the general situation in the South Asian countries had not foreboded any such collapse as had occurred in China. There had been neither a request nor any clear need for U.S. aid to prevent a possible Communist takeover. Moreover, in January, 1950, the British Commonwealth ministers

[19] W. Arthur Lewis, "Helping Underdeveloped Countries," in *Problems of United States Economic Development* (New York: Committee for Economic Development, 1958), p. 140.

evolved what became known as the Colombo Plan to provide joint Commonwealth aid for economic development to countries in South and Southeast Asia, with the exception of Afghanistan. In view of India's food deficit, however, the U.S. made a small *ad hoc* grant of $4.5 million to buy food grains. This amount was made possible under the unobligated China aid funds, as authorized under the China Area Aid Act. Later, in 1950–51, the Indian food problem worsened, and it was feared that another famine might be approaching. India therefore requested substantial grain imports from the United States. Unfortunately, the U.S. Congress was still piqued over India's neutral role in the Korean War. After prolonged debate and some delay, Congress passed the India Emergency Food Aid Act of 1951, which enabled India to purchase food grains on a long-term loan of $190 million. Though the Act was passed in FY 1951 the actual expenditure was incurred in FY 1952. The allocation of funds for this help came not from the Mutual Security Program's funds but from a special authorization.

Unfortunately, this first stage of Indo-American aid relations got off to a bad start; it looked, for a time, as though the two countries were working at cross-purposes. Of the original demand, a cut of some 60 per cent was imposed by Congress. According to competent observers, two factors contributed to this cut. Charles Wolf gives a fair and sober appraisal of the situation:

> The first consideration concerned India's foreign policies, and more particularly its policy on Korea. Assertively independent in its foreign policies generally, India had abstained from the original Security Council resolution of June 27, 1950, that recommended U.N. military assistance to the Korean Republic to help it deter aggression. India had officially criticized MacArthur's crossing of the 38th Parallel, and Nehru and India's U.N. delegates repeatedly called for Communist China's admission to the U.N. both before and after its intervention in Korea. As might have been expected, India's reaction to U.N. resumption of the air war in Korea in the summer of 1952 was sharply critical, and came at precisely the time when the Mutual Security Appropriation Bill was under debate in the Congress.
>
> To some in the United States, and especially in the Congress, this record, coming as a sequel to the $190 million food loan of 1951–52, seemed more like partisan belligerence than neutrality. The Congressional reaction was to discount the Administration's arguments for expanding aid to India, and to reduce it instead. If India showed neither understanding nor sympathy toward America's international problems, what was the value to the United States of showing sym-

pathy and ever-increasing generosity to India's domestic problems?
The other consideration affecting aid to India arose from the constraints imposed by the legislation under which the program was authorized. Unlike the economic and technical aid programs in Southeast Asia, those in South Asia were carried out under the continuing authorization of the Act for International Development repeated each year in the annual Mutual Security Act. As we have previously discussed, the AID had been enacted and the original Point Four Program launched with unrestricted optimism concerning the returns to be expected from low-cost technical services. When the Administration's 1953 proposals plainly showed that the Act was to be used, at least in the special case of India and Pakistan, for undertaking programs of substantial capital assistance as well, Congressional reaction was sharply adverse.[20]

Thus the very first phase of Indo–U.S. aid relations was marked by certain perhaps unavoidable misunderstandings of each other's foreign policies. Neither America nor India can be blamed; the villain of the piece was the Korean War, for the war was responsible for America's preoccupation with mutual security and military alignments—a preoccupation that pushed the Point Four Program to the background. India is partly at fault for not being able to understand the sinister, silent, and treacherous enemy that China really was.

Despite the fact that Indo-American aid relations began during the tenure of Ambassador Chester Bowles, whose ebullient liberalism seemed to reflect the spirit of the Point Four Program, there were unfortunate misgivings and suspicions on both sides. Ambassador Bowles hoped to deliver many things to India, but the whole philosophy of aid changed in Washington with the change in Administrations, and the Ambassador was called home. India felt rather let down. As Dr. John P. Lewis rightly points out:

> The resulting disillusionment only enhanced New Delhi's disenchantment with Washington's new view that foreign assistance should be regarded primarily as an instrument for reinforcing positions of allied military strength around the periphery of the Communist world—a policy in which the Government of India saw, besides faults of principle, inflammatory local possibilities in its provision of American arms to Pakistan. This American aid posture, adopted largely by the Truman Administration, was consolidated and stiffened in the Dulles era. Most objectionable to Indian ears was the Secretary's statement that neutrality as to the Western-

[20] Wolf, *op. cit.*, p. 145.

Communist struggle was inherently immoral. Friction between the two governments also was compounded by the Government of India's particularly voluble and doctrinaire advocacy of public enterprise during the middle fifties, a position that especially grated on the nerves of the Eisenhower Administration, which felt morally committed to the promotion of private enterprise overseas.[21]

The Second Phase

With the establishment in 1952 of the Technical Cooperation Mission (now the Agency for International Development), American aid to India entered its second phase. The Technical Cooperation Mission's objective was to "aid the peoples of economically underdeveloped areas to develop their resources and improve their working and living conditions by encouraging the exchange of technical knowledge and skills." The purpose of all TCM projects was to help India develop her human resources with necessary knowledge and training, thereby to increase productivity and reduce bottlenecks resulting from lack of technical knowledge, shortage of necessary skills, and lack of organizational experience.

Technical cooperation has three components: (1) to supply American experts and personnel to work on specific technical and economic problems in the Indian development program. Each expert is assigned to work in a training, demonstration, or advisory capacity (with an Indian counterpart) in a government office, a manufacturing plant, a training or an educational institute, a research institution, a professional or trade society, or on a demonstration project in a rural area; (2) to train, in the United States or a third country, Indian personnel associated with the American-aided projects to impart to them the technical knowledge and skills that will enable them to make greater contributions to their country's development; (3) to supply certain materials, such as textbooks and laboratory equipment. These are to be used in conjunction with technical training in India, particularly in demonstration projects.

In 1952, Point Four assistance was extended to India along with Pakistan, Afghanistan, Nepal, and Ceylon. The Technical Cooperation Mission started its work in India in 1952 with only sixty-four American technicians and professional personnel. In the same year, Secretary of State Dean Acheson, while presenting the

[21] John P. Lewis, *Quiet Crisis in India* (Washington, D.C.: The Brookings Institution, 1962), p. 253.

case for economic aid and technical aid for India and Southern Asia, observed:

> Poverty, disease, illiteracy, and resentments against former colonial exploitations are our enemies. . . . They represent turbulent forces which the Communist exploits at every opportunity. To achieve our objective of helping the people of this area maintain independent governments friendly to us, we must understand these forces at work in Asia, and we must assure that the forces of nationalism and of the drive for economic improvement are associated with the rest of the free world instead of with Communism.[22]

During 1953 and 1954 the amount of aid to India was increased, by more than 20 per cent, for India was considered a special case. Assistance to other countries in Southern Asia was proportionately reduced.

The Third and Fourth Phases

The years 1954–57 witnessed the third stage in Indo-American aid relations. In 1957, "Development Assistance" was terminated, to be replaced by loans from the newly established Development Loan Fund (DLF) and also, eventually, from the Export-Import Bank of Washington. That year also the first sales agreement between India and the United States was signed. This and subsequent agreements, particularly under P.L. 480, gave a special and welcome significance to this new phase of American assistance to Indian economic development. The concept and nature of American assistance during this period widened to include large amounts of commodity aid. India began to receive from the United States a considerable amount of a wide variety of semi-finished and finished capital goods and raw materials. These for the major part were food grains, fertilizers, steel, and railway equipment. During this period, there was a steady increase also in the number of American technical personnel. By 1957, there were 207 American experts in India under the TCM.

The fourth phase of American aid to India began in 1957 when India was faced with foreign-exchange difficulties in her Second Five-Year Plan. This stage witnessed the beginnings of American participation in the international aid-for-India consortium under the leadership of the World Bank. The original members of the Aid India Club were the World Bank, the United States, the

[22] *Mutual Security Act of 1951,* Senate Hearings, p. 5. Washington, D.C., 1952.

United Kingdom, West Germany, France, Canada, and Japan. (To these must now be added Austria, Belgium, Italy, and the Netherlands.) It was at this stage of India's development planning that the consortium, under American initiative, tried to raise about $2.5 billion for India. The situation was changing: The United States had established the new Development Loan Fund in 1957, her interest in aiding India was no longer tied to military considerations, and the Indian democratic planning experiment began to attract a wide circle of influential friends in and outside of Congress. On the whole, the climate of the Indo-American aid relationship became bracing.

The Fifth and Current Phase

The year 1959 ushered in the fifth and current phase—the healthiest and happiest so far—in Indo-American aid relations. Laudable efforts on both sides have contributed to the growth of better understanding between the two countries. First, there has been an increasing awareness on the part of India of the soundness of the U.S. aid-to-India philosophy. As Ambassador Ellsworth Bunker, quiet, effective, and able, pointed out,

> We have found that to help others is often the best way to help ourselves to progress. Another motivating cause, deep rooted in the American tradition, stems from our earliest colonial days when we learned that mutual aid was often the price of survival. Still another reason, I think, is the fact that because the people of my country have come from many lands they have a concern for the problems of other people and other countries. There is a deep urge to assist those who have been less fortunate than we in achieving political or economic independence. We believe, too, that the aspirations of people for a fuller, more significant life can best be achieved under democratic institutions; that democracy is a force which holds possibilities of unlimited progress for mankind. It is in this belief and in this spirit that we in America are ready to join hands with you in India in your great effort to achieve a better life for all your people.[23]

Second, the tumultous reception given President Eisenhower in Delhi in 1959 revealed the average Indian's extraordinary appreciation of America's help and support to India.

Third, India's difficulties with Communist China on her north-

[23] Ellsworth Bunker in his Foreword to *India's New Horizons* (New Delhi: USIS, 1959).

ern frontier became widely known, and America's quiet and unobtrusive assurance of sympathy and help against the common enemy endeared her to India.

Fourth, the United States created a new post by combining the offices of the Economic Minister in the United States Embassy and the Director of TCM (now AID). The combination of these two posts into one has ensured a much-needed integration in the American aid operations in New Delhi. The appointment of an extremely able senior officer, sympathetic to India, C. Tyler Wood, to fill the post, has resulted in a high level of coordination and a single and effective source through which all aid requests from New Delhi can be channeled.

Fifth, the government of India and the Planning Commission appear to have conceded the importance of the role of private enterprise in Indian economic development. The government has begun to take a more pragmatic approach to foreign private capital. Although calls for the creation of a "socialist pattern of society" have not ceased, the nation's economic ills and the maldistribution of economic power are no longer piled exclusively at the door of the private sector.

This new attitude was partly responsible for the efforts of the government to attract private capital from abroad, particularly from the United States. With this end in view, the Indian Investment Centre was set up by the government and was officially inaugurated on February 16, 1961, in New Delhi by the then Indian Finance Minister, Shri Morarji Desai. It is an autonomous body with a Board of Governors. Shri G. L. Mehta, an Indian businessman, is its Chairman.

Its major objectives are: (1) to promote wider knowledge and understanding in the capital-exporting centers of the world of conditions, laws, policies, and procedures pertaining to investment opportunities in India; (2) to advise and assist Indian industrialists, including those engaged in medium and small industries, on matters necessary to attract foreign private capital and/or techniques; (3) to advise and assist foreign businessmen on matters pertaining to investment in India, and for this purpose, if necessary, to establish branch offices abroad. The first foreign branch was opened in New York in 1962; (4) to undertake surveys of foreign investment possibilities and studies in relation to particular industries; and (5) to undertake by the diffusion of such knowledge and information, implementation of programs designed to encourage and promote the flow of private capital into India in a manner most helpful to the Indian economy and the Indian Five-Year Plans.

The government of India, through the Indian Investment Centre, has publicized the incentives offered by India to foreign capital. The government believes that foreign private investment has a necessary and important role to play in the country's development plans and that it should receive all the facilities that the indigenous capital enjoys. These are: (1) No discrimination is made between Indian and foreign capital, once foreign capital is admitted into the country. The government, however, expects all undertakings, Indian or foreign, to conform to the general requirements of its industrial policy. (2) The government will continue to provide facilities for the remittance of profits, and no restrictions will be placed on the withdrawal of foreign capital investments. (3) If and when foreign enterprises are acquired, compensation will be paid on a fair and equitable basis. (4) As a rule, the major interest in ownership and effective control of an undertaking is to remain in Indian hands. There is, however, no rigid or doctrinaire insistence on this rule, for the government does not object to foreign capital having control of a concern if it is found to be in the national interest. Each individual case is to be considered on its own merits. (5) The government does not object to the employment of non-Indians in technical posts when Indians of comparable qualifications are not available. However, the government expects and hopes that suitable Indians will be trained to fill such posts in the shortest possible period.[24]

Sixth, the election of John F. Kennedy to the Presidency and his appointment of a distinguished Harvard economist, John Kenneth Galbraith, as American Ambassador to India raised Indian hopes for a more sympathetic policy in the United States toward foreign aid to India, for both President Kennedy, as a Senator, and Professor Galbraith had gone on record as being in favor of large-scale aid to India. Galbraith had earlier visited India and studied Indian economic problems with special reference to the Five-Year Plans, and he was impressed with the progress that India had registered. As Ambassador, he was successful in promoting closer relations between India and the United States. The appointment of his successor, Chester Bowles, the present Ambassador, was also welcomed by Indians. Bowles, in his 1951–53

[24] *Investing in India: Indian Investment Centre* (New Delhi, 1961), p. 13.

tenure as American Ambassador to India, had proved immensely popular. The government of India could not have hoped for a better friend or a more dedicated liaison officer between the two countries.

Seventh, Communist China's massive and unprovoked attack on India's northern frontiers in October, 1962, had two immediate results: national integration in India and closer and more sympathetic collaboration between India and the United States. The common enemy made the Indians forget to some extent their internal differences based on caste, language, and religion. They rose as one man to defend India's sacred soil and sovereignty. The United States rushed military aid to strengthen the Indian army in defending the country's frontiers. India's request for military aid was received warmly and supplied promptly, and India has reason, in view of the unfortunate past relations vis-à-vis Communist China, to be grateful to America both for the aid and for not saying "we told you so."

4. *AMERICAN AID AND INDIAN AGRICULTURE*

The Peasant: His Problems and His Prospects

The plight of the Indian peasant has been drawn only too often. His poverty is both a cause and a consequence of his station in life. He is illiterate and suffers from poor health. He lives in a squalid mud hut devoid of hygiene and sanitation. His food, despite the fact that he is the primary producer, is coarse and unnutritious. He is in chronic debt to the state, the landlord, when there is one, or the local moneylender. The monetary demands made on him by his social and religious obligations—marriages, festivals, and funerals—accentuate his financial misery.

The land he cultivates is in an equally miserable condition, unless he is fortunate enough to own an irrigated section of it. Over the years, thanks to the steady growth of population and the traditional Hindu laws of inheritance, the land has been fragmented and subdivided into numerous, uneconomic patches. Cultivated in a primitive and unscientific fashion, it has lost much of its inherent fertility: It has been giving for centuries without receiving anything in return. The monsoon determines the peasant's destiny; drought or deluge, the peasant suffers. When the monsoon fails, famine stalks the land; thus, his crop is a gamble in the rains. Erosion is a major problem, crop rotation is not the common rule, and, in some areas, there are no fertilizers, natural or artificial.

The ecology of the Indian cultivator does not brighten the picture. The types of land tenure, despite recent progressive legislation, range from near-agrarian slavery and share-cropping to peasant proprietorship. Landless tenancy seems to be the lot of the majority of the world's farmers, and India is no exception. Rural credit must cover the cost not only of seeds, plows, manure, fertilizers, cattle, and fodder, but also of marriages and funerals.

These problems, however, are not insoluble. They can be met with the aid of soil conservation, afforestation, irrigation, better implements, better seeds, the use of organic and inorganic fertilizers, better control of pests, fewer but better livestock, the consolidation of holdings, and the creation of rural credit facilities. The implementation of these apparently simple reforms would require nothing short of a social and economic revolution in the countryside, but without such a revolution the Indian farmer will never come up to American, Danish, or Swedish standards of productivity and prosperity. To accomplish this revolution, our present efforts must be multiplied a thousandfold.

All efforts at agricultural development in the underdeveloped countries can be grouped under two broad categories: measures that contribute toward an increase in the yield per acre, and measures that help to bring new land under cultivation.

The yield per acre and the yield per head of agricultural population differ rather widely from country to country and between regions within a country. The yield depends largely on the condition of the soil, the climate, the rainfall, and the technological stage of the art of farming. The differences in yield per acre between, say, the United States and India are impressive and understandable in view of the great cultural and technological differences between these two countries. There are some significant differences between the Asian countries themselves. For example, Japan raises twice as many food crops per acre as China, and China's yield is nearly double that of India. If the yield per acre in each of these countries is taken to be representative of the average fertility of the land, the differences in output become all the more striking, since there are no major institutional or technological differences in farming practices between India, China, and Japan. The problem is to make an acre in India yield as much as an acre in Japan and eventually to make it yield as much as an acre in the United States, Canada, or Sweden.

Even in a country of advanced agricultural practices, such as the United States, the last word on agricultural development has not been said. Recently, Dr. Charles E. Kellogg of the U.S. Department of Agriculture asserted that the yield per acre in the United States could be considerably increased and that American farmers are not yet making full use of the materials and techniques readily available to them. How the adoption of hybrid corn has increased the yield per acre in the United States corn belt by as much as a fifth is well known. If the same can be done on lands where yields are already high, it should be possible to do at least as well in such low-yielding areas as India. Tables 2 and 3 compare yields per acre and per capita in India and nine other countries and show the very low productive capacity of both farmers and land in India:

TABLE 2

COMPARISON OF FOOD CROP YIELDS, 1950

Crop	*Country*	*Percentage of World Production*	*Yield per Capita (in lbs.)*	*Yield per Acre (in lbs.)*
Rice	Burma	3.6	686	1,216
	China	31.8	n.a.	2,248
	India	19.6	185	1,048
	Japan	7.9	318	3,821
Wheat	Australia	3.6	1,484	909
	Canada	7.5	1,832	979
	India	3.8	3	591
	Pakistan	2.3	100	733
	U.S.	24.9	538	1,079
Raw sugar (cane and beet)	Cuba	20.0	2,622	4,567
	India	5.7	33	3,063
	Mauritius	1.2	1,956	6,132
	Pakistan	5.2	31	3,100
	U.S.	5.2	25	3,701

SOURCE: *India in World Economy* (New Delhi: Government of India, 1950).
n.a. not available

As the accompanying tables indicate, India occupies a rather unsatisfactory position in world agricultural production. Both the per capita yield (probably due to the large population) and per acre yield are comparatively low. But the soil cannot be blamed, for, during the period 1950–61, when relatively better methods of cultivation were adopted and more fertilizers employed, there is unmistakable evidence of improvement in India's agricultural yield, despite heavy fluctuations from year to year. (See Table 4.) The cumulative rate of growth was about 3.5 per cent per annum and was much higher than in any previous decade. The decade 1940–50 produced an average annual yield of food grains of 50 million tons, a figure that increased year by year. The yield in 1960–61 was 76 million tons. These figures strongly suggest that, with intensive cultivation, more chemical fertilizers, and greater irrigation facilities, the cultivated land in India is capable of yielding much more than it does at present.

TABLE 3
COMPARISON OF FOOD CROP YIELDS, 1962

Crop	*Country*	*Percentage of World Production*	*Yield per Acre (in lbs.)*
Rice	Burma	5.2	1,453
	China	n.a.	n.a.
	India	34.6	1,351
	Japan	10.4	4,199
Wheat	Australia	3.1	1,020
	Canada	3.3	660
	India	5.1	780
	Pakistan	1.8	680
	U.S.	15.8	1,440
Raw sugar (cane and beet)	Cuba	7.5	5,400
	India	5.8	3,775
	Mauritius	1.2	6,009
	Pakistan	n.a.	3,080
	U.S.	10.1	4,840

SOURCE: *World Agricultural Production and Trade: Statistical Report* (Washington, D.C.: Department of Agriculture, 1963).
n.a. not available

Measures should be taken to bring new land under the plow. Although there is no "new" land as such in India, there is, according to official statistics of the pattern of land utilization, some "cultivable but uncultivated" land available. This land is neither fertile nor easily accessible for settlement. It is no doubt near-barren, and it probably demands more than the usual investment to make it productive. But in view of the country's persistent food shortage, no land other than fallow and forest can be left un-

TABLE 4
INDEX NUMBERS OF AGRICULTURAL PRODUCTION
(1949/50 = 100)

Group	*1950/51*	*1955/56*	*1960/61*
All crops	96	117	135
Food crops	91	115	131
Other crops	106	120	142

SOURCE: *The Third Five-Year Plan—A Draft Outline* (New Delhi: Planning Commission, 1960), p. 17.

cultivated—no matter how great an investment is needed. Table 5 shows the pattern of land usage in India according to the official cadastral surveys.

TABLE 5

PATTERN OF LAND UTILIZATION IN INDIA, 1950 AND 1960
(*In Millions of Acres*)

	1950/51	*1959/60*
Total area	806.3	806.3
Total area for which statistics are available	702.5	726.1
Forests	100.0	130.1
Not available for cultivation	117.4	114.7
Other uncultivated land, excluding fallow lands	122.2	97.4
Fallow lands	69.5	59.8
Net area sown	293.4	324.1
Total cropped area, including area sown more than once	325.9	372.8

SOURCE: *India: 1963* (New Delhi: Ministry of Information and Broadcasting, 1964), p. 201.

American aid to Indian agriculture revolves around the twin approach of making cultivated land yield double or treble, and of bringing all the available cultivable and near-cultivable land under the plow. This twin approach could transform Indian agriculture from a losing, pathetic, traditional way of life into a commercial, economic, and successful proposition.

U.S. assistance to Indian agricultural development has touched almost every major area of rural reconstruction. However, only a few significant projects that reveal how the aid has been crucial in attacking certain fundamental defects in Indian agriculture will be examined here.

Supplying Food to India

Of the total U.S. aid to India since her independence in 1947 over one-half has been in the form of P.L. 480 Food for Peace Commodities. In 1962, the total amount of these American-supplied agricultural commodities was the equivalent of 160 pounds of food grains for every man, woman, and child in India, amounting to some 30 rupees for every inhabitant in India. This impressive agricultural aid has come to India through the India Wheat Loan of 1951; Section 402 of the Mutual Security Act (Public Law 665); and Public Law 480, Titles I, II, and III. Tables 6 and 7 present the various commodities received by India and their value in dollars and rupees under each of these agreements.

TABLE 6

VALUE OF AMERICAN AGRICULTURAL COMMODITIES COVERED BY AGREEMENTS WITH INDIA, 1951–61

(In Millions of Dollars)

India Wheat Loan of 1951	189.7
Section 402 of Mutual Security Act (P.L. 665)	67.8
P.L. 480, Title I	
First agreement, August 29, 1956	354.5
Second agreement, June 23, 1958	55.3
Third agreement, September 26, 1958	259.8
Fourth agreement, November 13, 1959	297.9
Fifth agreement, May 4, 1960	1,369.8
Sixth agreement, May 1, 1962	39.3
Seventh agreement, November 26, 1962	46.6
Eighth agreement	5.1
P.L. 480, Title II	4.9
Miscellaneous relief grants	5.5
P.L. 480, Title III	116.8
Total	2,813.0

SOURCE: *Food for Peace* (Madras: USIS, 1962).

The Wheat Loan. Almost two-thirds of all U.S. assistance to India since fiscal year 1951 comes under the Food for Peace Program. The first instance of American aid being extended to India was in August, 1950, when a grant of $4.5 million to purchase American food grains was offered during a food shortage. The grant was authorized under the China Area Aid Act of 1948.

When India's food shortage became critical again early in 1951, India requested more assistance. Congress passed the India Emergency Food Aid Act of 1951 and approved, under this legislation, the first loan to India in June, 1951. The loan, $189.7 million (Rs. 90.3 crores), was given to India for the purpose of financing the purchase of 2 million tons of wheat from the United States. The loan, with 2.5 per cent interest, is repayable in dollars. The Act provides, however, that the first $5 million of interest paid by India is to be turned back to her for the rehabilitation and development of her universities and institutions of higher learning. The United States Information Service administered this project, known as the India Wheat Loan Educational Exchange Program. For details, see Chapter 7.

TABLE 7

COMPOSITION OF AGRICULTURAL COMMODITIES COVERED BY U.S. AGREEMENTS WITH INDIA, 1951–61[a]

Commodity	*Unit*	*Quantity Stipulated in Agreements*	*Quantity Imported by India Through June, 1961*
Wheat and flour			
Wheat Loan of 1951	Ton	2,000,000	2,000,000
Section 402 of Mutual Security Act	"	636,000	636,000
Five agreements under P.L. 480, Title I	"	26,400,000	13,230,000
P.L. 480, Title II	"	10,000	10,000
Total wheat and flour	"	29,046,000	15,876,000
Rice			
P.L. 480, Title I	"	1,580,000	639,000
P.L. 480, Title II	"	10,000	10,000
Total rice	"	1,590,000	649,000
Corn and sorghum			
P.L. 480, Title I	"	832,000	832,000
Total food grains	"	31,468,000	17,357,000
Cotton			
Section 402 of Mutual Security Act	U.S. bale	86,000	86,000
P.L. 480, Title I	"	1,150,000	1,150,000
Total cotton	"	1,236,000	1,236,000
Tobacco			
P.L. 480, Title I	Ton	4,000	4,000
Non-fat dry milk			
P.L. 480, Title I	"	24,000	24,000
P.L. 480, Title II	"	4,000	4,000
Total non-fat dry milk	"	28,000	28,000
Soybean oil			
P.L. 480, Title I	"	3,000	3,000

SOURCE: *Food for Peace* (Madras: USIS, 1963).

[a] This table does not include commodities imported under Title III of P.L. 480 and "miscellaneous relief grants" given to India in 1951.

Mutual Security Act: Section 402. In 1955, the Mutual Security Act (Public Law 665) was amended so that a portion of U.S. technical and financial aid to India could be supplied in the form of agricultural commodities. Under Section 402, 636,000 tons of wheat and 18,000 tons of cotton worth $67.8 million (Rs.32.3 crores) were supplied to India during U.S. fiscal years 1955, 1956, and 1957.

The rupee proceeds from the sales of these commodities were to be spent on certain mutually agreed-upon development projects. Of the proceeds, Rs.40 million have been earmarked for a number of technical-cooperation missions, for the visits of Indians to the United States, and for the salaries of American technical personnel in India. Another Rs.198 million were credited to the Rihand Dam Project, discussed in Chapter 5.

Under the Mutual Security Act, the U.S. Government also assists private American aid by paying the ocean freight for relief shipments of nonsurplus agricultural commodities. As of the beginning of 1960, American philanthropic and voluntary agencies had purchased $5.7 million worth of supplies and equipment and shipped it to India at the expense of the U.S. Government.

Public Law 480. The Agricultural Trade Development and Assistance Act (P.L. 480), enacted in July, 1954, did not come into operation in Southern Asia until U.S. fiscal year 1956. Under Title I of P.L. 480, the President is authorized to sell agricultural commodities for foreign currencies (not necessarily surplus agricultural commodities, for the foreign purchasers may buy from the most advantageous source in the United States).[1] Title II permits the free donation of supplies by the President to foreign countries to meet famine and other urgent relief requirements. Title III permits U.S. agricultural commodities to be used (a) for bartering in exchange for strategic and other raw materials, and (b) for donation to nonprofit, voluntary agencies that assist needy persons both in and outside the United States. The Cooley amendment to P.L. 480 sets aside 25 per cent of the sales proceeds under Title I for loans to private industry.

TITLE I. India signed her first agreement with the United States under P.L. 480 in August, 1956. The total value of commodities actually imported under this first agreement was $354.55 million. A second agreement for wheat and other grains valued at $55.28 million was signed in June, 1958; a third agreement, signed only three months later, came to $259.81 million worth of supplies; in November, 1959, a fourth agreement, involving 2,997,000 metric

[1] Section (d) under Title I allows a portion of the local-currency sales proceeds to be set aside for buying goods and services for friendly countries. United States "triangular trade" transactions include purchases for India of Japanese electrical goods, clay products, and fertilizers with Japanese yen, French francs, and Italian lira. These products are resold in India and the sales proceeds contribute toward supporting U.S. operations in India (total $6 million as of 1962).

tons of wheat, 210,000 metric tons of rice, 350,000 bales of cotton, 226 metric tons of tobacco, and 100,000 metric tons of coarse grains, valued at $29.787 million, was signed. The fifth, representing the biggest agricultural-commodities agreement ever signed between any two countries, was concluded in May, 1960. It supplied India during 1960–64 with 16 million tons of wheat and 1 million tons of rice. The total value of the fifth agreement comes to $1,370 million. The total value of Indian imports from the United States under these five agreements amounted to $2,337 million, through 1960. Three more agreements have since been signed under Title I, bringing the total value to $2,428.3 million.

TITLE II. Under this title, India received donations for relief in emergency years 1956 and 1957 of 10,000 tons each of wheat and rice and 3,000 tons of dry milk, with a total value of $4.9 million (Rs.2.3 crores). In October, 1961, India received a gift of 1,250 short tons of dry milk for her flood victims.

TITLE III. As of August 31,1961, India received, in donations, $161.8 million worth of food grains, milk powder, and other agricultural commodities. These were distributed to the poor and needy by voluntary agencies. Through the Cooperative for American Relief Everywhere (CARE), the American people donated Rs.3 crores in 1961–62 to assist the School Mid-day Meals Project in Madras State. When Ambassador Galbraith turned over the first CARE shipment of dry milk to the Chief Minister of Madras State, he addressed those assembled for the ceremony as follows:

> There can be little question that a noon-day meal does more to ensure school attendance than the most efficient officers. . . . It is good that we have light in our lamps. It is even better that we have light in our children's eyes. I hope that those who look at the power plants and transmission lines of the Five Year Plans will also spare a glance for children who are better fed and better read as the result of the progressive vision of the people of Madras.[2]

More than 1 million school children studying in 27,000 schools in Madras State receive free lunches under the Mid-day Meals Project. According to Dr. Allan Kline, the Director of CARE in India, the project is the largest of its kind in the world.

In October, 1961, Ambassador Galbraith inaugurated a similar

[2] *Food for Peace* (Madras: USIS, 1962), p. 8.

project for free lunches in Kerala State schools; he announced at that time that American commodities will also be made available to schools in the Punjab. Since then, CARE school-feeding programs have also been initiated in the states of Andhra Pradesh and Rajasthan. Some 4 million school children benefit by the program in these five states.

The only difference between India's purchase of food grains under P.L. 480 and normal commercial purchases is that the purchase is made out of funds subsequently placed at India's disposal by the United States. Eighty-seven per cent of the sales proceeds under P.L. 480 go toward the economic development of India. One-third of the proceeds are given as grants; a larger portion is loaned to the Indian Government for development projects; and 6.9 per cent of the total is loaned to private industry. The remaining one-eighth of the total supports U.S. Government agencies in India.

As of October 31, 1961, Rs.570.1 crores had accumulated from the sales of agricultural commodities, of which Rs.475.6 crores have been allocated for loans and grants to the Indian Government and private enterprise.

P.L. 480: GRANTS. Apart from agriculture, P.L. 480 grants as of December 31, 1961, were given for health (malaria eradication, Rs.8 crores, All-India Institute of Medical Sciences, Rs.2.90 crores); industry (Indian Institute of Technology, Rs.0.45 crores, Indian Investment Center, Rs.0.22 crores, craftsmen training, Rs.1.0 crore), transportation (national highways, Rs.20 crores); and higher technical education (Rs.2.0 crores). Rs.5.94 crores has been donated to river-valley development schemes.

Grants to agriculture are a double form of aid, for the money is derived from the sales of food greatly needed in India to prevent inflation of food prices. The Uttar Pradesh Agricultural University, the Dairy Development, Soil and Water Conservation Program, and the Exploration of Groundwater Resources Project have all benefited from P.L. 480 grants.

The Third Five-Year Plan (1961–66) includes the establishment of fifty-five new milk-supply projects. The United States has provided equipment for a milk-processing plant and three milk-collection centers near Amritsar (the Punjab); three rural creameries at Aligarh (Uttar Pradesh), Barauni (Bihar), and Junagadh (Gujarat); pasteurizing and bottling plants at Bhopal (Madhya Pradesh) and Trivandrum (Kerala); and milk-supply schemes at

Balgachia (West Bengal) for greater Calcutta. P.L. 480 funds (Rs.3.6 crores) have been allocated to fifteen additional milk projects and will cover the entire estimated cost for two years of India's Third Five-Year Plan. A number of American dairy experts have also been made available by the U.S. Technical Cooperation Mission for dairy-development projects in India.

Soil erosion is a serious problem in India. By proper soil conservation, the amount of silt filling up the reservoirs of river-valley projects can be reduced and the useful life of reservoirs can be greatly increased. Floods can be controlled and moderated, and timber and fuel resources can be increased. A grant of Rs.2 crores from P.L. 480 funds met costs during the first two years of the Third Five-Year Plan for the conservation of 1,140,000 acres in the various catchment areas. It is estimated that 15 million acres of the 37 million in the various river-valley projects will require soil conservation. American advisers have been assigned to the Central Conservation Board of the Ministry of Food and Agriculture, as well as to seven research and training centers around the country.

India today uses, for irrigation, about 20 per cent of the underground water annually available. The Technical Cooperation Mission has allocated $18,644,842 for the construction of 3,000 tube wells in Uttar Pradesh, Bihar, and Punjab states.[3] The funds were used for technical assistance and specialized equipment needed for the projects. Under a second TCM agreement, 287 exploratory wells were sunk in various states with the aid of $4 million worth of United States equipment and assistance in the training of a large number of Indian personnel. On October 31, 1961, a grant of Rs.80 lakhs (8 million rupees) was made available from P.L. 480 funds to cover the cost of 200 exploratory tube wells.

P.L. 480: LOANS. The bulk of P.L. 480 loans has been made to twelve river-valley projects that will develop power resources and provide irrigation in Andhra Pradesh, Bihar, Bombay, Madras, Mysore, Orissa, Rajasthan, and Uttar Pradesh. These projects are expected to provide 1.4 million kilowatts of power as well as abundant water for the irrigation of more than 11 million acres. Besides Rs.5.9 crores in grants, the projects have been given loans of Rs. 124.1 crores under P.L. 480. Table 8 breaks down the total Rs.130 crores distributed.

[3] A tube well is about 300 feet deep and 16 inches in diameter. It is powered by an electric or diesel pump and can irrigate about 300 acres a year.

TABLE 8

AMERICAN AID TO RIVER-VALLEY PROJECTS IN INDIA, 1951–63

(*Amount in Crores of Rupees*)

Project		
Chambal (Rajasthan)	27.1	
Hirakud (Orissa)	4.6	
Damodar Valley (Bihar, West Bengal)	7.5	
Mahi Right Bank Canal (Bombay)	2.0	
Kakrapara (Bombay)	3.0	
Nagarjunasagar (Andhra)	29.5	
Kosi (Bihar)	17.0	
Bhadra (Mysore)	7.9	
Tungabhadra (Andhra Pradesh)	7.1	
Mahanadi Delta Irrigation (Orissa)	5.2	
Kundah (Madras)	7.6	
Koyna (Bombay)	11.4	
Total	130.0	($273,210,000)

SOURCE: *Indo-U.S. Aid Programme* (New Delhi: USIS, 1964).

In addition to P.L. 480 rupee loans and grants, the Agency for International Development supplied $70,000 worth of technical assistance to river-valley projects, as well as a grant of $14 million for the purchase of heavy construction equipment; the Development Loan Fund extended a credit of $32.4 million for the projects. A brief examination of a few of these river-valley projects is necessary to obtain an idea of their significance in the over-all development of Indian agriculture.

The Kosi is Bihar's "river of sorrow." It causes considerable damage to life and property by continually changing its course. Flowing through one of the most densely populated areas of the country, the river's wandering torrents destroy many lives and devastate the land and crops during virtually every monsoon season. A three-stage project has been designed to harness the river's unruly floods and channel them to irrigate some 1.5 million acres of parched land. First, a barrage, completed in June, 1962, was built across the Kosi River about three miles above Hanumannagar in Nepal. The second unit of construction, embankments 150 miles long, have been completed. The third stage, the Eastern Kosi Canal, is now being built to divert water from the barrage. When the entire project is completed, the Kosi's turbulent waters will not only have been controlled but will contribute to the fertility of Bihar's soil.

The Damodar Valley Project has been designed to some extent

on the lines of the famous Tennessee Valley Authority in the United States. It consists of three thermal-power stations at Bokaro (Bihar), Durgapur (West Bengal), and Chandrapura (Bihar)—the last two financed entirely by American loans—four storage dams, an extensive power-transmission grid, and an irrigation barrage at Durgapur. The Durgapur barrage will irrigate nearly 1 million acres. From P.L. 480 funds, Rs.7.5 crores have been loaned to this project.

The tallest and widest masonry dam in the world is being built across the Krishna River at Nagarjunasagar in Andhra Pradesh with the help of a loan of Rs.29.5 crores from P.L. 480 funds. The reservoir will have the largest storage capacity of any in India (9.3 million acre feet) and will render the irrigation of some 20.6 million acres possible. It is estimated that as a result of this irrigation the increased food is likely to amount to 800,000 tons.

At Hirakud in Orissa State, the world's longest mainstream dam is being built across the River Mahanadi. The United States has granted a loan of Rs.9.8 crores toward the construction of this dam. The reservoir will contain 6.6 million acre feet of water and it will make possible the irrigation of some 570,000 acres in the Sambalpur and Bolangir districts in Orissa State.

A P.L. 480 loan has also been extended to the government-owned Trombay Fertilizer Factory in Bombay. Rs.13.4 crores are expected to meet the local costs of the plant, which began operating in 1962–63. The factory's production of 97,500 tons of urea and 254,000 tons of nitrophosphate fertilizers will save India about Rs.12 crores of foreign exchange now being spent annually to import fertilizers. The factory has also been credited $30 million from the Development Loan Fund for the import of equipment.[4]

Technical Cooperation Mission. Apart from the $4.5 million grant to meet India's food crisis in August, 1950, and the Wheat Loan of 1951, the history of U.S. aid to India begins in fiscal year 1951 with the activities of the Technical Cooperation Mission. The primary purpose of technical aid is to increase productivity by developing India's human resources. Through joint projects initiated by the government of India and approved by the Ministry of Finance and the U.S. Technical Cooperation Mission (now the Agency for International Development), Indians acquire techni-

[4] This is the only direct contribution of the Development Loan Fund to agriculture, although it has extended loans for the import of steel to be used in the public and private sector—steel essential to agricultural projects.

cal knowledge, skills, and organizational experience in both India and the United States.

The government of India contributes toward rupee costs involved in the projects, such as the cost of local construction, domestic transport, salaries of American personnel in India, and living expenses of Indians sent abroad for training. On the request of the Indian Government, the United States contributes American experts in a training, demonstration, or advisory capacity for specific technical and economic projects. The United States also provides training facilities for Indians either in America or other countries outside of India. When necessary, a limited amount of supplies and equipment is provided for demonstrations and training purposes by American technicians in India.

In the first eleven years of the development program (fiscal years 1952–62), the United States sent a total of 1,593 technicians and experts to India. More than one-third of these were sent for projects in agriculture and natural resources. In the same period, more than 3,000 Indians went abroad for training; of these, 846 to study agriculture.

Since these numbers represent only a drop in the bucket, "training of trainers" has been emphasized in recent years. The Uttar Pradesh Agricultural University, whose program is described on pp. 99ff., was established in 1958 as an institute where teaching and research would be coordinated to meet the diverse requirements of agricultural development in India.

Between 1951 and 1952, United States economic and technical aid doubled in Southern Asia. "Obligations in India, which in 1951 were just $5 million, or 7 per cent of the regional total, in 1952 were nearly $53 million, or 35 per cent of the regional total."[5] Most of this was in the form of technical aid. Because the accent of the First Five-Year Plan was on agriculture, the first project agreed upon after the signing of the Indo-American Technical Cooperation Agreement in January, 1952, was the acquisition and distribution of fertilizers. Under this agreement, $17,307,000 was obligated to India. Since that time, technical cooperation has touched upon almost every aspect of agricultural and natural-resources development in India.

The importance of fertilizers for India's agricultural output can hardly be exaggerated. The yield per acre of India's overworked, handkerchief plots of land is very low. In relation to that of China

[5] Wolf, *op. cit.*, p. 127.

and Japan, it is expressed by the ratio 1:2:3. The best natural fertilizer, cattle manure, is used for fuel. Since 1951, however, India's Sindri Fertilizer Plant has made rapid strides. During the First Five-Year Plan, the plant was producing 300,000 tons of nitrogenous fertilizers; production is expected to exceed 1 million tons by the end of 1966. Production of phosphatic fertilizers is expected to increase from 67,000 tons in 1960 to 400,000 tons by the end of 1966.

Under the Indo-American aid program, fertilizers were imported and distributed to farmers. Proceeds from fertilizer sales were credited to a separate fund for the acquisition of certain other types of fertilizers for demonstration purposes and for a survey of the Sindri plant. A contract to expand this plant has been entered into by the government of India.

In 1952–53, 215,000 tons of fertilizer were imported. The program in 1954 was concerned only with importing new types of fertilizer—5,000 tons of urea and 5,000 tons of ammonium sulphate-nitrate—to be tested under Indian conditions. In 1955, 44,000 long tons of fertilizer, including urea, ammonium sulphate, sulphate-nitrate, and nitro-chalk (calcium ammonium nitrate), were imported for use, and an additional 14,500 tons for demonstration purposes. In 1956, 400,000 cultivator demonstrations were conducted to acquaint Indian farmers with the importance of phosphorous for crop fertilization; during the same year, 4,250 tons of fertilizers were distributed free to farmers.

Whereas fertilizers are important, the soil to be fertilized and the seeds to be planted in it are important too. The All-India Soil Testing Service has been sponsored by the Technical Cooperation Mission from the very beginning; twenty-four laboratories are now in operation, and demonstrations are given to agricultural extension workers in various training centers. Two three-month courses were held on the use of atomic energy for agriculture at the Indian Agricultural Research Institute. The American conservation experts assigned to the Central Conservation Board of the Ministry of Food and Agriculture at New Delhi have introduced hybrid seed for maize and sorghum, and the TCM has assisted in setting up, in Coimbatore, a collection of the 1,200 varieties of sugar cane available in the world. Thus, all known sugar protoplasm is available to Indian plant breeders. Annually since 1955 the TCM has tested American hybrid seeds in the Punjab and other states and has shown through these tests that food production can be increased in those areas.

Under the third TCM agreement, $556,000 was obligated for plant protection and locust control. Coordinated locust-control plans are carried out on a regional as well as a national scale by the United Nations Food and Agriculture Organization. India receives aid from the United States and the United Nations; in turn, she aids other countries in fighting the pest.

India's Central Anti-locust Unit has many skilled entomologists who attack locust swarms with many techniques—both ancient and modern. The Indo-American project augmented existing facilities by supplying jeeps, power sprayers, and wireless communication sets. The project was expanded to cover other forms of plant protection, and, in 1954, fumigants were provided to demonstrate how to protect stored grain.

India's irrigation program has received TCM assistance through its participation in tube-well, river-valley development, and ground-water exploration projects. Another project (Water Resources Survey and Minor Irrigation) received $414,000 toward the purchase of equipment outside India for use in surface-water studies. In order to collect basic data on rainfall, stream flow, underground water, and so forth, a survey was made in the states of Hyderabad, Madhya Pradesh, and Maharashtra. The equipment necessary for this survey—current meters, sounding reels, sump pumps, casing pipe, and earth-moving equipment—was provided by the TCM.

TCM aid went also to a project in Agricultural Information Production and Training designed mainly to provide equipment for the All-India Agricultural Information Program, which employs about 15,000 village extension workers in community projects. These workers need reference material and audio-visual production and teaching aids to relay information on the latest agricultural findings. TCM support was also extended to the Indian Council of Agricultural Research, which is the centre for coordinating and supervising the agricultural-information program. Through fiscal year 1959, $400,000 from TCM was designated for these purposes.

With the aid of U.S. agricultural experts, a study was made of research, education, and public administration in agricultural economics. Equipment from outside India needed for research in agricultural economics, such as calculators, card punchers, tabulators, verifying equipment, and books, was supplied by TCM prior to June 30, 1961, at a cost of $152,000.

The largest allocation by TCM for Indian agriculture was made for the acquisition of iron and steel. It is estimated that the amount of iron and steel needed to make simple farm implements is 275,000 tons a year, yet at the time of the First Five-Year Plan, India could allocate for this purpose only 120,000 tons a year from her limited national supply. The United States helped India to acquire, through TCM, 135,000 long tons of iron and steel from outside sources; $19,770,000 was obligated for this purpose. The iron and steel acquired under the agreement became part of India's steel pool and was distributed to blacksmiths, farmers, and farm-implement factories.

Since 1954, a training center for the use of agricultural machinery has been operated by the Central Tractor Organization on a 200-acre farm at Budni in Madhya Pradesh. The United States provided a technician and tractors and other farm equipment. A second technician was assigned to the Tarai State Farm (which has since been attached to the U.P. Agricultural University) to demonstrate the efficient use and servicing of farm equipment.

With new seeds, fertilizers, agricultural methods, and machinery, a surplus of produce is hoped for. In June, 1962, S. K. Patil, then Union Minister of Agriculture, observed in the lower house of Parliament (Lok Sabha) that India's granaries were full. "The food situation today is as it was never before in the history of India," he reported.[6] Food production rose consistently during the last three years of the Second Five-Year Plan (1956–61). The food-grains output in 1959–60 amounted to 74.7 million tons; in 1960–61 it rose to 79.3 million tons; and during the 1961–62 agricultural year it was estimated at 80.5 million tons—in spite of the fact that the weather in those years was not exceptionally favorable. India's annual food production now falls short of domestic consumption by only about 3 million tons.

In 1954, a demonstration project was designed to determine the feasibility of using grain elevators to replace the traditional Indian method of storing grain in individual bags or even in pots. By 1957, a project was formulated to evaluate the various modern methods of storing and handling food grains. The first elevator was installed at Hapur (Uttar Pradesh) in 1959. A second one was planned for Calcutta, and prefabricated metal buildings were being constructed near Madras and Cochin. A grain reserve of 2 million tons is planned. TCM provided the services of a grain expert, an agricultural engineer, and an entomologist. U.S. assistance

[6] "Granaries—Today and Tomorrow," *The Eastern Economist* (New Delhi), June, 1962, p. 1,272.

for these installations came to $1.4 million through fiscal year 1961. As of December, 1961, India had been given Rs.10.3 crores from P.L. 480 funds for this project.

TCM's contribution to India's fishing industry has been significant. Two technicians were assigned to the Deep-Sea Fishing Station at Bombay to train crews in modern fishing techniques. Sixteen fishing vessels, nets, ice plants, and other modern equipment were also supplied by TCM. The catch of the two refitted trawlers increased from 27 tons to 48 tons a trip. A third American expert was assigned in an advisory capacity to the Fisheries Section of the Food and Agriculture Ministry, while another technician was assigned to fisheries extension.

Originally, the project covered the purchase of three new trawlers, diesel engines for small fishing craft, and the overhaul of trawlers in use. It was extended to cover inland fishing as well, however, because of the development of the river-valley projects. An inland fisheries extension-training center in New Delhi was equipped by TCM. In 1956, TCM provided 20,000 pounds of nylon twine and nets to be sold, leased, or given to fisheries cooperatives, 6 jeeps, 2 sets of film on fisheries, 4 purse-sein fisheries experts, and various technical services. In all, TCM contributed 8 technicians, training for 21 participants, and $2.6 million (Rs.1.2 crores) worth of equipment to the industry by 1961.

For the improvement of India's cattle, TCM provided assistance to 78 out of 150 artificial-insemination centers in India in 1960. It advised in the laying out of grazing management projects and assigned an adviser to the Ministry of Food and Agriculture to help organize village cattle markets and larger, more efficient market centers. For these, $348,000 were obligated through June, 1961.

To help improve the quality and quantity of swine, TCM contributed two technicians and some equipment. TCM contributions toward poultry improvement included the importation from the United States of 30,000 day-old chicks and 8,640 hatching eggs. These birds now serve as the basic breeding stock on state poultry farms, which in turn supply poultry to the demonstration centers. Equipment has also been furnished to 5 regional farms and 300 development centers.

Technical assistance to the river-valley projects (amounting to $70,000)—excluding the grant of $14 million for equipment—includes aid in establishing two Heavy Equipment Training Centers, one at Kotah (Rajasthan) and one at Nagarjunasagar

(Andhra Pradesh). Heavy earth-moving and construction equipment had to be imported for these projects; the training centers, however, will supply expert operators and mechanics to care for the equipment.

Technical advice and equipment have been supplied to India's Ministry of Irrigation and Power, which directs the river-valley projects. Two walking excavators (draglines) worth $680,000 (Rs.32 lakhs) were provided, as well as technical personnel to demonstrate their use in constructing canals and to train Indian personnel to operate and maintain the draglines. The heavy equipment provided directly for the projects in 1952 and 1953 came to $7.2 million (Rs.3.4 crores).

The sum total of U.S. assistance for agriculture under the Technical Cooperation Mission through March, 1962, including developmental grants (not repayable) and loans (repayable in rupees or dollars), came to $504.7 million (Rs.240.3 crores). Of the total, $348.6 million (Rs. 166.0 crores) was in grants. We shall have occasion to refer to the work of the Technical Cooperation Mission in the next few chapters. Enough has been said here to show the wide variety of projects that have come to its attention.

Development Financing

Development financing covers the purchase and importation of capital goods and equipment and related services for basic development programs. Loans and grants from the U.S. are provided by several agencies. From fiscal years 1951 through 1957, development financing was part of the Indo-American Program. During this period, obligations came to $307.8 million (Rs.146.6 crores), of which $177.8 million (Rs.84.7 crores) represented loans. An amendment to the Mutual Security Act in 1954 required that at least 30 per cent of development financing must be in loan form (until that time it was all in grants), and, from fiscal years 1955 through 1958, loans to India totaled $130 million (Rs. 61.7 crores). Amortization installments are small during the early years of the loans and increase steeply thereafter. If repayment is in rupees, the interest charge is 4 per cent; if in dollars, it is 3 per cent.

It was also in fiscal year 1955 that Section 402 of the Mutual Security Act of 1954, as amended, was added to provide for a large portion of development assistance to be drawn from the rupee proceeds from sales of surplus American wheat and cotton. Under development assistance, Indian agriculture was aided by the importation of equipment for projects such as ground-water exploration, ground-water irrigation, and river-valley development. A portion of the funds (called "nonproject") financed the importation of fertilizers and iron and steel. After 1957, the needs of development assistance were met by the Development Loan Fund; as we have already mentioned, this fund aided Indian agriculture by extending a credit of $30 million to the Trombay Fertilizer Factory and providing loans for the importation of steel for both the public and private sectors.

Uttar Pradesh Agricultural University

A major barrier to Indian agricultural development through the years has been the absence of education in the latest agricultural and allied sciences at the rural peasant level, where it is most needed. Indian education was largely classical and literary under the British; when agricultural colleges were established, they catered to the city youth who desired to become white-collar officers in the state government agricultural departments—officers notoriously unwilling to soil their hands. Hence, the latest agricultural knowledge remained with the educated administrators and did not percolate to the tiller of the soil. U.S. aid to Indian agriculture has sought to rectify this serious drawback by helping to found agricultural universities modeled after the American land-grant colleges. The first such university to be established in India is the Uttar Pradesh Agricultural University at Rudrapur, which opened in 1960. The relevance of these agricultural universities to Indian agricultural development can be best appreciated against the historical background of their American prototypes.

A hundred years ago when the United States was in the throes of the Civil War (1861–65), the country was predominantly agricultural, much as India is today. Nearly 80 per cent of the population was rural and an average farmer produced enough for two people (today an average U.S. American farmer produces enough for twenty-five people). The yield per farmer and per acre was small, storage was difficult and expensive, and the farmer's per capita income was relatively low.

American university education followed the European pattern, much as Indian education was and is patterned after the British. It was a classical education that had little to offer either the farmer or the artisan. Agricultural knowledge was traditional and was handed down from generation to generation. It was not considered dignified enough to be taught on the university level. Empirical and commonsensical agricultural knowledge was useful, of course, but it was inadequate to the needs of developing agriculture in a vast country.

The American farmer and his representatives in Congress demanded educational institutions where scientific agricultural knowledge would be imparted. In response to this request, Senator Justin S. Morril of Vermont introduced the necessary legislation. The Morril Act, also known as the Land-Grant Act, received the assent of President Lincoln in 1862. The Act provides for the grant of land to each state on the basis of 30,000 acres for each member of Congress. The land thus granted was to be sold and the proceeds invested in government bonds at 5 per cent interest. The income secured was to be used for:

> the endowment, support and maintenance [in each state] of at least one college where the leading object shall be, without excluding other scientific and classical studies, . . . to teach such branches of learning as are related to agriculture and the mechanic arts in such manner as the legislatures of the states may prescribe in order to promote the liberal and practical education of the industrial classes in the several pursuits and professions in life.

In 1887, the Hatch Act, which established agricultural experiment stations throughout the country, was passed. The land-grant colleges, which number sixty-eight today, work in close association with the experiment stations, and together they are responsible for the coordination of all agricultural research activities throughout the country.

In 1914, a half-century after the establishment of the land-grant colleges, Congress passed the Smith-Lever Act, which allocated funds for extension work in agriculture and home economics. The Land-Grant Act had brought science to agriculture and made farmers as knowledgeable about farming as possible. The Hatch Act had established the agricultural-experiment station, where the latest knowledge in making agriculture as productive as possible could be demonstrated. The Smith-Lever Act brought this combined knowledge to the home and the kitchen. The present extremely high level of productivity in U.S. agriculture and the high nutrition standards of the people (as well as the countless gadgets that bring comfort and convenience to the American home and kitchen) are the product of these three vital Acts. It is this rewarding and cumulative experience that the United States Government shared with India when she helped to set up the Uttar Pradesh Agricultural University in Rudrapur.

The development of agricultural universities in India on the model of American land-grant colleges, goes back in a sense to 1948. During that year the government of India appointed the Indian University Education Commission under the chairmanship of Dr. Radhakrishnan, to report on and suggest reforms in university education to meet India's current and future needs. The Commission studied the land-grant college and recommended its adoption in India. Subsequently, the governments of the United States and India signed a "Program Agreement" in April, 1954, popularly known as Agreement 028, to cooperate on this matter.

In 1955, an Indo-American team of prominent agricultural educationists was organized to study the agriculture, veterinary colleges, and research institutions in India and the United States. They recommended a program directed toward the establishment of a few leading agricultural institutions where teaching, research, and extension education would be coordinated to meet the diverse requirements of agricultural development in India.

In 1956, Dr. H. W. Hannah of the University of Illinois submitted a report called "Blueprint for a Rural University in India." The Uttar Pradesh state legislature enacted a law establishing the U. P. Agricultural University in 1958, and the university was inaugurated in July, 1959, marking a new era in Indian university education.

At the university, students learn the theory of agriculture and then put what they have learned into practice on the university's 16,000-acre farm. Students have an opportunity to earn while they learn, for that most valuable lesson—the dignity of labor, particularly manual and physical labor—is inculcated. There are no peons (*chaprasis*) on the campus to run errands. The students run their own errands. They also hold jobs as postal clerks, telephone operators, farm workers, laboratory assistants, and helpers in the various departments of the university.

The Agricultural University is the first institution in India to offer an integrated program in agricultural education, research, and extension work. It incorporates the best and the latest in American educational policy and technique and has also adopted many American academic procedures, among them the course, credit, and advisory systems. As in American universities, the curriculum is broken up into separate courses, each of which is attended separately and examined separately. The student is not judged by a comprehensive examination at the end of his whole course—an examination that decides his fate. Different courses are taken for different credits, ranging from one to four. The more credits a student obtains the greater the scholastic progress toward the completion of the curriculum. The requirements for the degree are not expressed in terms of years, as in other Indian universities, but in terms of the number of credits needed and completed. Therefore, a bright student can obtain the degree earlier than an average student. The gifted and the below-average student need not plod on together for a specific number of years.

The U.P. Agricultural University has several constitutent colleges: the College of Agriculture, the College of Veterinary Medicine, the College of Agricultural Engineering and Technology, and the College of Basic Sciences and Humanities. Three additional colleges are proposed: a College of Home Science, a Postgraduate College, and an Agricultural Teacher-Training College.

American financial assistance to the Agricultural University has taken three major forms: (1) the exchange of professors; (2) dollar grants for the supply of scientific equipment to the various laboratories; and (3) payment of the nonrecurring (capital) expenses of the university. The equipment bought with U.S. dollar grants includes animal cages, balances, barometers, centrifuges, distilling apparatus, electronic tubes, forceps, heating ovens, incubators, microscopes, refrigerators, sterilizers, transformers, and so on. The university's rupee expenses are met by grants from the sale proceeds of agricultural commodities supplied to India under U.S. Public Law 480 and Section 402 of Public Law 665. The United States Government envisages that the total American aid to the university from June, 1960, to October, 1965, will amount, in grants, to $6,332,000 (Rs. 30,142,000).

Other Agricultural Universities in India

The U.P. Agricultural University serves today as a model for other states to set up similar agricultural universities. The Punjab, Rajasthan and Andhra Pradesh have set up their own agricultural universities, and other states are on their way to passing legislation enabling them to do the same. It is hoped that, before the end of the Third Five-Year Plan, every state in the union will have its own agricultural university.

Food for Peace

America's supply of much-needed food grains has helped maintain the stability necessary for peaceful and democratic economic growth. George McGovern, Director of the American Food for Peace Program, observed in a February, 1962, tour of India that:

> This is a stirring moment in the long history of friendly relations between India and the United States. . . . Today India has emerged as a great independent world power. . . . It has one of the most far-reaching plans for the development of its people and resources. In that plan, I am proud to say that American wheat and rice have played a vital part. Of the $4,000 million in U.S. aid that has come to India since independence, over one-half has been in the form of P.L. 480 Food for Peace commodities. . . . The total tonnage of food grains in the P.L. 480 program and earlier agreements such as the Wheat Loan of 1951 provide for the supply to India of over 31 million tons.[7]

The total amount of these American-supplied agricultural commodities is the equivalent of 160 pounds of food grains for every man, woman, and child in India. The total value exceeds Rs.12,000 crores, or about 30 rupees for every inhabitant of India.

[7] *American Embassy News Letter* (New Delhi: USIS, February 14, 1962), p. 2.

5. *AMERICAN AID AND INDIAN INDUSTRIALIZATION*

INDUSTRIALIZATION: THE WORK OF THE FUTURE

ALL THE UNDEVELOPED and underdeveloped countries regard industrialization as the sovereign remedy for most of their economic ills. Many of these nations look upon a policy of rapid and large-scale industrialization as a relatively quick solution to their problems of poverty and low levels of consumption. And certain over-populated and underdeveloped countries consider industrialization as an answer to their problems of population pressure on land and of surplus labor in the belief that, with the rapid development of heavy industries, they can siphon off their unwanted labor from the overcrowded soil to the new urban factories, thus promoting more employment, higher wages for more people, and an increasing demand for goods and services. In a word, in all developing countries, industrialization is considered a major, if not the only panacea for the ills of poverty, population pressure, and technological backwardness.

In the words of the Planning Commission of India:

> Rapid industrialization is the core of development. But if industrialization is to be rapid enough, the country must aim at developing industries which make the machines needed for the larger number of industries in the field of consumer goods and intermediate products. This is possible only if substantial expansion is undertaken in iron and steel, non-ferrous metals, coal, cement, heavy chemicals and other industries of basic importance.[1]

Although it is conceded that many countries could doubtless benefit by rapid industrialization, and could thus produce for themselves various manufactures that now have to be imported and that thus involve a loss of foreign exchange, it is doubtful

[1] *Draft Outline of the Second Five-Year Plan* (New Delhi: Planning Commission, 1956), p. 7.

whether all the present-day underdeveloped countries have the necessary prerequisites to build up an industrialized economy. And granting that these prerequisites are available in some measure, it is uncertain whether such a policy of industrialization would not be more expensive to the country on the whole in the long run. Of course, there is always compensation in terms of national status, prestige, and power.

The minimum prerequisites for industrialization are raw materials, capital resources, technological know-how, skilled labor, and a market. It is known on the basis of geological surveys that India has considerable natural resources, which, if explored efficiently, could enhance her present national income several times over and ensure a high degree of prosperity for her people.

Whether a country or region has or does not have sufficient natural resources is a geological accident. Some countries are handicapped by the inability to explore such latent resources as they may have. This inability itself constitutes a sign of underdevelopment. There is some truth in the description of India as a "beggar sitting on a bench of gold." An underdeveloped country does not have the technological know-how to organize a thorough geological survey of her terrain.

That India has a huge reservoir of labor—unskilled and semiskilled—is well known. But this huge manpower is today considered more a liability than an asset—more a mass of hungry mouths than pairs of skilled hands. A large investment in education and health is needed to make these hands creative and productive. Once the raw materials are unearthed and fed into factories to produce much-needed goods, India's now relatively idle labor force (annually increasing because of the rapid population growth) would be an asset rather than a drawback. The development process must be able to provide employment to the people that will enable them to achieve a higher standard of living to save a little of their income and thus increase the country's investment potential.

As for a market, once the level of national and per capita income is increased significantly, Indian industrialists need not seriously explore the overseas markets, for providing the basic wants, and in time the growing needs of some 460 million people should keep them more than busy. This should bring into effect a beneficent and gainful chain reaction of increased employment, higher wages, a greater demand for goods and services, and greater production and productivity to meet the demand. The present dismal picture, in which 460 million Indians own fewer automobiles than 11 million Australians for want of sufficient purchasing power, can be radically altered.

There are, however, two serious obstacles in the path of large-scale Indian industrialization: the dearth of required capital resources, and the lack of technological know-how. As for capital, the government of India has tried all the conventional means of raising as much as possible through internal taxes and levies. It has borrowed from and received grants and gifts from various friendly countries, particularly the United States. India has also received substantial loans from the various specialized agencies of the United Nations. In recent years India has tried to attract private foreign investment in Indian private industrial undertakings. There was some initial hesitancy on the part of the government in welcoming private foreign capital, but this has largely been overcome. In fact, in 1956, the Planning Commission in a draft outline of the First Five-Year Plan, welcomed in principle the free flow of foreign capital. The Planning Commission is of the view that, when finance is the main handicap in the progress of industries, a free flow of foreign capital should be welcome, particularly since it would ensure the supply of capital goods and technical know-how and make it possible to utilize foreign-patented processes. "From the point of view of industrial development," the Commission observed, "it would be best if foreign investments in the country take the form of equity capital."

It is interesting to note in this connection President Eisenhower's observations in his public address at New Delhi on December 13, 1959. He said, "I do not think India can achieve its full potential without the acquisition of more capital than you now possess. The best means for a nation, determined to maintain its independence, are private investments from outside, governmental loans from others, and, where necessary, grants from other friendly nations. . . . India is becoming one of the greatest opportunities of our times—an investment in the strengthening of freedom."

India's technological backwardness is the second major barrier to her plans for rapid industrialization. Despite the low wages paid for labor, the cost of production in an underdeveloped country is relatively high because of the primitive and obsolete methods of production. However, this situation can be altered. Technological know-how and scientific knowledge know no frontiers and are not the monopoly of any single nation, though certain nations are more advanced than others in acquiring, exploring, and applying such knowledge. The United States, the Soviet Union, the United Kingdom, and West Germany, have made great strides in only a few decades. Given the necessary help in setting up the required educational and training institutions, India can overcome this particular handicap in her plans for large-scale industrialization.

American assistance to Indian industrialization may be said to have begun with the signing of the Indo-American Technical Cooperation Agreement on February 5, 1952, though assistance from various American sources had been received by India before that date. Ever since the Development Loan Fund has been established, continuous and systematic assistance has been provided toward industrializing India.

As a result of the agreement between India and the United States, a program of technical assistance and cooperation to be financed jointly by the two governments was initiated in 1952. Nowhere has this financial and technical cooperation been of greater significance than in the field of Indian industrialization.

> The essential purpose of the Indo-American Technical Cooperation Programme is to make knowledge, techniques, men and materials of one country available for the economic and social development of the other. As with the Colombo Plan and the United Nations Technical Assistance Programme, the basic intent is to help raise standards of living. The assistance given to India is mainly technical and developmental, and comprises a five-pronged approach: One, the use of American technicians or experts who demonstrate new techniques or methodology under the various projects; two, the additional training of Indian technicians abroad, who upon their return to India carry forward work already undertaken by American counterparts; three, the procurement of demonstration equipment not available within India for pilot projects; four, the payment of costs for contracted services; and five, substantial assistance in the form of food stuffs, steel and capital equipment.[2]

Through the first two Five-Year Plans and up to the middle of the Third Five-Year Plan, more than a hundred major projects were taken up under the Technical Cooperation Program. The projects are too numerous for a detailed discussion here. Only a dozen that have directly and significantly contributed to the Indian industrialization program are discussed in this chapter.

[2] *Indo-American Technical Cooperation: 1952–1956* (New Delhi: USIS, 1957), p. 5.

Before discussing these projects, let us recall the industrial priorities outlined by the Second Five-Year Plan: (1) increased production of iron and steel and of heavy chemicals, including nitrogenous fertilizers, and the development of the heavy engineering and machine-building industries; (2) expansion of capacity in other developmental commodities and producer goods, such as aluminum, cement, chemical pulp, dyestuff, and phosphatic fertilizers, and of essential drugs; (3) modernization and re-equipment of important national industries already in existence, such as jute and cotton textiles, and sugar; (4) fuller utilization of installed capacity in industries where wide gaps exist between capacity and production; and (5) expansion of capacity for consumer goods in view of the requirements of common production programs and the production targets for the decentralized sector of industry.

Iron and Steel

Shortage of steel has been a major obstacle to the attainment of India's economic objectives. Whereas the normal annual production was approximately 1.1 million tons at the beginning of the First Five-Year Plan, the estimated demand now is for more than 3 million tons. Steel output must, of course, be increased enormously if India is to think in terms of rapid industrial development.

Initially, the U.S. assistance program provided 336,345 long tons of steel for use by the Indian Railways, by industries that manufactured hospital equipment, oil drums, containers, pipes, tubes, and machinery, and by the river-valley development program. A steel pool was established to facilitate the distribution of imported steel.

A steel-casting foundry—an essential prerequisite for developing a successful system of railways—for the manufacture of large steel castings was established at Chittaranjan, West Bengal, as an ancillary project to the Chittaranjan Locomotive Works. The bulk of the work in the foundry consists of manufacturing locomotive underframes, twin-seam cylinders, and manganese steel railway crossings and points. All these heavy steel castings, hitherto imported from abroad, are now produced in India.

Aside from supplying steel, the United States has given considerable aid in training steel engineers in the new steel plants in the public sector at Bhilai, Durgapur, and Rourkela. According to a recent modest estimate, India needs at least 2,000 engineers and technicians with specialized steel experience and training, men who until a few years ago were unavailable in India. While the training of some engineers for the Bhilai (Russian) steel plant was undertaken by the Soviet Union, the engineers for the other two steel plants received training under the American steel-training project. The Ford Foundation undertook the training of 285 men in the United States with a practical in-plant training course at a cost of $1.6 million.

The Ford Foundation was assisted in this project by the Technical Cooperation Mission. The steel-training course consisted of academic training in some American universities as well as in-plant training at the American Iron and Steel Institute. The TCM trained 100 men from India every year for 3 years at a cost of $373,000 per year; the Ford Foundation paid for the academic part of the program at a cost of $150,000 a year for 3 years. The government of India paid the travel costs and other incidental charges within India. Through 1961, the United States provided training for more than 300 Indians at the Illinois Institute of Technology in Chicago and at the Carnegie Institute of Technology in Pittsburgh. This project was altered in 1962 to provide for 4 American engineers to work at Hindusthan Steel to direct a within-India training program.

Exploratory Lignite Excavation and Development

Madras State requires annually about 3 million tons of coal, but the supply in the state has always been less than 2 million tons. Yet, the South Arcot District in the state is said to possess a hundred square miles of lignite or "brown coal." It is estimated that the reserves of lignite in the South Arcot deposit run to some 2 billion tons. Their exploitation, it is said, would make India more or less self-sufficient in iron and steel.

Various efforts at exploration have been under way since 1945; from 1951 to 1955, a lignite engineer from the U.S. Bureau of Mines worked with Indian mining engineers and geologists assembling technical data about the mine. In 1953, the Indo–U.S. program set up an exploratory excavation project to determine the possible costs of mining and the best way to utilize the lignite deposits. As a result of the explorations, a pilot excavation was begun to help determine the physical feasibility of both large-scale mining operations and of providing sufficient amounts of lignite for tests and experiments. A pilot processing plant, a power plant, laboratory equipment, and technical reference books (equipment valued at $577,000), as well as the services of 5 American technicians, were provided by the TCM. For this aid $579,000 were obligated till the end of 1961.

The integrated Neyveli project, which has been chosen for implementation, envisages the mining of 3.5 million tons of lignite annually for thermal-power generation (250 MW), fertilizer production (70,000 tons of nitrogen), and the production of carbonized briquettes (380,000 tons). Under the Third Five-Year Plan, the thermal power capacity will be increased to 400 MW, and for that purpose the mine output is to be increased from 3.5 to 4.8 million tons.

Mining and Excavation

American aid has also been available to certain other areas of the mining sector of the Indian economy. The Oil and Gas Commission of the government of India, a pioneering body for estimating the petroleum resources of the country, the possibilities of their optimum exploitation, and the size of the demand for petroleum products in India, owes its existence to a large extent to American initiative. An initial grant of $55,000 made in 1959 has covered the administrative costs of the Commission as well as the participation of American experts in the Commission's scientific inquiries. India's coal industry has also received substantial amounts at various stages of the Indo-American aid program. This aid totaled $315,000 through 1961.

Improvement of Rajasthan Power Facilities

Lack of rain and a sustained water flow as well as scarcity of animal power make Rajasthan a "powerless" state. Existing power units are so old and in such bad repair that breakdown in power supply has become rather common. The lack of power has prevented both the adequate irrigation of the parched acres in Rajasthan and the much-needed industrialization of this backward state. American aid is aimed at renovating the existing thermal stations and extending the transmission and distribution lines throughout Rajasthan State. A total of 20,000 kilowatts of generating capacity has been successfully installed so far under the program, for which $1,046,000 has been obligated.

The thermal capacity available for the state was only 15,000 kilowatts at the beginning of the First Five-Year Plan, but grew to 100,000 by the end of the Second Plan. The Third Plan proposes to increase the availability of power to 900,000 kilowatts but, since even this falls short of the power needs of the state, the government of India is exploring the possibility of creating an atomic power station in Rajasthan.

Scientific Research

In order to promote general scientific research and strengthen existing research organizations and technical-service departments in India, the United States Government sanctioned in 1954 the expenditure of $2 million. This amount and the program of scientific development were administered by the Ministry of Natural Resources and Scientific Research. With this aid, the National Physical Laboratory at New Delhi received electronic and precision-testing instruments, and the National Chemical Laboratory at Poona received library and laboratory equipment. The Fuel Research Institute at Jealgora, Bihar, received a pilot plant and the necessary scientific equipment to operate it. Three engineers at the Central Electronic Engineering Research Institute at Pilani, Rajasthan, received special training in India and the United States.

In 1955, the Geological Survey of India and the Indian Bureau of Mines received a grant of $525,500 for the development of their research and training programs. The Geological Survey supplied with geophysical, petrological and mineralogical equipment for its laboratories and with photogrammetric equipment for making maps. The Bureau of Mines was provided with equipment for handling low-grade manganese and chrome ore.

Through 1961, the Central Leather Research Institute at Madras, the Central Glass and Ceramic Research Institute at Jadavpur, West Bengal, and the Central Drug Research Institute at Lucknow have all received technical assistance to the value of $2.9 million.

The Irrigation Research Institute at New Delhi received $85,000 for research equipment and other technical requirements. The Fuel Research Institute (where research is being done to discover new and cheap sources of fuel in order to save the manure now used for domestic fuel) received $25,000 in 1958–59. The Indian Council of Scientific and Industrial Research, which administers India's network of national laboratories, was granted $45,000 during the same period.

The need for highly skilled scientific workers is surpassed by the need for skilled craftsmen. To meet this need, a Craftsmen Training Institute has been set up with American aid and the technical cooperation of the Dunwoodie Industrial Institute in

Minneapolis, Minnesota, to train annually some 450 craftsmen. The U.S. Government has provided the services of 9 American technicians. Over-all assistance amounted to $900,000, through 1963.

In 1958, the TCM undertook a Natural Resources Development Program to evaluate the magnitude of the natural resources available in the country and the most efficient way to exploit them. Another scheme of a similar nature—the Mineral Survey and Development project—was also undertaken by the TCM at the request of the government of India. These projects have proved invaluable in estimating the availability of the nation's natural resources and projecting their exploitation.

National Productivity Council

The National Productivity Council was established in 1958 with American advice and assistance with the avowed objective of promoting productivity consciousness and efficiency of operation of Indian industry. The Council, headquartered in New Delhi, has four Regional Productivity Councils and thirty local centers in industrial towns. The central and regional councils are to be the base for a campaign for more efficient use of industrial resources through better management and lower cost of production, which in turn can mean lower prices for the consumer, higher earnings for the worker, and greater returns for the entrepreneur.

American assistance through 1963 included the services of 13 American technicians for in-country training, besides 4 short-term consultants. The AID contribution through 1963 totaled $4.2 million. By the end of 1964 more American technicians had arrived in India under the same program. The program has enabled about 250 Indian managers and technicians to go to the United States for training. Thirty-seven productivity teams of about 10 each have been sent abroad to examine the various techniques employed in raising industrial efficiency and productivity and to determine their suitability for India.

American aid in this area has included the provision of experts in production quality, personnel management, production technology, etc. Major emphasis was placed on assistance in such areas as light consumer goods, light engineering products, and newsprint production. American productivity teams and individual experts have also advised the Indian textile, steel, cement, machine-tool, and foundry industries. Mobile blacksmith and machine-shop vans were provided for demonstration purposes. TCM obligated $1,892,000 for industrial technical services through 1961.

Small Industries

Both the Second and Third Five-Year Plans emphasize heavy industries, but the role and importance of cottage and small industries in the over-all rural and national development have not been ignored. The development of small industries can contribute substantially toward the solution of the country's unemployment problem as well as promote national self-sufficiency in consumer goods. When the government of India started the Regional Small Industries Institute during the Second Five Year Plan, American aid was readily available in the shape of modern machinery and equipment to the Okhla Industrial Estate in New Delhi. Six American technical experts were assigned to plan the layout of the estate and to assist in constructing its pilot production and development center. Technical consultants were also made available to the Regional Institute and Service Centers. American aid in this direction amounted to $801,000 through 1961.

The magnitude of electric-power generation is a major index of a country's economic progress. India's power needs are enormous and there are many rivers that can be harnessed to meet these needs, but the country, particularly in the rural areas, has, by and large, starved for electricity. The lack of both financial and technical resources has been the major obstacle in the generation of adequate electric power.

The newly created Central Water and Power Commission is responsible for the development of the nation's water and power resources and has received considerable help from the TCM. Apart from the supply of valuable up-to-date technical publications, documents, and reports, the services of eleven senior American engineers have been made available to the Commission. A separate project providing technical and advisory services to the Commission received an initial allocation of $100,000. (For U.S. assistance to power-project development in India, see Table 9.)

The Commission has rightly given some priority to rural electrification in India's planned economic development, for cheap electricity is vital for the success of tube-well operation, the development of cottage industries, and other basic community needs. American aid has also furnished the necessary foreign exchange for the purchase of equipment not available in India. An initial provision of $3 million (added to India's own Rs.350 million) has brought electricity to some 30 million rural inhabitants.

TABLE 9

U.S. ASSISTANCE TO THE DEVELOPMENT OF POWER IN INDIA, 1957–63

(*In Millions of Dollars*)

Dollar grants	15.0
Rupee grants	9.9
Total grants	24.9
Dollar loans	147.1
Rupee loans	314.6
Total loans	461.7
Grand total	486.6

SOURCE: *Fact Sheet on U.S. Economic Assistance to India* (New Delhi: USIS, 1964).

Rural electrification is only one among the many significant by-products of the various river-valley projects. Nearly all of the multipurpose river-valley projects for generating power, irrigating thirsty acres, and controlling floods, have received substantial American aid in heavy equipment, technical know-how and experts' services. The massive cost of these projects has been met by American aid. By June, 1961, India had received U.S. grants and loans totaling $486.6 million (Rs.231.6 crores) for the development of power resources. Most of the foreign-exchange costs of these various river projects have been covered by TCM-AID funds and loans from the Development Loan Fund. The local-currency costs have been met by the government of India and by P.L. 480 and Section 402 P.L. 665. Almost 10 per cent of all rupee sales proceeds have been obligated for power development.

It is unnecessary to list all the river-valley projects, but reference must be made here to two of the major ones: the Rihand and the Sharavathi.

The Rihand Valley Development Project was the first major water-resources development scheme to receive American aid. The reservoir resulting from the Rihand Dam in Uttar Pradesh helps to prevent floods, provides water during the dry season, and produces electric power (250,000 kilowatts of capacity). It pumps water to irrigate nearly 2 million acres of land. This project received rupee loans totaling Rs.19.8 crores under Section 402 of P.L. 665, $6 million for importing heavy construction equipment, and $78,000 worth of services of technical consultants. The American contribution came to more than half of the total cost of this project.

The Sharavathi Project is a major power-development scheme to harness the Sharavathi River in Mysore State. The scheme is designed to tap the power potential of the Sharavathi waters, which flow west down the Jog Falls to the Arabian Sea. The project is expected to be completed in three stages. The first stage provides for the erection of two turbine generators capable of producing 178,000 kilowatts of energy. The United States has given a loan of Rs.7 crores from P.L. 480 funds, another loan of $8.4 million in foreign exchange channelled through the Development Loan Fund, has been promised for this stage. The second stage of the project visualized the installation of five more generators to produce 445,000 kilowatts. The United States has agreed to finance the entire cost through a loan of Rs.17.2 crores from P.L. 480 funds and a Development Loan Fund credit of $21.5 million. In the third stage, three more generators will be added to bring the total installed capacity to 890,000 kilowatts. It is also planned to utilize the tail-race flow to produce additional power. On completion, Sharavathi will become one of the largest hydroelectric power projects in Southern Asia.

Electrical Distribution Systems and Maintenance Training Centers

Generating sufficient electric power is one thing but maintaining its uninterrupted flow is another. The breakdown of power supply is not unknown even in advanced countries unless expensive double transmission lines are maintained. In India, where the power supply is limited, breakdowns are common for various reasons and they entail heavy industrial loss. Certain American techniques have solved this problem.

In the words of C. Tyler Wood:

> At the present time it is necessary for double-circuit transmission lines to be established in India to assure uninterrupted supply of power to the consumer. In the case of single-circuit lines, power has to be cut while repairs are carried out. This involves a lot of inconvenience, loss of production and reduced earnings to industries consuming electricity. India is undergoing a process of expanding her power output phenomenally and the cost of installing networks of double-circuit transmission lines would seriously curtail the electricity-generation program.
>
> By using a special technique and safety tools it is possible to effect repairs to transmission lines without endangering the lives of the

men during the work even when the lines are "hot," i.e., while high voltage current is flowing through them. The U.S. Technical Cooperation Mission has provided two instructors and equipment to pilot training schools at Ganguwal and Bangalore where electricians from various states are taught the new technique and furnished with full sets of tools.[3]

The project cost the United States $355,000 (Rs.16.6 lakhs) as of June, 1959. The government of India has allocated $84,000 (Rs. 4 lakhs) to the two centers during the period of U.S. collaboration and also pays part of the salaries of the American technicians.

In all, about 8 projects with a total capacity of 1,197,000 kilowatts are financed in full by U.S. dollar and rupee loans, without

TABLE 10

INDIAN POWER PROJECTS WHOSE ENTIRE ANTICIPATED COST IS MET BY THE U.S.

	Capacity in Kilowatts	*DLF Loans[a] in Millions of Dollars*	*Rupee Loans[b] in Rupees in Crores*
Thermal			
Chandrapura Thermal Power Station (Damodar Valley)	250,000	30.0	20.5
Durgapur Thermal Power Station Extension (West Bengal State Electricity Board)	120,000	20.0	3.4
Barauni Thermal Power Station (Bihar)	30,000	3.8	1.3
Kanpur Thermal Power Station Extension	15,000	1.6	1.0
Talcher Thermal Power Station	250,000	33.0	8.5
Amlai Thermal Power Station (Birsingpur District)	60,000	8.4	6.6
Total thermal	725,000	96.8	41.3
Hydroelectric			
Barapani Hydroelectric Power Project (Assam)	27,000	2.5	6.2
Sharavathi Project, Stage II	445,000	21.5	17.2
Total hydroelectric	472,000	24.0	23.4
Grand Total[c d]	1,197,000	120.8 (*Rs.* 57.5 *crores*)	64.7 (*$135.9 million*)

[3] C. Tyler Wood, "Indo–U.S. Economic Cooperation," *The Hindu* (Madras), June 12, 1960.

any sort of contribution from the Indian government. Thirteen other projects, producing a total of 1,609,400 kilowatts, are financed jointly by the two governments. In addition, the Development Loan Fund has given a credit of $10 million for the purchase of power-generating equipment. Grants and loans from P.L. 480 funds have been extended to a number of other river-valley projects, including Chambal, Hirakud, Damodar Valley, Nagarjunasagar, Bhadra, Tungabhadra, Kundah, and Koyna, all of which will make significant contributions to India's much-needed power production. And power means rapid industrialization.

Tables 10 and 11 present the various power projects that receive partial or total aid under the Indo-American program and the magnitude of "power" they are expected to generate.

In addition, by an agreement signed on December 23, 1960, the U.S. Export-Import Bank has authorized a further credit of $50 million (Rs.23.81 crores) to buy equipment and capital goods in the United States for projects in both the public and private sectors in India.

SOURCE: *Indo-American Economic Cooperation* (New Delhi, 1964). Mimeographed paper.

[a] To meet foreign-exchange costs.

[b] From sale proceeds of U.S. agricultural commodities in India, under P.L. 480, to cover local-currency costs.

[c] The total cost of the eight projects amounts to $256.7 million, or Rs.122.2 crores.

[d] The ninth power project to have its cost met entirely by U.S. aid was announced on April 11, 1962. The Pamba Kakki (Sabarigiri) Hydroelectric Project in Kerala State will receive a loan of $20.2 million (Rs.9.6 crores) from the U.S. Agency for International Development to meet foreign-exchange costs and a loan of Rs.15.3 crores from U.S. P.L. 480 funds. (Total Rs.25 crores.)

A tenth project was added to the list when Ambassador Galbraith announced a U.S. Government loan of $17.9 million to cover the full foreign-exchange cost of a 125 mw. generating unit that will expand the Trombay Thermal Power Station. The loan agreement was made with the Tata Power Companies by the government of India and will be repaid over 40 years with no payment during the first 10 years. During the first decade, there will be a service charge of .75 per cent. When repayment begins, the interest charged will be 3½ per cent.

Three more U.S. A.I.D. loan agreements were concluded in November, 1962: $8.4 million (Rs.4.0 crores) for the Ramagundam Thermal Power Project; $16.0 million (Rs.7.6 crores) for the Delhi "C" Thermal Power Station Extension; and $25.1 million (Rs.12.0 crores) for the Satpura Thermal Power Station.

TABLE 11

INDIAN POWER PROJECTS WHOSE PARTIAL ANTICIPATED COST IS MET BY THE U.S.

	Capacity in Kilowatts	*Percentage of U.S. Aid to Total Cost*	*TCM Grant (Millions of Dollars)*	*TCM or DLF Loan (Millions of Dollars)*	*Rupee Loan (Rupees in Crores)*
Thermal					
Delhi Thermal Plant Extension	30,000	60	–	4.0[a]	–
Ahmedabad Electric Company	30,000	not fixed	–	3.9	–
Rajasthan Power Plant	7,700	18	1.0	–	–
Total thermal	67,700	–	1.0	7.9	–
Hydroelectric					
Rihand Project	250,000	40	6.0	–	15.8
Sharavathi Project, Stage I	178,000	48	–	8.4	7.0
Chambal Project	92,000	–	–	–	–
Hirakud Project	232,000	–	–	–	–
Damodar Project	104,000	–	–	–	–
Nagarjunasagar Project	187,500	–	–	–	–
Bhadra Project	33,200	15	8.0[b]	–	67.0[c]
Tungabadra Project	45,000	–	–	–	–
Kunda Project	180,000	–	–	–	–
Koyna Project	240,000	–	–	–	–
Total hydroelectric	1,541,700	–	14.0	8.4	89.8
Grand total	1,609,400	–	15.0	26.3	89.8
			(Rs.7.1 crores)	*(Rs.12.5 crores)*[d]	*($188.6 million)*[e]

SOURCE: *Fact Sheet on U.S. Economic Assistance to India* (New Delhi: USIS, 1964).

[a] The only loan from TCM; the rest of the loans in the column are from DLF.

[b] The figure includes grants made to the Mahi right-bank canal, Kakrapur Kasi, and Mahanadhi Delta, which have no power potential at present.

[c] 93 per cent is in loans, 7 per cent in grants.

[d] Includes a $10 million DLF loan to purchase equipment.

[e] Total U.S. aid is $229.9 million (Rs.109.4 crores).

Since the $150 million loan to India agreed upon in 1958, the number of loans has increased to 8. The Export-Import Bank loans totaled $246.9 million (Rs.117.6 crores) as of December 31, 1961: $153.7 million (Rs.73 crores) are for the private sector, and $93.2 million (Rs.44.3 crores) are for the public sector. (See Tables 12, 13, and 14.)

TABLE 12

EXPORT-IMPORT BANK LOANS TO PUBLIC SECTOR IN INDIA, 1951–63

(*In Millions of Dollars*)

	Value of Orders Placed	*Amount Drawn from Credit*
Equipment for irrigation project	3.5	2.378
Equipment for Dandakaranya project	2.5	0.245
Equipment for power projects	2.2	0.305
Equipment for iron-ore mining	3.8	2.180
Equipment for National Coal Development Corporation	19.4	13.247
Equipment for Neyveli Lignite Corporation	1.1	0.570
Equipment for Dugda Coal Washery	6.0	3.886
Equipment for roads and bridges	3.0	0.158

SOURCE: *American Aid to India* (New Delhi: USIS, 1964). Press release.

TABLE 13

EXPORT-IMPORT BANK LOANS TO PRIVATE SECTOR IN INDIA, 1951–63

(*In Millions of Dollars*)

	Value of Orders Placed	*Amount Drawn from Credit*
Equipment for textile industry	24.0	6.856
Equipment for engineering industry	4.6	2.305
Equipment for machine tools for various industries	4.5	1.928
Equipment for chemical industry	18.9	4.491
Equipment for automobile industry	10.4	4.009
Equipment for aluminum industry	5.7	—
Equipment for private manganese and iron-ore industry	0.8	0.726

SOURCE: *American Aid to India* (New Delhi: USIS, 1964). Press release.

Investment Institutions and Indian Industrialization

India's private industry also benefits from U.S. loans through the Industrial Finance Corporation, a government of India corporation with a U.S. Government loan as capital. The IFC extends medium- and long-term loans to private Indian industry. It also facilitates and promotes investment of private foreign capital in India. The first loan (under DLF) signed in December, 1960, for $10 million has since been fully allocated to Indian industries. A pharmaceuticals factory in Bengal, a plastic chemical plant in Maharashtra, and a paper mill in Mysore have benefited.

TABLE 14

EXPORT-IMPORT BANK GENERAL LOANS TO INDIA, 1957–61

	Amount (in Dollars)	*Date Authorized*
Sundatta Cotton Seed Utilization, Ltd.	60,000	March 29, 1957
National Rayon Corporation	1,800,000	October 4, 1957
First line of credit to government of India	150,000,000	February 27, 1958
Hindustan Aluminium, Ltd.	13,650,000	January, 1960
Air India International (first loan)	4,100,000	September 8, 1960
Second line of credit to government of India	50,000,000	December 23, 1960
Orient Paper Mills, Ltd.	18,500,000	January 6, 1961
Air India International (second loan)	8,100,000	June 19, 1961
East India hotels	717,000	July 27, 1961
Third line of credit to government of India	25,000,000	Subject to approval
Total	271,927,000	

SOURCE: *Fact Sheet on U.S. Economic Assistance to India* (New Delhi: USIS, 1962), p. 16.

The second loan, of $20 million, was agreed upon in March 30, 1962. It will provide, as did the first, the foreign-exchange component of credits extended to Indian private industries. The loans are to be repaid in dollars, but the terms of the loans will be set at 40 years (repayable period) and the credit fee is only .75 per cent. In addition, the IFC has received a loan of Rs.10 crores from P.L. 480 funds ($21 million).

Other investment institutions to benefit from American aid are the Refinance Corporation of India (RCI), the Industrial Credit and Investment Corporation of India (ICICI), and the Indian Investment Centre (IIC). The IIC was granted Rs.0.2 crores ($420,000) from the rupee-sales proceeds of U.S. agricultural commodities under P.L. 480. The first two received loans of Rs. 26.2 crores ($55 million for the RCI) and Rs.17.5 crores $38.8 million for the ICICI) under Title I of P.L. 480 on December 31, 1961.

Many factors inhibit foreign investment in India. Foreign investors by and large are not familiar with Indian laws, policies, and the general conditions of the changing but expanding Indian market. Also, Indian officials and industrialists are not familiar with foreign capital sources. Adequate literature on the subject is rather meager. There are no fully documented publications put out by India to familiarize potential foreign investors with the situation and to save them costly investigations and negotiations.

The Indian Investment Centre, which has its headquarters in New Delhi, (a branch in New York, and other branches being opened in Bombay, Calcutta, Madras, Tokyo, Brussels, and Amsterdam), helps in locating foreign capital sources. It prepares prospectuses and helps in negotiations between foreign investors and Indian industrialists. Besides the P.L. 480 grant, the IIC has received a grant of $713,000 from the United States and the services of American specialists.

Since one of the major obstacles in the establishment of new enterprises in India is the difficulty of mustering adequate domestic capital resources, the American-financed investment institutions aid development by extending loans to small and medium-sized industries.

The Refinance Corporation of India extends loans to private commercial banks. These banks in their turn extend loans to productive private medium-sized companies, i.e., companies with total resources not exceeding Rs.2.5 crores, and loans not exceeding Rs.50 lakhs. Thus, RCI stimulates more effective participation of Indian and foreign private banks in financing Indian private industrial enterprises.

The ICICI, like the Industrial Finance Corporation mentioned above, makes medium- and long-term loans directly to various industrial concerns in India. It also guarantees loans from other private investment sources, underwrites new issues of stocks or bonds, and assists businesses with equity preparation. The Development Loan Fund has contributed support to the ICICI in the form of a $5 million loan. ICICI has nearly 1,800 shareholders, including British and American subscribers.

Altogether, Rs.385.3 crores have been programmed by the United States Government for investment institutions in India. Table 15 shows the total loans and grants to Indian investment institutions by source, to 1963.

Non-Project Loans

As India's economic development proceeds apace, the nature of external-assistance requirements has shifted from the financing of specific capital projects to the financing of equipment to maintain such projects and the importing of raw materials for use in domestic consumption. Three loans have been extended by the United States Government to help India finance "maintenance imports." The first loan agreement was signed on October 26, 1961, under the DLF and was used for the import of $20 million worth of nonferrous metals. Two further loans, one concluded on February 28, 1962 (under the U.S. A.I.D.), for $100 million and a second for the same amount on March 30, 1962, will finance the import of raw materials and machinery (steel, fertilizers, synthetic tire-cord yarn, sulphur, wood pulp, automobile parts, machine tools, etc.).

TABLE 15

U.S. GOVERNMENT GRANTS AND LOANS TO INDIAN INVESTMENT INSTITUTIONS, BY SOURCE, 1951–63

(In Rupees in Crores)

Source	*Loans*	*Grants*	*Total*
P.L. 665, Section 402	19.9	4.0	23.9
P.L. 480, Title I	223.4	66.2	289.6
Fund B[a]	7.5	64.3	71.8
Total	250.8	134.5	385.3

SOURCE: Based on a report of the Indian Investment Centre in New Delhi, 1963.

[a] Proceeds of Mutual Security Act dollar aid. They are owned by the Indian Government and were generated by commercial sales of dollar commodities granted to India and from reimbursal transfer of aid-financed equipment from the central government to revenue-earning public enterprises such as railways. Furthermore, repayments of AID-financed loans from the central government to state governments for imports accrue to Fund B.

P.L. 480 Cooley Amendment Loans

The Cooley Amendment, as we noted in the discussion of P.L. 480, provides for the setting apart of 25 per cent of the rupee proceeds from the sale of agricultural commodities for loans to private industry falling under two categories: American firms in India or Indian firms associated with American firms, and Indian firms aiding in the disposal of American agricultural commodities (private warehouses, flour mills, etc.). The Export-Import Bank extends Cooley loans in India at the rate of 6 per cent for up to 10 or 12 years; they therefore do not compete with commercial bank loans.

Under the five P.L. 480 agreements with India, Rs.77.6 crores have been set aside for loans to private Indian and American industries, of which Rs.14.18 crores have been given as shown in Table 16.

In brief, Table 17 provides the latest figures as of June 1, 1961, on the amount of American aid for industrial development.

Table 16

American Aid to Private Industries in India, 1951–63

(In Rupees in Crores)

Otis Elevator of India, Ltd.	0.10
Good-Year Tyre & Rubber Co. of India, Ltd.	2.25
Mysore Cements Limited (M/s. Sarangapani Mudaliar/Kaiser, Inc.)	0.55
Hindustan Aluminium Limited (M/s. Birla/Kaiser, Inc.)	1.00
Synthetics & Chemicals, Ltd. (M/s. Kilachand/Firestone, Inc.)	5.42
Merck, Share & Dohme Private, Ltd.	0.50
Ex-Cell-O (India) Private, Ltd. (M/s. Amerind Engineering Co./ Ex-Cell-O, Inc.)	0.20
Premier Tyres, Ltd. (Joint enterprise with Dayton Rubber, Inc.)	0.30
Seshasayee Paper & Board, Ltd. (M/s. Seshasayee/Parsons & Whitemore, Inc.)	2.00
Lederle Laboratories (India), Private, Limited	0.25
Gabriel India Private, Limited (M/s. D. C. Anand/Gabriel of Detroit)	0.05
Carrier Air Conditioning & Refrigeration Private, Limited (M/s. Voltas/Carrier Air Conditioning, Inc.)	0.37
Madras Rubber Factory, Ltd. (Factory is being set up in	
Total	14.18
collaboration with Mansfield Rubber Co. of Ohio.)	0.25
Wyeth Laboratories Private, Limited (American Home Products Corporation)	0.17
East India Hotels, Ltd. (M/s. Oberoi/Intercontinental Hotel Corporation, Inc.)	0.77

Source: "Cooley Fund Loans," in *U.S. Economic Assistance to India* (New Delhi: USIS, 1964).

Table 17

American Aid to Indian Industrial Development, 1951–61[a]

(In Millions of Dollars)

Purposes	
Capital equipment for such industries as jute, cement, automobile, rayon, paper, etc.	298.2
Mineral development	21.2
Financial institutions	25.0
Industrial research organizations	12.3
Nuclear engineering and research	1.4
Electric-power generation	162.1
Rural electrification and electrical distribution systems	3.4
Steel supply	145.8
Total	669.4

Source: *Fact Sheet on U.S. Economic Assistance to India* (New Delhi: USIS, 1961).

[a] Only the foreign-exchange component.

The rupee loans from the sale proceeds of U.S. agricultural commodities amount to $2,337.3 million (Rs.1,112.6 crores), more than half of which has been given for Indian industrial development.[4] The private sector has received about Rs.77.3 crores through the Cooley Amendment to P.L. 480 (figures as of June 1, 1961).

The First Five-Year Plan allocated Rs.173 crores for industry, Rs.127 crores for power, and Rs.266 crores for multipurpose power projects. The three together totaled 28.5 per cent of the total outlay for the First Plan. The Second Plan allocated Rs.690 crores for industry and minerals and Rs. 913 crores for irrigation and power; these allocations together comprise 35.5 per cent of the total outlay. Thus both plans together expended Rs.2,269 crores (approximately). We can compare this with the amount given by the U.S. to India, which runs to more than Rs.600 crores for industrial, mineral, and power development. It is obvious that the United States has contributed about 25 per cent in the total achievements of the first two Five-Year Plans.

While India's industrialization since she became politically free is not spectacular, she has taken greater strides during the last fifteen years than she had during the earlier half-century, thanks to many factors, chief of which is American aid. During this brief period, India's over-all industrial production has doubled, steel output tripled, and electric-power output quadrupled. The production of capital goods has increased fourfold.

Although India has received aid of various kinds from many friendly nations, American aid is perhaps the most significant from the point of view of India's rapid and large-scale industrialization. During the period under survey, American machinery components, spare parts, raw materials, and other help worth Rs. 560 crores ($1,170 million) have reached India. Foreign-exchange assistance to the value of Rs.200 crores for power development and Rs.130 crores for transportation facilities have been received.

The "multiplier" effect generated by the American nonproject loans aids the over-all development of the country. C. Tyler Wood cites the following apt example with reference to conditions in India:

> Let us take a tyre factory which represents an enormous investment of capital. India produces natural rubber, but needs to import carbon

[4] The exact amount is not available for the part utilized for power and industry.

> black, an essential item in the manufacture of tyres. The unavailability of carbon black will drastically curtail production and make it difficult for the economy to benefit fully from the investment of the resources and skills tied up with the factory. The value of carbon black may account for a small percentage of the cost of rubber tyres but without this key item the latter cannot be produced. India will manufacture carbon black ultimately but in the meantime the foreign aid used in making the chemical available contributes many times its value to the natural economy. The absence of such key supplies will cause unemployment, deny a market to Indian producers of raw material, and bring about a slackening in the rate of expansion of the country's economy as a whole.[5]

In a word, Indian industrialization, in the short period of about a dozen years, has not only taken firm roots but has taken rapid strides, thanks largely to American aid and cooperation.

[5] C. Tyler Wood, "U.S. AID Helps India's Resurgence," *The Hindu: Survey of Indian Industry* (Madras, 1963), p. 29.

6. AMERICAN ASSISTANCE FOR BETTER HEALTH IN INDIA

All enlightened governments and societies recognize that health is of fundamental importance to national and human progress. A people's health is of the greatest importance in the nation's economic, social, and cultural development. The health of a citizen, whether he works in a field or a factory, at home or in an office, is of paramount consideration in terms of individual productivity and national wealth.

It is now widely recognized that health is not merely a negative state of the absence of disease, but a positive state of integrated well-being in which an individual's physical, mental, and emotional capacities develop harmoniously. The health of a community does not depend merely upon the healthy habits of an individual but on a wide variety of economic, social, and educational factors, in fact the total cultural milieu. The attitudes, habits, and programs of individuals, societies, and governments all affect the health of a nation.

Despite the tremendous importance of health, almost all the underdeveloped countries, where health problems are acute, tend to give relatively low priority to public health, sanitation, and environmental hygiene. One suspects that the reasons for this are not so much the paucity of funds and technical personnel, but rather a blind imitation of the advanced countries, giving low status to the health minister in both central and state cabinets and low priority in the allotment of funds. In advanced countries, health problems of the kind encountered in India and other underdeveloped countries were solved, by and large, decades ago; there is, therefore, no need for these countries to spend large sums of money on health or to accord the health minister the status of a major member of the cabinet. But in India, where cholera, smallpox, and malaria are still prevalent and where problems of providing a pure water supply and adequate sanitation are enormous, the low priority given to public-health matters is difficult to understand.

The government of India has shown an awareness of the major problems of public health in the country. There is no need to repeat here the nation's vital statistics, for her high general mortality, infant mortality, and morbidity incidence are well known. The First Five-Year Plan summed up admirably the distressing health situation in India:

> The epidemic diseases together account for 5.1 per cent of total mortality. India continues to be the largest reservoir of these epidemic diseases. More than half the deaths are recorded under fevers by the reporting agency, which has no means of proper diagnosis of the cause of death. Respiratory diseases are numerically the next important group. There is a large prevalence of bowel disorders and parasitic infections. It is estimated at about one million. It is similarly estimated that about 2.5 million active cases of tuberculosis exist and about 500,000 deaths take place every year. The present low state of public health is reflected in the wide prevalence of disease and the high rate of mortality in the country as a whole and in particular among vulnerable groups such as children and women in their reproductive age period. A large part of this represents preventable mortality.
>
> The output of the industrial worker in India is low compared with that of the worker in other countries. The productive capacity of the agricultural worker is comparatively low. The loss caused by morbidity in working time is enormous. To this must be added the expenditure to the individual and to the state in the provision of medical care.
>
> The causes of this low state of health are many. The lack of hygienic environment *conducive* to healthful living, low resistance, which is primarily due to lack of adequate diet and poor nutrition, lack of proper housing, safe water supply, proper removal of human wastes, and the lack of medical care, curative and preventive, are some of the more important factors, besides lack of general and health education and low economic status. These are serious impediments to rapid progress. The country's financial resources are limited, trained personnel are lacking and the whole programme of health development is bound up with a broader programme of social improvement.[1]

It is obvious that the Indian health problem is of enormous proportions and calls for tremendous financial and technical re-

[1] *The First Five-Year Plan,* pp. 489–90.

sources. It must be pointed out, however, that the problem is not unusual. The present advanced countries had to face similar problems. Once India musters enough money and methodology, she can be made into a healthy and clean country. India's present filth and morbidity can and must be eliminated.

Resources are limited, however, so priorities have to be set and realistic targets outlined. India has asked for American help in certain strategic areas of her over-all health problem, such as malaria eradication, filaria control, provision of national water supply and sanitation, and health and medical education.

Malaria Eradication

As already pointed out, in the years before 1947 there were in India an estimated 100 million cases of malaria and 1 million resultant deaths every year.

What is malaria? Malaria is an intractable and incapacitating disease spread by the female anopheles mosquito. The proboscis of the female anopheles is strong enough to pierce the human skin, through which she draws the blood meal required to produce fertile eggs. The male anopheles is harmless, for his proboscis cannot pierce the human skin. From her human host, the female mosquito draws, along with the blood, malaria parasites. These parasites then go through a cycle of development, lasting about a week or ten days in the body of the mosquito. At the end of this period, the parasites collect in the salivary glands of the mosquito to be injected into the blood stream of her next victim. She is unharmed by the sojourn of the parasite in her digestive tract.

Once the one-celled malaria parasite bores its way into the victim's blood cell, it begins to multiply. The temperature rises and the invaded blood cell ruptures, shedding the parasites into the blood stream to seek out and infect new red-blood cells. As the process repeats itself, frequently recurring fevers alternate with chills. The victim now has the debilitating and persistent disease, malaria.

According to Dr. John Leathers, a pioneer in the field, "Malaria is one of the greatest scourges inflicted upon humanity. It is a menace to any people or country in which it has a decided incidence; in the number of deaths caused either directly or indirectly, the sickness and suffering, the loss of time and efficiency, the expense, the lowered vitality of the afflicted, and the reduction of the valuation of property, malaria is without rival among the diseases afflicting mankind."

The incidence of malaria in India was so high in some areas that serious economic activity was virtually impossible. For instance, the disease held up the construction of the railroad in eastern India linking Vizianagar with Raipur for a period of forty years. The Terai in Uttar Pradesh, a relatively fertile region, was rendered virtually uninhabitable for years by malaria. During the first year of construction of the Sarda Canal Headworks, an important irrigation project in Uttar Pradesh, work could not progress during the entire year because 96 out of every 100 workers were down with malaria.

A few decades ago malaria was so prevalent in India and other parts of the world that its conquest was considered well-nigh impossible. Dr. Walter Sinton, writing in 1936, observed that "the problem of existence in very many parts of India is the problem of malaria. There is no aspect of life in this country which is not affected, either directly or indirectly, by this disease. It constitutes one of the most important causes of economic misfortune, engendering poverty, diminishing the quantity and quality of the food supply, lowering the physical and intellectual standards of the nation, and hampering increased prosperity and economic progress in every way." In a word, the cost of malaria to the economy of India in loss of manpower, in medical expense, and in lessened agricultural and industrial productivity has been estimated in the past to be as high as $500 million a year.

In 1952, the government of India gave the fight against malaria the highest priority in its health program and launched a vigorous Malaria Control Program with the help of the Technical Cooperation Mission. Control units were organized under the direction of the National Malaria Institute at New Delhi. In the first three years of the Indo-American program, 125 units were organized, each extending protection to 1 million persons. By 1955, the number of units was raised to 136.

In 1958, the control program was converted into the Malaria Eradication Program, for the discovery during World War II of DDT and BHC, two synthetic insecticides, assured the program definite success. If the spraying program is completed before the malaria mosquito develops immunity to the presently known insecticides, it has been demonstrated that eradication is technically feasible. It is now a question of getting enough men in the field with sufficient supplies of insecticides. To this end, India became an active member of a world-wide campaign to eradicate malaria. The U.S. Congress authorized for this specific purpose the expenditure of special-aid funds (under Section 402, Title IV, of the MSP Act).

Some $90 million (Rs.43 crores) was provided up to 1962 for the supply of DDT, dieldrine, jeeps, trucks, power sprayers, hand sprayers, training of staff, building and research equipment, and the services of three American malariologists. In addition, P.L. 480 rupee grants were made to the eradication project to a total of Rs.31 crores ($65.1 million).

The government of India has spent more than Rs.120 crores for local expenses. This program has received aid from other quarters, such as the World Health Organization, which provided $1.5 million worth of DDT in 1958 and fellowships at a cost of $300,000 annually, and UNICEF, which provided some financial and technical assistance in the construction of the DDT plant in India.

The result? The incidence of malaria has been reduced by 98 per cent. The dramatic decline in the number of malaria patients is demonstrated by the fact that, during 1961–62, out of some 12 million blood smears collected from fever patients throughout the country, only 1 out of 400 turned out to contain malaria parasites. The project, on an accelerated program, will continue until 1965, when it is hoped that malaria in India will be no more than a bad memory.

Control of Filariasis (Elephantiasis)

After malaria, filariasis is the second most devastating of the mosquito-borne diseases affecting the nation's health and economy. This infection (or group of infections) is caused by round, delicate, threadlike worms, or filariae. The human filariae include two common types, Bancroft's and Malayan. The female worms give birth to minute snakelike embryos called microfilariae, which gain access to the cutaneous blood stream or lymphatic vessels and are picked up by bloodsucking flies and mosquitoes. Bancroft's filariasis is prevalent all over the tropics and subtropics, but the Malayan filariasis is confined to India, Indonesia, and China.

The objectives of the government's nation-wide filaria-control program during the Second and Third Five-Year Plans are to provide treatment to infected persons, protect people in endemic areas, and eventually prevent the disease from spreading to new areas. The first phase of the program is directed at curing some 5 million people living in the hyperendemic filarious areas. Some American aid is directed toward evaluating procedures and techniques of attacking filaria that can be used on a nation-wide basis. American assistance also includes the latest training facilities for Indian technicians in parasitology and entomology—skills that will help in the fight against filariasis.

Thirteen control and twenty-two survey units have also been set up in twelve states to collect facts, detect the endemic areas, and map the campaign. During the Second Five-Year Plan, forty-six control units were set up in much the same pattern as the malaria-control units. Besides continuing these units during the Third Five-Year Plan, a plan to set up filaria clinics at the teaching hospitals in the affected areas has been approved by the government. Larger schemes for adequate drainage facilities are also planned.

Up to 1960, the U.S. Government provided about $2.2 million toward the fight against filaria. But these efforts have not been as rewarding as in the fight against malaria, for the simple reason that the diagnosis of filaria is itself relatively recent. Nevertheless, America is bound to bring to this attack the latest available knowledge and equipment.

National Water Supply and Sanitation

Apart from malaria and filaria, water- and filth-borne diseases constitute a major public-health problem in India. Since less than 10 per cent of the country's total population is served by protected water supply, the incidence of such diseases as cholera, dysentery, and typhoid is high. They account for some 50 million cases of illness and 2 million deaths annually.

The problem of providing an adequate supply of pure water is complicated by the fact that about 80 per cent of the population live in villages, where, apart from a short supply of the much-needed protected water, the people have to be educated to keep pure the sources of the available natural water supply.

The government of India has tackled this problem along two different lines. During the first Five-Year Plan, 10,000 villages and 25 municipalities received a good water supply and proper sanitary arrangements at a cost of Rs.37 crores under the rural water-supply scheme. Rs.12 crores were allocated for urban water supply and sanitation. With the growing importance of urban areas, attention and priority were diverted from the rural areas and, in the Second Five-Year Plan, were directed toward water supply and sanitation for towns and cities. Rs.58 crores were allocated for this purpose. About 650 water-supply schemes, with an estimated cost in excess of Rs.100 crores, were undertaken to serve the needs of some 12 million of the urban population.

The U.S. Government has provided India with scientific equipment and the services of experts. U.S. public-health engineers, sanitarians, and specialists in water supply have all aided India as consultants. The supply of U.S. equipment to India has included pumps, well-drilling rigs, trucks, jeeps, air compressors, galvanized iron pipes, cast-iron water pipes, and so forth.

For water supply and sanitation during the decade covered by the first two Five-Year Plans, the government of India incurred an expenditure of Rs.122 crores. For this project, American assistance through TCM came to about $6 million (Rs.33 crores) and about Rs.2 crores were available from the Ford Foundation. American assistance came to a quarter of India's total expenditure on rural health, sanitation, and water supply—a sizable and significant contribution.

Health Education

Public-health problems are solved only in part in laboratories, by preventive measures, and with curative drugs. No national-health policy can succeed without the active and informed cooperation of the people. The people must be aware not only of what the government is doing and why certain measures are advocated and adopted, but also of basic health and sanitary practices. A plan of health education that will inculcate good habits ranging from personal hygiene to disposal of household garbage is needed.

As a step in this direction, a cooperative program of health education was undertaken by the government of India and the Technical Cooperation Mission. This involved training health instructors and setting up Health Instruction Training Centers. The major task in health education is to train instructors to work in rural areas and on community-development projects where the task is formidable.

The Health Instruction Training Centers were set up under the joint cooperation of the government of India, the Ford Foundation, and the Technical Cooperation Mission. These centers are at Poonamallee in Madras State, Singhur in West Bengal, and Najafgarh in Delhi. The Center at Poonamallee has attracted considerable attention by its successful program of health education among the illiterate people in rural areas.

The total TCM expenditure came to $27,000, a modest amount

for a pioneering venture. The Ford Foundation granted $353,105 for the construction of residential accommodations for the staff and full operating expenses for the first two years, one-half of these expenses for the third year, and one-quarter for the fourth year. The balance is met by the state governments.

Medical Colleges and Allied Institutions

A nation's health depends upon a variety of factors, all the way from a mother's knowledge of infant care up to the quality of medical education, research, and medical personnel. The quality of medical education and training has of late begun to suffer in India as the number of medical colleges has increased to meet the growing demand for the services of physicians, surgeons, and technicians. More colleges mean more highly trained personnel for faculty, more buildings, and more scientific equipment, all of which are lacking for financial and other reasons.

The need for impeccable standards is great in any realm of human endeavor, particularly in medical education and clinical training. The need for continuous replenishment of ideas and knowledge is obvious in any intellectual pursuit, but its absence is a particularly grave disadvantage to a physician. A medical person must have ready access to the latest medical literature (without having to worry about cost) and opportunities to observe new techniques (in an advanced center in one's own or a foreign country) and to meet, exchange information with, and learn from specialists at national and international conferences. These facilities are particularly important for the basically competent but overworked and undertrained physicians and surgeons in India and other underdeveloped countries. As the Bradshaw lecturer told the Royal College of Surgeons in 1956, "The situation for practicing physicians is truly frightening; if he has been qualified for five years and has not been reading regularly or has not attended postgraduate medical instruction, he is distinctly out of date. . . . If ten years, he is dangerously misinformed. The situation of many who left medical school twenty years ago and are still relying on the instruction that they received as students is almost medieval. . . ."

American aid has tried in a small way to meet some of these problems. One of the major needs has been for well-trained professors to staff the growing number of medical colleges, and TCM has sponsored the Medical Education Project to help to overcome the shortage. The project was initiated in 1958 and is expected to continue through 1965. Under this scheme, 27 American medical specialists have visited India to work with medical colleges in 7 states, as well as in the All-India Institute of Medical Sciences in New Delhi. The specialists include professors of preventive and social medicine, biochemistry, anatomy, pharmacology, and surgery, as well as experts in biostatistics and hospital administration. At the same time, about 300 members from the faculties of various medical institutions all over India were sent to the United States for advanced training. In the first three years of the project, definite emphasis was placed on preclinical fields, including social and preventive medicine.

India is just beginning to manufacture specialized and modern medical and surgical equipment, and American aid has brought to Indian medical institutions spectrophotometers, centrifuges, incubators, blood-cell calculators, ultimate-analysis apparatus, vacuum ovens, extraction apparatus, sterilizers, microscopes, and X-ray and other laboratory, hospital, and research equipment. TCM spent on this project, up to June, 1961, $789,000.

The project has also provided scientific equipment for demonstration purposes, teaching aids, apparatus, and specialized office equipment in order to enhance the effectiveness of American technicians working in India. The estimated cost of the project through its termination at the end of 1964 was $3,729,000. Of this total, more than $2 million went for participant training; the balance was used to pay for the services of American experts and the needed commodity imports.

Nursing Education

Apart from the general support to various medical colleges, particularly those at Baroda, Hyderabad, and Trivandrum, American aid has been helping India to overcome the critical shortage of trained nurses. India needs about 176,000 trained nurses for hospitals, schools of nursing, and public-health and allied activities. The number of nursing schools and colleges is grossly inadequate for India's needs, and, even where such institutions exist, the quality and duration of the course of study and the training offered is generally far below desirable standards. In 1958, only two colleges were providing the necessary training in "general nursing." American aid has helped to develop colleges of nursing at the university level, and today six states have colleges of nursing. American nursing educators have worked with their Indian counterparts in revising and upgrading the curriculum in various medical colleges and schools of nursing and in improving nursing services. In addition, some nurses from these schools have been sent to the United States for advanced training.

A secondary objective of the project is to have greater emphasis placed by the union and state ministries and departments of health on the public-health aspects of nursing. To demonstrate the value and effectiveness of the State Advisory Nursing Service, American nurses have been assigned to the Madras and Rajasthan states and the central government to prepare Indian nurses for advisory services. They will demonstrate the importance of organizing community groups and teaching home nursing, child care, and nutrition.

The entire project may cost more than $2.1 million over a ten-year period. Twenty-six American technicians will be working in India, and 76 Indian nurses will go to the United States for advanced training. Equipment worth about a million dollars is being furnished to the Indian institutions involved in this project.

The All-India Institute of Medical Sciences

The All-India Institute of Medical Sciences at New Delhi has been designed not only to provide undergraduate and postgraduate instruction to students in medicine and related subjects, but to carry on basic research. The hospital attached to the Institute has 650 beds and an outpatient department. The Institute will serve as a national center for clinical teaching and research as well as a research source for preclinical departments. The cost of constructing and equipping the center and the hospital has been met by American grants of P.L. 480 funds and aid from the Rockefeller Foundation.

American Contribution to Better Health in India

American assistance toward better health in India cannot be evaluated merely in terms of dollars and cents, drugs and medicines. America's pilot projects, demonstration ventures, and pioneering ideas have created an awareness of what can be done, even with limited resources. Once health education shows the people of India the possibilities of better health it will have a beneficent chain reaction.

Today, fewer Indians suffer from malaria; fewer die of typhoid and tuberculosis. The number of medical and nursing colleges has increased, as has the number of physicians, surgeons, and nurses. The incidence of morbidity in India, while still high compared to the advanced countries, has definitely fallen during the last fifteen years.

The greatest contribution was the Ford Foundation's attempt to raise rural health standards. In doing so, the Foundation revealed a rare understanding of the real crux of the rural problem.

The American contribution toward bettering Indian health has been an eye-opener to the Indian Government. It has, to some extent, diverted the nation's attention from the long-term process of industrialization to the immediately rewarding sphere of better health, hygiene, and sanitation. The advanced countries have moved from the machine age to the age of automation, but, in India, man must continue to be a greater asset than the machine. The importance of healthy citizens in the over-all economic and cultural development of the nation cannot be overstressed.

7. *AMERICAN AID TO INDIAN EDUCATION*

EDUCATION: THE HOPE OF THE FUTURE

FROM EARLIEST TIMES, according to the available historical evidence, India has paid considerable attention to education, and in the traditional social hierarchy the teacher enjoys an honored place. However, the education that was imparted through the centuries, down to the advent of the British, was predominantly academic, literary, and religious, as it was in many parts of the world, and was restricted to the elite of the population.

With the establishment of British rule, however, a Western pattern of education was introduced to India. This education was theoretically open to all classes of the population, but, for political and economic reasons, it was actually confined to privileged groups in the new urban centers of India. To receive an education was a rare privilege, and the gap between the minority of the educated and the vast majority of the illiterate and ignorant continued as wide as ever. Thus, when India attained independence and adopted a democratic and republican form of government, the task of educational reconstruction and expansion was a formidable one.

Democracy and a vast, uneducated population are incompatible. It is unrealistic to expect a country that has had no free compulsory educational system to run a parliamentary democracy intelligently and effectively. Representative political institutions cannot succeed when they are dependent for their existence on the choices of an illiterate electorate. It is true that the mass mind can operate in a literate and educated society quite as powerfully as in one that is illiterate and uneducated, as we see today in the totalitarian countries. But, in a country where the government is chosen by a free electorate, education must be regarded as a precondition of the exercise of democratic rights.

In 1947, India's educational picture was grim. Less than 15 per cent of the population was literate in the mother tongue. Only a quarter of the children between 6 and 11 could go to school; about a fifth of those between 12 and 16 had high-school facilities. The total number of students in colleges and universities was about 250,000 out of a population of some 350 million. As for scientific and technical education, the number of institutions and students attending them was inconsequential.

The unhappy import of this educational picture was not lost on the government of India. If uneducated people and an effective democracy did not go together, neither did an illiterate population and rapid industrialization and economic development. The First Five-Year Plan correctly evaluated the situation when it pointed out that:

> Education is of basic importance in the planned development of a nation. The educational machinery will have to be geared for the specific tasks which the nation sets itself through the Plan so as to make available in the various fields personnel of suitable quality at the required rate. The educational system has also an intimate bearing on the attainment of the general objectives of the Plan inasmuch as it largely determines the quality of the manpower and the social climate of the community. In a democratic set-up, the role of education becomes crucial since it can function effectively only if there is an intelligent participation of the masses in the affairs of the country. The success of planning in a democracy depends also on the growth of the spirit of cooperation and the sense of disciplined citizenship among the people and on the degree to which it becomes possible to evoke public enthusiasm and build up local leadership. It is essential for the successful implementation of the Plan that the educational program helps to train the people to place responsibilities before rights and to keep the self-regarding outlook and the force of the acquisitive instinct within legitimate bounds. The educational system should also satisfy cultural needs, which is essential for the healthy growth of a nation. The system should stimulate the growth of the creative faculties, increase the capacity of enjoyment and develop a critical appreciation of arts, literature and other creative activities.[1]

Insofar as widespread public education is essential for economic development, effective political participation, and cultural advancement, it would seem that we should give high priority to education and invest a large portion of our budget and foreign aid on our schools and colleges. A nation's educational system is

[1] *The First Five-Year Plan,* p. 525.

the key factor in the development of its human and material resources. There is no doubt that a country's economic development is directly dependent on the latest knowledge, the skills, and the healthy attitudes engendered by a sound educational system.

The Third Five-Year Plan highlights the role of education in the over-all development of a nation. The planners observe that:

> Education is the most important single factor in achieving rapid economic development and technological progress and in creating a social order founded on the values of freedom, social justice and equal opportunity. Programmes of education lie at the base of the effort to forge the bonds of common citizenship, to harness the energies of the people, and to develop the natural and human resources of every part of the country. Developments of the past decade have created a momentum for economic growth; yet there are large deficiencies in the sphere of education, which must be removed speedily if progress is to be sustained and enduring.[2]

American assistance to Indian education has kept in view the implications of the foregoing observations of the Planning Commission and has supported key and strategic projects at all educational levels.

During the years since 1950, American specialists have aided primary and secondary education as well as higher university, technical, and scientific education. It is unnecessary to list all the educational projects receiving aid, for the extent of the coverage can be understood by selecting a few representative projects. However, it must be pointed out that, in relation to other sectors of the economy, American governmental assistance in this field is relatively small, although American foundations have played a major and significant role in aiding Indian education. Official aid is predicated upon the specific request of the government of India.

Aid for Primary and Secondary Education

A total of $1,944,000 was obligated through 1961 by AID for Extension Training for Secondary School Teachers. The 54 Extension Training Centers were devoted to the development of an in-service education program. Five American specialists assisted the program in the fields of curriculum and organization, social stud-

[2] *The Third Five-Year Plan* (New Delhi: Planning Commission, 1962), p. 573.

ies and sciences, and improved methods of examination and evaluation. The centers received books, teaching aids, and vehicles. A complementary project was set up in Educational Administration. The services of an American specialist in this field were supplied to the government's Central Institute of Education at New Delhi. The assistance also covered the supply of books and periodicals dealing with all aspects of educational administration. Besides the dollar aid, a grant of Rs.30 crores was made from P.L. 480 funds to the government of India, up to 1962, for the improvement of elementary education in India. The second phase of this program provided assistance in developing a vocational curriculum in the multipurpose secondary-school program. Five American specialists served on the project, which also received, up to 1962, commodities worth $167,000.

Aid for Adult Education

The program of adult education is in a sense part of the primary-education program, for both involve instruction in the rudiments of reading and writing. Apart from the services of specialists, material aid for this program has included periodicals and books, audio-visual equipment, and station wagons.

A nongovernmental project, the Literacy Village in Lucknow, founded in 1953 by Mrs. Welthy Fisher, an American, received a grant of Rs.720,000. This center trains teachers specializing in adult education. A major activity of the center is the training of writers who can prepare materials that new readers can enjoy. (Without such material, the newly acquired reading skills quickly deteriorate and sometimes even disappear.) The center has so far trained some 4,000 teachers. It also produces such adult-teaching aids as filmstrips, puppets, and taped dramas.

Aid to Higher Education

Higher education in India, including colleges and universities, professional and technological institutes, research laboratories, and advanced training and research centers in a variety of fields, has received American assistance through several general and *ad hoc* channels, mainly the Fulbright Program, the Smith-Mundt grants, the Wheat Loan Program, the Participant Training Program, and the Indian Specialist Program of the TCM (now AID). Private American aid to Indian education has come also through foundations and universities as well as certain other academic bodies.

The Fulbright Program

The Fulbright Educational Exchange Program went into effect in India in February, 1950. To administer it, the United States Educational Foundation in India was established in New Delhi in 1950. What are the objectives of the Foundation? It is obvious that cross-cultural education through the international exchange (here Indo-American) of students, researchers, and professors is of lasting value in a world torn by political and economic tensions and ideologies. This objective was spelled out by the Board of Directors of the USEFI after the program had been in operation for a few years.

> The United States Educational Foundation in India seeks to contribute to better understanding and closer relations between India and the United States, specifically by increasing the number of Indians and of Americans who have direct knowledge of both countries, and by providing indirect knowledge to larger numbers through students and professors in the universities of both. To this end, the Foundation proposes to exchange the representatives best qualified to present the cultural and social value of each country.
>
> The Foundation proposes, further, to increase the knowledge available by providing additional opportunities in Indian studies to American students, and in American studies to Indian students. Universities in both countries will be encouraged to offer new courses in these areas.
>
> A further objective of the Foundation is to aid Indian education: first to strengthen the universities by assisting them in specific subjects which are new or weak, and in which American education has notable development; and secondly to cooperate in the reorientation and reconstruction of secondary education.
>
> On the other hand, the Foundation seeks to provide opportunities to American scholars to make first-hand studies in India of their various subjects, and also to enjoy the experience of teaching in Indian universities.

The Fulbright Program is financed from the funds derived from the rupee proceeds of the sale of American war-surplus property and agricultural-surplus commodities to the government of India. The maximum amount available for expenditure annually by the Foundation is the rupee equivalent of $600,000. The funds available to the USEFI are in nonconvertible rupee currency, however, which means that the Foundation cannot pay for the expenses of Indians in the United States. Part of the necessary dollar funds is made available by U.S. Congress authorization under the Smith-Mundt Act. American universities and foundations cooperate in the program by offering a limited number of scholarships, fellowships, and assistantships. The USEFI is managed by a Board of Directors consisting of the American Ambassador, who is honorary chairman, five Indian members appointed by the government of India, and five American members appointed by the American Ambassador.

The Foundation promotes Indo-American relations primarily through a balanced mutual-educational program and the exchange of students and scholars. Grants are made to Indian professors for lecturing or for advanced research at American colleges and universities, to postgraduate students and high-school teachers for studies and research in the United States, and to Americans in comparable categories for work in India. The Fulbright grants to Indians cover their round-trip transportation to the United States. In certain cases, full or partial dollar-maintenance fellowships for students are available from the U.S. Government under the Smith-Mundt Program and from American universities through the Institute of International Education.

This program has been successfully implemented since 1950, despite the difficulties inherent in an undertaking of this size. And, as Dr. Dawes has commented on its future:

> In a world in which both the value of education in itself and the importance of understanding between nations have risen to new heights, educational exchange under a bi-national agreement holds a unique position of opportunity and realization. In such a world, the United States Educational Foundation in India will be looked to for leadership; its role will be of expanded proportions not only in terms of money but in relation to the whole area of education in the United States and in India."[3]

The Wheat Loan Program

In the first United States Government aid agreement with India, namely, the Indian Emergency Food Aid Act of 1951, provision was made for American aid to higher education in India. The first $5 million paid by India as interest on the loan was reallocated in the Treasury of the United States for a program of educational reform and rehabilitation of institutions of higher learning in India. The program involved the exchange of persons and the pro-

[3] Norman Dawes, *A Two-Way Street* (Bombay: Asia Publishing House, 1962), p. 176. A detailed description of the operation of the Fulbright Program during the last decade is given in this book.

curement of books, apparatus, and scientific equipment. Thus began the Indian Wheat Loan Educational Exchange Program in 1951, under the administration of the United States Information Service.

All three parts of the program (the procurement of book and scientific equipment and the exchange of persons) are executed through consultations between the officers of the Wheat Loan Program in New Delhi and officials of the Ministry of Education, the Ministry of Scientific Research and Culture (now combined), and the University Grants Commission.

The book-procurement part of the program involves more than merely presenting a few books to an institution. It is part of a large-scale educational program of assistance and advice. Grants for this purpose may range from $25,000 to $75,000; they are given to an institution on the recommendation of the government of India. For instance, the biggest telescope between Cairo and Tokyo has been erected at the Nizamiah Observatory at Hyderabad with funds provided by the Wheat Loan Program. The cost of the telescope was $250,000 or about Rs.12 lakhs.

The Exchange of Persons part of the program is designed to promote some specific improvement or reform in some area of Indian education. Here, as elsewhere, the project has been a two-way proposition. For instance, a group of Indian educators went to the United States to study the pattern of American undergraduate education, and in return some American educators visited India to advise the Indian universities on certain contemplated reforms.

Under the program, 145 Indian educators have toured the United States to observe the American educational system and American institutions, and 31 American professors have come to advise and teach in Indian universities in their specialized fields.

A total of $5 million has been spent or programmed in grants as follows:

Scientific equipment	$1,824,275
Books	1,376,513
Exchange of Persons	1,005,614
Purchase of books from the government of India and the state governments for the Library of Congress	75,000
Administration	652,000
Contingency fund to cover unexpected cost increase	50,000
Total	$4,983,402

Home Science Education and Research

A quarter of a century ago "home science" was not considered important enough to be included in the curriculum in women's colleges in India. Of late, however, its importance in promoting more attractive homes, scientific nutrition, and better child care is readily granted. Much of the credit for this welcome change must go to American initiative and assistance.

American assistance to various home-science education and research projects falls into two phases. The first phase (1955–58) provided help in developing and strengthening home-science courses in eight selected Indian universities. The services of eleven American professors of home economics were provided; twelve Indian participants were given higher training in the subject at the University of Tennessee. Commodities to aid in teaching and research valued at $91,604 were also supplied.

The second phase (1958–62) involved assisting four regional demonstration centers to plan, develop, implement, and evaluate teacher-training programs in home science at all educational levels. The services of eight American home-science experts and supplies for classroom and laboratory purposes worth $40,000 were provided.

Technical Secondary Schools

A weakness in Indian technical education has been that it begins only at the college level. That is, there is no preparation at the high-school level for a student who plans to be, say, an engineer. The choice of a profession is usually made after graduation from high school. American assistance has pioneered in developing technical education at lower levels. With U.S. aid, India set up, in 1956, twenty-six multipurpose technical secondary schools. In these schools, students spend half a day in the classroom and the other half in the workshop—an adaptation of the Wardha Scheme of craft-centered education. The curriculums of some of the teacher-training institutions are coordinated with the multipurpose technical high schools.

Scientific and Technical Education

American assistance has touched almost every aspect of the complex and vast problem of Indian education—from adult illiteracy to advanced scientific research—but no aspect has received such special attention as technical education.

The literary bias and lack of technological and scientific orientation of Indian college and university education have already been touched upon. For an underdeveloped country that has embarked upon large-scale industrialization, nothing is of greater importance than advanced technological education, for there is a direct and fundamental relationship between the availability of competent and qualified engineers and rapid industrial development. New and modern engineering colleges must be created, and existing technical institutions expanded and upgraded. The government of India and the Five-Year Plans have therefore rightly accorded the highest priority to higher technical education.

In 1954, the United States began to assist India to develop her engineering colleges and technical institutes. A grant of Rs.79 lakhs provided American professors to train faculty members of Indian engineering colleges. In 1958, 300 lecturers from India's engineering colleges were sent to the United States for postgraduate training. The institutions that participated in the program included the Bengal Engineering College in Howrah, the College of Engineering in Guindy, the College of Engineering in Poona, the Indian Institute of Technology in Kharagpur, and the University of Roorkee in Uttar Pradesh. The University of Wisconsin and the University of Illinois participated in the program.

The Indian Institute of Technology

Of all the technical institutions that have risen with the help of foreign collaboration in India, none has been planned with as much care, foresight, and technical know-how as the Indian Institute of Technology in Kanpur. The institute has been designed, along with three others, to serve many needs. It stands on a 1,050-acre site and is planned to provide the most modern and effective technical education available anywhere in the country. American aid to this institute began in 1959 when a team of six U.S. engineering educators under a contract with the American Society of Engineering Education completed a survey of Indian engineering education. This survey included recommendations to the Agency for International Development and the government of India for the organization and operation of the institute; it also outlined the role that the U.S. Government was willing to play in its development. A second survey team, from Educational Services, Incorporated, arrived at the end of 1961 to examine at first hand the requirements of the Kanpur Institute. The Institute will receive technical aid from a consortium of nine American universities and engineering institutes. A director, two administrative assistants, twenty professors of engineering, technologists and science specialists, and ten short-term technical consultants will be supplied.

By 1963, the United States assisted the Kanpur Institute to a total of $6.2 million for equipment and advisory services. By 1966, when the Institute is expected to be in full operation (though teaching has already begun), American aid is likely to total $14 million. Besides dollar aid, the Institute will have received P. L. 480 rupee grants totaling Rs.1.9 crores ($4 million). The government of India on its part has not only provided the land for the Institute but has committed $17.4 million (Rs.8.7 crores) for recurring expenses. For the years 1964 and 1965, the U.S. Government has promised a total assistance of about $8 million.

The Kanpur Institute is expected to become, in a quarter of a century, the Massachusetts Institute of Technology of Asia. It is hoped that this Institute will be instrumental in raising the standards of technological education and in promoting advanced technological research throughout India.

Indian Specialists Program

Several other projects in the over-all field of education have received American aid. These include the National Institute of Education in New Delhi; rural institutes in different parts of the country; the National Institute of Basic Education at New Delhi; training in educational administration of Indian educational leaders in selected centers of the country; and the Indian Specialists Program.

The Indian Specialists Program enables Indian specialists in diverse fields to study and travel in the United States. Financed by the U.S. State Department, the program is devised especially to give the Indian expert some insight into American life. To achieve this end, he is encouraged and provided opportunities to enter into the life of the American community in which he lives, no matter for how brief a period. Travel throughout the country is arranged for him in connection with his special interests. All his expenses, including international travel, travel within the United States, tuition fees, and living costs, are met by the State Department. His minimum assignment is for four to five months and the emphasis is on specific training to provide him with the maximum practical experience.

The Indian Specialist Program is implemented under two separate titles: the Foreign Leader Program, and the Foreign Specialist Program. Up to 1962, 127 and 144 Indians, under these two categories respectively, received grants to visit the United States. The total amounts expended on these two programs were $647,700 and $734,400 respectively.

International Farm Youth Program

This program was inaugurated in 1948 and is administered in the United States by the Extension Service of the Department of Agriculture, the Land Grant Colleges, and the National 4-H Clubs. In India, the Director of Training in the Extension Services of the Ministry of Agriculture supervises the project. Indian and American farmers between twenty and thirty years of age travel to each other's country and live and work on farms for a period of four to six months. The project is financed by combined contributions from the State Extension Services, private foundation grants, and grants from industrial houses and interested individuals.

Conclusion

It may be difficult to evaluate the impact of American aid on Indian education in precise terms. American money and equipment are important. But even more important are American ideals, and it is in reflecting these ideals that the American professors and other specialists who have willingly imparted their knowledge and skills to Indians have played a commendable part.

The ideals of American education can be summed up very briefly. The philosophy of American education is predicated upon the worth and dignity of the individual. It is opposed to dogmatism and authoritarianism of all kinds. American education stresses freedom of choice. The student is taught to think and to make his own choices. He is guided in discovering his abilities and aptitudes, and he is free to pursue the goals for which he is best suited. The American educational system provides free and compulsory education to all its citizens up to the age of seventeen. It also presents a curriculum variegated enough to meet a wide range of aptitudes, talents, and intellectual needs. American ideals include the growing equality of educational opportunities to all, regardless of race, religion, nationality, sex, or financial resources. If Indian educators and students have absorbed some of this American ideology of freedom in education, American aid will bear ample dividends for generations to come in India.

8. *AMERICAN AID TO COMMUNICATION AND TRANSPORTATION*

COMMUNICATIONS and transportation provide the important basic infrastructure essential to long-range national economic and social development. Channels of communications are the nerve threads that knit the country together, roads are the blood stream that give life to the country. Their importance can hardly be overemphasized.

India's three Five-Year Plans have fortunately been well aware of the importance of greatly increasing the existing meager transportation and communications facilities. Regional economic development relieves the strain on the transportation system on the one hand, but, on the other, makes further demands on it. For instance, a fertilizer factory in a port city will do away with the necessity for transporting the fertilizer from the docks, if it was hitherto being imported. But, at the same time, increased internal production will be meaningless if the fertilizer cannot be moved rapidly from the factory to the demand centers. In general, the cumulative effect or even a small measure of economic development results in a greater demand for transportation and communication facilities, and this demand is precisely what India is experiencing at present. The industrialization of the country that has already taken place as a result of certain improvements in transportation is resulting in heavier demands for better and more transportation and communication facilities.

The transportation system in India can be conveniently divided into national highways, railways, and airways.

National Highways

In ancient times, travel by "road," the only travel available, must have been an arduous adventure. There were no roads in the modern sense of the term, but there were dusty "highways" for armies to march on and pilgrims to use in visiting the far-flung sacred cities. The roads in India received some attention before and during the Mughal rule, but they were developed, in the main, by the British. As with many necessities of national life, only a little money and effort was spent on them, and India has never had a national network of modern multi-lane highways such as exists in the United States and some European countries. However, the major cities are connected by national highways and most cities have tolerable roads, although these do not meet the growing demands of the country. In a country where the private car is a luxury and where even the bus is a relatively new phenomenon, road-building naturally received low priority. Even modern, bustling cities like Calcutta, New Delhi, Bombay, and Madras have roads that are far from satisfactory.

Roads in India have to bear the burden of a great variety of vehicles, some of them as outmoded as the handcart and the bullock-drawn cart, which are both ubiquitous in India. There has not been sufficient awareness of the fact that the cart and the horse and carriage are anachronisms in the age of the jet. Nor is the freedom of cattle to wander on roads and highways conducive to transportation efficiency.

In 1957, India received a TCM loan of $28,000 for the purpose of purchasing truck and jeep parts to be assembled in India. In 1958, India received $29,000 toward the construction of a few new highways and bridges. The Development Loan Fund's Loan No. 2 (June, 1958) stipulated that $25 million of the total $35 million allocated for private enterprise be set aside for road transportation; it was used for the purchase of automobile parts and equipment. In 1960, the Export-Import Bank provided India with a $3 million loan to import equipment for the construction of roads and bridges. The Development Loan Fund extended a loan in June, 1960, of $13.1 million for buying automobile and truck parts in the United States to be combined with components manufactured in India to produce jeeps, station wagons, and Dodge one-ton and three-ton trucks. And, in December, 1962, AID agreed to loan Hindusthan Motors, Ltd., and Tata Engineering and Locomotive Company, Ltd., $15.8 million and $13.7 million respectively for the production of road-transport vehicles. A second AID loan of $38 million was granted for the import of automobiles, jeeps, parts, and for the construction of roads and bridges.

It is to be hoped that road construction will receive more attention in the current development plans of the various state governments. The problem is not only to increase road mileage and broaden the existing (for the most part, one-lane) roads, but to improve the quality and durability of road surfaces. City roads as well as the intercity highways are constructed in such a poor fashion that a single monsoon leaves them full of hazardous holes. An objective of the Third Plan is to complete the 787 national-highway improvement schemes begun under the Second Plan.

The Third Five-Year Plan provides for the extension of surfaced roads as well as an increase in the number of road vehicles. The Plan's targets are to increase the road mileage from 144,000 in 1961 to 164,000 by March, 1966. During the same period, the Plan provides for the production of 30,000 passenger cars, 60,000 commercial vehicles, 10,000 jeeps and station wagons, and 48,000 motorcycles, and scooters. American assistance to this sector of the Indian economy will go a long way to achieving these targets.

Railway Rehabilitation

For more than a century, India's network of railways has been the lifeline of her communication system. India's railways were the biggest commercial venture undertaken by the British. The Indian railway system, one of the major pillars of the economy, is the largest in Asia and the fourth largest in the world. It is the nation's largest nationalized enterprise, with nearly 35,000 miles of track. It carries about 80 per cent of the country's freight traffic and about 70 per cent of the passenger traffic. Some 5,000 passenger trains run daily between 6,400 railway stations. The system employs 12 million workers.

When India became free in 1947, the Indian railways were the most damaged part of India's total national assets. Wartime damage to locomotives, coaches, and wagons, the strains and losses of partition, and the fact that there had been no replacement of any kind in a decade combined to pose a formidable problem of rehabilitation and expansion. In 1951, at a time when greater demands than ever were being made on the railways, there were more than 1,000 locomotives, about 6,000 coaches, and about 2,000 wagons that needed to be replaced.

The task before the First Five-Year Plan was primarily one of recovery and rehabilitation. This meant both the encouragement of indigenous manufacture and the large-scale import of necessary equipment. American aid here became crucial. Nearly 20 per cent of the total American aid received by India during 1952–56 was used for the modernization and expansion of her surface-transport facilities.

During the First Five-Year Plan, India bought with her own resources more than 2,000 locomotives. America supplemented this supply in 1954 with 100 new locomotives and 2,500 broad gauge freight cars. In 1955, the United States provided India with 3,700 freight cars. In 1956, India received 255,000 tons of steel and 4,000 tons of rail for the expansion and rehabilitation of her railroads. Above all, there was a need for a detailed survey of the entire railway-transportation system in order to formulate long-range plans for expanding the system in relation to other modes of transport and to meet the ever-increasing pressures from agriculture, industry, and trade. To meet this need, the United States Government sent two survey teams of American railroad experts to India. The first team surveyed the existing situation, studied future demands, and suggested methods of achieving phased optimum capacity. The second team examined the feasibility of using combined rail-sea shipment of bulk commodities, thus relieving the pressures imposed on the railways by increased movement of coal.

Total U.S. Government aid given for the rehabilitation and expansion of Indian railways, including equipment, amounted to $63,062,200 up to 1956. Through June, 1961, America had obligated in all $74,442,000 for Indian railroad development.

The Development Loan Fund made three substantial dollar loans for railway expansion in India up to the end of 1960. The first railway-loan agreement was concluded on June 23, 1958, for a total of $40 million, which was shortly reduced to $30 million. (The reduction was added to the third railway-loan agreement.) The first loan was for the acquisition of steel components for railway cars, coaches, diesel locomotives, and bridges. By the end of 1960, $18.87 million had been drawn from the loan. The second DLF railway-loan agreement was concluded in December, 1958. It authorized $35 million for the acquisition of rolling stock, steel, and electrical-signaling and other equipment. The entire amount has been drawn and utilized for these purposes. The third railway-loan agreement was concluded on December 5, 1960, for the acquisition of equipment for centralized traffic control and for diesel and electric locomotives. The loan amounted to $50 million, including the $10 million transferred from the first railway loan. The most recent loan agreement for Indian railway development was concluded on March 8, 1962, for $35 million (Rs.16.7 crores). India has to repay this AID loan in dollars over a period of 40 years, with an initial 10-year grace period, at an interest rate of .75 per cent.

Airways

India occupies a favorable geographic position for the development of air transport, both internal and international. From the national point of view, the country's vast distances and good weather assure civil aviation an important role to play in the future development of the country. From the international point of view, India occupies a strategic position in the international skyways, linking East Asia and Australia on the one hand, and Europe and America on the other. The modern air force has become a major arm of India's defense system. Though India has become aviation-conscious only in recent years, she has made considerable progress.

The first American grant to Indian aviation was for the development of aviation ground facilities. In the words of an official publication,

> India occupies an important geographic position in the international aeronautical communications pattern. Numerous operational messages are received, sent and relayed by the communications centers at Calcutta, Bombay, Delhi and Madras. Radio teletype facilities established under the Indo-American program have permitted the decommissioning of the much slower manually operated radio corresponding telegraph circuits.
>
> The project has provided additional assistance for modernization and expansion of telecommunication, navigational and meteorological aids. This includes installation of 10 duplex radio teletype network terminals, one ground-controlled approach radar (GCA) facility for handling traffic in bad weather at Bombay, and at least 10 very high frequency semi-directional range (VOR) facilities for use at short-range navigational aids. A storm-warning radar system has been provided at Calcutta for use by the Indian Meteorological Department.
>
> Subsequently, it was proposed to provide modern electronics equipment for the Civil Aviation Training Centre at Allahabad in order to ensure that personnel receive training in the same type of equipment they will later have to maintain.[1]

Besides these training facilities for more than 200 Indian technicians, American aid includes training opportunities for a limited number of Indian personnel in the United States in flight inspection, electronics engineering, and air-traffic control. A total grant

[1] *Indo-American Technical Cooperation, 1952–1956* (New Delhi: USIS, 1957), pp. 38–39.

of $2,536,500 was made to cover these items of the project up to 1961.

Air India International has received both technical assistance and loans to buy the latest planes. To help AII set up modern administration procedures, an experienced American airlines executive was "loaned" to India for a short period. Another American specialist in stores and inventory management was loaned for six months to examine the management, organization, and operations of Air India and to make recommendations for improvement. Aid in the amount of $33,500 covered the services of these two specialists.

In 1960, the Export-Import Bank authorized a credit for $4.1 million to the government of India to assist in the purchase by Air India of one Boeing 707 and necessary spare parts. This loan carries an interest of 5.75 per cent per annum and is repayable in 14 approximately equal semiannual installments beginning at the end of 1961. Air India also received from the same bank a second loan of $8,100,000 to buy additional aircraft. A consortium of five American banks extended a credit of $11.2 million to Air India during 1959–60 for the purchase of three Boeing jets.

Development of Telecommunications

In 1959, at the invitation of the government of India, the Technical Cooperation Mission carried out a mass-communications training program for Indian technical personnel in the field of telecommunications, wireless systems, etc., with the aid of American experts. The project received $56,000.

The Posts and Telegraphs Department of the government of India has established a Telecommunications Research Laboratory in New Delhi to carry out research on improved methods in its technical work. Through new designs, improved manufacture of equipment, and more efficient maintenance methods, the public can be assured of better and more efficient telecommunication services. The TCM assisted in this project by providing a nucleus of modern precision-testing and measuring equipment for line communications systems, technical books and periodicals, and the services of a telecommunications engineer to assist in setting up the laboratory and in training research personnel. The total amount provided for this project was $47,000.

American assistance has also been received by All India Radio and by the Posts and Telegraphs Department for training its personnel and for modern scientific equipment. The Development

Loan Fund has supplied two loans to India. The first loan, $18 million, was for obtaining structural and other steel for various nonprofit public-utility projects under the Second Five-Year Plan. The Ministry of Communications used $10 million of the loan to procure electric lamp posts and steel plates. The second loan for $25 million was granted in December, 1960, for procuring structural and other steel products for the Posts and Telegraphs Department.

Although there is much yet to be accomplished in improving and developing transport and communication facilities, a few major strides have been taken in the right direction. During the last fifteen years, the number of trains has been more than doubled and the railway track has been extended. Today there are 35,000 miles of it. A locomotive factory at Chittaranjan in West Bengal and an integral coach factory at Perambur in Madras are making their contribution to the progress of Indian railway travel. Highways have also improved and the total surfaced roads today amount to about 150,000 miles. The pace has been slow but the targets set up in the Third Five-Year Plan will be achieved. Air transport has caught the imagination of the people. Although it is still expensive enough to be a luxury, it is being patronized increasingly by the small segment of the Indian population to whom the value of time has assumed new importance.

In the years ahead the development of transportation and communications will become both the cause and consequence of the over-all economic development of the country. For, as the country advances, it is bound to make increasing demands on these services, in turn, the expansion of these services will contribute to faster economic growth. To the development of this important infrastructure, American assistance in men, material, and money has been vital.

9. *MISCELLANEOUS AMERICAN AID*

A NUMBER of small but worthwhile projects and institutions in several states have received grants—big and small—from the United States.

Indian economic development largely implies the reconstruction of rural India, since India lives in her villages. After numerous experiments and pilot projects attacking the problems of India's villages, it is now realized that only a multipronged approach can yield lasting results. The village needs to be approached simultaneously from the points of view of education, health, sanitation, hygiene, and agriculture. The multipurpose "village worker" can be an effective means for combating the villagers' apathy, ignorance, and poverty. A "village worker" is one who is specially trained to carry to the villagers new but practical ideas on all aspects of social welfare and agricultural-extension work. America has contributed not only the dynamic idea of extension work but also her experience in implementing the program among American farm families.

The Community Development Program thus conceived received considerable financial support from the Ford Foundation, but American governmental aid (TCM, now AID) has also been substantial. In 1956, some 560 Community Blocks and about 600 National Extension Service Blocks, covering 126,857 villages with a total population of 82 million were set up to receive aid of various kinds. American commodity aid for this project included 1,994 jeeps, 236 station wagons and trucks, 30 health vans, 163 tractors (some with bulldozers), 38 road rollers, 350 trailers, and 1,000 film projectors, valued at $7,884,368. The Community Development Program as a whole received from American aid through 1961 funds amounting to $13,519,000.

Social Work

Allied to the community-development program is the social-welfare education project to which AID contributed the services of a child-welfare worker for the Delhi School of Social Work and consultants to the Indian Conference of Social Work. The 1955–56 program provided specialists in social research, group and field work, child welfare, and community organization. These specialists were assigned to various schools of social work, including those at Baroda, New Delhi, Hazaribagh, Lucknow, and Madras, and were provided with the necessary teaching and testing equipment as well as technical books and periodicals. Through June, 1961, the project received $583,000 from AID funds. The supply of American consultants to Indian universities which requested such assistance continued in 1962–64.

Building Material Development

The problem of housing in India, as in many other underdeveloped countries, is the problem of finding low-cost building materials that are close at hand. Early in the aid program a project was initiated to develop low-cost housing suitable for Indian conditions. For demonstration and provision of low-cost construction and materials, $47,000 was obligated from AID funds. When an exhibition on the subject was sponsored by the government of India in New Delhi in 1954, American technicians helped officials of the Ministry of Works, Housing and Supply to organize it, and an American technician contributed the design for a special exhibit called the "growing house," the initial cost of which is small, but which, as its name suggests, can gradually be expanded into a permanent and comfortable home.

The Central Building Institute at Roorkee in Uttar Pradesh has been carrying on research to find cheap building materials. To help the Institute workers find an answer to their problem, AID has provided them with a laboratory and a pilot plant to experiment with indigenous materials. As of June, 1961, a total of $165,000 was obligated for the Building Materials Development project. The project is ultimately expected to establish a premixed plaster industry and the manufacture of lightweight cement asbestos sheets.

Central Labour Institute

One of the objectives of the Second Five-Year Plan was to improve the working conditions and raise the living standards of the industrial laborer. This objective was to be achieved by strengthening the trade-union movement and improving government services for labor. Plans were formulated for increasing real wages, providing apprenticeship and vocational programs for workers, developing stable industrial relations and expanding the number of trained labor leaders.

The AID projects in this field were coordinated with these broad aims of the government of India. To help establish the Central Labour Institute in Bombay, $83,000 was obligated as of June, 1959. The funds were used to purchase laboratory equipment and technical books and to provide exhibits for the Institute, which includes a center for visual demonstration, an industrial-hygiene laboratory, and a library. The Institute, which also serves as a meeting ground for government, management, and labor groups, has the over-all objective of improving the safety, health, and welfare of industrial laborers.

Bombay Craftsmen Training Centre

As the pace of industrialization increases, the need for trained and competent industrial craftsmen as well as instructors grows. To meet this demand the government of India has established the Craftsmen Training Centre at Bombay with American financial and technical aid.

The Centre is designed to train 212 instructors in a nine-month course, and 236 industrial craftsmen who receive a two-year course of study and work. An AID-financed contract with the Dunwoody Industrial Institute at Minneapolis, Minnesota, is providing the services of 9 technicians to formulate training programs and assist in their initial operation. American assistance through 1963 totals $900,000.

Trades Training Centres

In 1956, 570 Trades Training Centres were established by the central and state governments all over the country. At the request of the government of India, AID helped to coordinate them, introduce modern equipment, and improve the skills of the teaching staff. Nine Indian instructors from these centers received training for one year, first at Cornell University and then at various American industrial plants. In addition, the United States provided the project with an industrial-training expert. The equipment supplied includes electrical and construction machinery, lathes, drills and other machine tools, metal-working machinery, planimeters, etc. Altogether a sum of $641,000 was obligated for these purposes as of June, 1959.

One of the earliest of the labor projects undertaken by AID and the government of India was a series of studies in industrial hygiene during 1951–53. The project continued till 1955 with demonstrations, investigations, and training in regulating the thermal environment of workers. Special laboratory equipment was provided in Ahmedabad to determine the relation between thermal environment and productivity in order to set standards of industrial hygiene. In 1956, more equipment was supplied along with the services of an industrial-hygiene expert and a thermal-environment consultant. A sum of $14,000 was spent for these studies through 1961.

Public Administration

Modern India has a need for streamlined public-administrative procedures and for a new type of training for her civil servants. Although American aid to public administration has not been one of the major AID projects, some assistance has been provided both by sending American experts to India to observe and make suggestions and by sending selected Indian administrative personnel to the United States for special training. A grant of $55,000 was made to meet the expenses of this project.

Two minor grants were made for allied subjects. When a new Statistics and Reporting Section was established to process operating statistics for the Foreign Aid, Economics and Budget Division of the Department of Economic Affairs in the Ministry of Finance, AID equipped the section with modern machines for processing, tabulating, and reproducing data for Indo-American projects. This installation also served as a demonstration center for other ministries in the government of India. A sum of $13,000 was obligated by June, 1961, for improved operating statistics and reports.

The Indian Statistical Institute at Calcutta, a professional training and research body in statistics as well as the processing center of statistics collected for national sample surveys, obtained the services of two American specialists—one a statistical quality-control expert and the other an electronics-equipment specialist. Several hundred books and periodicals were supplied to the Industry and Management Research Unit of the Institute. AID assistance came to $12,000 through June, 1961.

Peace Corps

The Peace Corps was established by an Executive Order of President John F. Kennedy on March 1, 1961. It was designed to enable individual American citizens to work directly with people in other countries on economic, educational, or social problems in those countries. The major objective of the program is to promote international peace through personal relationships and the development of mutual understanding. This objective makes a strong appeal to the idealism and altruism of the average American. Peace Corps Volunteers are sent to a country only on that country's request, to work on projects approved by both the host country and the Peace Corps. The Peace Corps functions as an independent agency within the Department of State and is financed by Mutual Security Funds allocated each year by the U.S. Congress.

What can the Peace Corps Volunteers do? First, the Volunteers are trained as teachers, community-development workers, agricultural-extension workers, sanitation engineers, construction foremen, medical assistants, mechanics, and so on. They are not highly specialized technicians; they are merely coworkers. By living with their hosts the Volunteers gain an insight into a foreign country such as few, if any, Americans have ever had. The Peace Corps Volunteer is representative of an American seldom seen by the people of the host country. He is neither a tourist nor a wealthy resident. He works beside the nationals of the host country and lives on a level comparable to theirs.

In 1963, there were more than 5,000 Peace Corps Volunteers on active service overseas in 46 countries. Of these, 26 volunteers arrived in India in December, 1961, to work as agricultural consultants in Punjabi villages. They have been working in Rohtak, Batala, Khanna, Jagroan, Nabha, Galib Khan, and neighboring villages.[2]

Some of these volunteers hold degrees in agriculture, and all of them have had some experience on family farms in the United States as well as a ten-week orientation course (including lessons in Punjabi) to qualify them for Peace Corps work in the Punjab. One of the volunteers makes the rounds of fifteen villages on a bicycle to assist one of the Indian Government village-extension officers. Speaking from his own experience in farming in the United States, the volunteer is able to convince Indian farmers, despite his broken Punjabi, of the possibility of increasing crop yields through the use of insecticides and fertilizers. The same

[2] In 1965, at the request of Amdhra Pradesh and Kerala state governments, eighty additional Peace Corps volunteers were assigned to these states.

volunteer also introduced the idea of over-all economic plans for individual farmers so that they can see where their profits occur and where they can economize or spend more, instead of earning and spending haphazardly.

Two other volunteers are making a trailer workshop that can be hitched on to a jeep and taken from village to village to repair farm implements. Another volunteer advises farmers on raising poultry, while another is helping some farmers to set up small industries.

Though the program has been in existence for only four years, its impact has been rewarding. According to the Punjabi farmers, the advice of the Peace Corps Volunteers on such questions as hybrid seed and artificial fertilizers has already increased their farm yields by 25 per cent. This is only a welcome beginning. When more states ask for more volunteers and utilize their willing and informed services, some constructive and valuable work will get done. What is more, Indo-American understanding is bound to grow, and a welcome image of young affable America is bound to rise among the common people of India.

10. PRIVATE AMERICAN AID

PRIVATE American aid includes all kinds of nongovernmental assistance to persons, private projects and institutions, and the government of India. Such assistance comes from a wide variety of sources, all the way from munificent grants from large and wealthy foundations to small but nevertheless welcome donations from individual Americans to Indian causes they consider worthy of support. And between these two extremes lies a whole spectrum of private agencies, institutions (academic and otherwise), and organizations and philanthropic bodies in the United States that offer aid of one kind or another to India.

It is difficult to find a single consolidated record of all these acts of private charity and public philanthropy. As the donors do not always publish their benefactions, it is difficult to estimate the magnitude of their gifts and grants; nor is it easy to identify the fields of activity to which such donations are made. The difficulty is increased by the fact that the recipient does not always have to account for the receipt of funds to a central public body, and does not have to account at all if the donating body is a private family foundation. For example, when an American foundation or a wealthy American grants travel funds to enable an Indian scholar to attend an international conference abroad, the receipt of travel funds does not normally find its place in any public accounting—hence the difficulty of identifying all the sources of private American aid to India, its magnitude, and its purpose. However, governments, statutory bodies, and registered associations are exceptions, for they do publish in their annual balance sheets an account of funds received from abroad.

Such information as is available comes from four general sources: foundations, universities, church bodies, and other private philanthropic agencies.

Foundations

The United States is a land of foundations. A foundation in its broadest sense is an instrument for spending private wealth for general public welfare. According to an American author, "A foundation may be defined as a nongovernmental, nonprofit organization having a principal fund of its own, managed by its own trustees or directors, and established to maintain or aid social, educational, charitable, religious or other activities serving the common welfare."[1]

Foundations are tax-exempt, and almost all foundations are registered as legal entities and publicly account for the genesis, growth, distribution, and the over-all expenditure of their funds.

It is estimated that there are more than 12,000 foundations in the United States.[2] These are individual, family, and institutional foundations with assets ranging from a few thousand to a few billion dollars. Their fields of interest range from the welfare of stray cats and the distribution of ice cream to Sunday School children to advanced medical research and the promotion of lasting international peace. Although foundations present an infinite variety, they are generally classified as general-research foundations, special-purpose foundations, community foundations, company-sponsored foundations, and family foundations. Some foundations make grants for only local or state projects. That is, the money can be spent only locally or within the particular stipulated state. Some are restricted for national purposes within the United States. And a few are global in scope, outlook, and expenditure. Foundations can be classified by the subjects in which they are interested and which they would like to promote.

In 1960 there were ten American foundations with assets of more than $100 million each. These were, in order of the magnitude of their assets, the Ford Foundation, the Rockefeller Foundation, the Duke Foundation, the Hartford Foundation, the Carnegie Corporation of New York, the Kellogg Foundation, the Sloan Foundation, the Lilly Endowment, the Commonwealth Fund, and the Danforth Foundation. Of these, the Ford Foundation tops the list and has today estimated assets to the value of about $3.3 billion. The Rockefeller Foundation has assets totaling $650 million.

Of these ten large foundations, the Ford and the Rockefeller foundations have taken a serious and abiding interest in promoting India's welfare through generous grants to persons, projects,

[1] F. Emerson Andrews, *Philanthropic Foundations* (New York: The Russell Sage Foundation, 1956), p. 11.

[2] Ann D. Walton *et al.*, *The Foundation Directory* (New York: The Russell Sage Foundation, 1960), p. x.

institutions, and the government in a wide variety of nation-building activities. The Danforth Foundation and the Duke Foundation have also given some aid to India through scholarships and a few *ad hoc* grants. Besides these major foundations, a few smaller ones have taken some interest in aiding India's over-all educational and social advancement through scholarships for Indian students to obtain advanced education in the United States and through grants to Indian colleges, universities, and research institutes for equipment and research projects. These are the Asia Foundation, the Hopkins Fund, the Cowles Foundation, the Hazen Foundation, and the Watumull Foundation. Although other foundations may make occasional grants to certain projects in India, it is difficult to trace these as they have no offices or representatives in India, and the reports of their activities are not easily available.

The Ford Foundation. The Ford Foundation, the world's richest, was established in 1936 in New York by Henry Ford, the automobile manufacturer, and his son, Edsel Ford, as a private, nonprofit, tax-exempt, philanthropic corporation. Its sole objective is the "advancement of human welfare." In 1950, this objective was spelled out as the promotion of international understanding and world peace, the strengthening of democratic institutions and processes, the advancement of economic well-being, the expansion and improvement of education, and the enlargement of scientific knowledge and understanding of man.

For the first fifteen years after its establishment, the Foundation's grants went mainly to charitable and educational institutions in Michigan, the donors' home state. In 1950, it began to operate on a national scale and today its philanthropic activities embrace many needy and underdeveloped countries all over the world.

Early in 1951, Paul Hoffman, then President of the Ford Foundation, accepted the invitation of Prime Minister Nehru to visit India and discuss ways in which the Foundation could help in India's development plans. From the first years of India's First Five-Year Plan, the Ford Foundation has worked in close cooperation with the government of India, with the United States Government, and with the various United Nations and other international agencies for India's development. The objectives of the Ford Foundation's work in India are twofold. One is the over-all long-range objective of strengthening the democratic process and fostering peace; the second is the more immediate objective of attacking problems of poverty, illiteracy, hunger, and disease.

During the first few years the Foundation's programs were concentrated entirely on agricultural development to help India overcome its food shortage, which was causing famine conditions. In recent years, the Foundation's program has expanded; it now includes community development, extension training and agricultural production, small-scale industries, industrial design and development, business management and education, manpower, mobilization, labor-relations research, legal education and research, family-planning, communications research, and so forth.

The *modus operandi* of Ford Foundation aid to India is simple and follows the procedure of most foundations. Once the project and the budget are approved by mutual consultation, funds are transferred directly to the government of India, or, if they are for a private project, to its administering body. Generally, the government projects supported by the Foundation are planned, directed, and administered by the government of India and they are designed to continue as permanent parts of the government program even after the Foundation aid ceases. The general pattern is for the Ford Foundation to pay all costs the first year, half the second, and one-third the third year; the government—state or central—makes up the balance and bears the full responsibility thereafter.

So far two-thirds of the Ford Foundation grants have gone to government projects while a third have been given to private agencies and institutions. Of the latter, the projects are expected to continue after the termination of grants with private Indian support.

During the last twelve years the Ford Foundation has given more than $50 million to various projects in India. It is impossible to list all the projects that have received some kind of aid, financial or personnel. Nor is it necessary. A full account of all the aid given by the Ford Foundation since 1951 would demand a book. Fortunately, the office of the Foundation in India does bring out periodically a publication listing all the grants made to various projects supported by the Foundation in India,[3] as does the Foundation's head office in New York.[4] However, a few major projects that have received substantial support from the Ford Foundation

[3] *The Ford Foundation and Foundation-Supported Activities in India* (New Delhi, 1955).

[4] *The Ford Foundation Annual Report* (New York).

during the last few years are agricultural village extension work, rural public health training centers, centers for training village-level workers, in-service training program for rural development, public health education and environmental sanitation, village planning and rural housing, community development, small industries, primary and secondary education, social-science research (in universities), public administration, urban-planning teams, American training for Indian steel engineers, the National Institute of Industrial Design, and international cultural exchange. These projects, selected at random, give a picture of how the Foundation has strengthened and supported certain vulnerable spots in the Indian rural economy, higher education, and cultural institutions.

The Rockefeller Foundation. The Rockefeller Foundation was endowed by John D. Rockefeller, Sr., and chartered by the State of New York in 1913 "to promote the well-being of mankind throughout the world."

His only son, John D. Rockefeller, Jr., continued his father's interest in philanthropic causes and devoted his life to the development of the various endowments that his father had created, the biggest of which was the Rockefeller Foundation.[5] He became the first President of the Foundation, serving until 1917, when he was elected Chairman of the Board, a position he held until 1940 when he retired at the age of sixty-five.

Before 1929, the Foundation's activities were mainly concerned with research and cooperation with governments in the control of hookworm disease, malaria, and yellow fever; the improvement and development of general public-health organizations; and developing medical, public-health and nursing education in the United States and abroad through grants for education and research and for institutions and individuals engaged in the pursuit of these objectives.

In 1929, the Rockefeller Foundation was merged with the Laura Spelman Rockefeller Memorial, a fund established by Rockefeller in 1918 in memory of his wife and dedicated to the advancement of social sciences, child growth, and parent education. After 1929, the Foundation's activities became world-wide in scope. Major emphasis was placed on the advancement and application of

[5] For an excellent and authoritative account of Rockefeller philanthropies, see R. B. Fosdick, *The Story of the Rockefeller Foundation* (New York: The Rockefeller Foundation, 1952).

knowledge in medical sciences, public health, natural sciences, agriculture, the social sciences, the humanities, and international understanding.

The Foundation received from the founder more than $240 million as capital funds. Today, through investments and interest, the book value of the assets of the Foundation exceed $650 million. The Foundation has been appropriating about $35 million annually during the last decade for its activities all over the world.

The Rockefeller Foundation was probably the first American foundation to show any serious interest in India. Its association with India dates back to 1916 when its public-health workers on the International Health Commission collaborated in surveys of the incidence of hookworm in India. Since 1920, the Foundation has maintained at least one resident representative in India, and since 1947, when India achieved her independence, there have been a dozen specialists from the Foundation working in different parts of India.

The Foundation has always placed a great premium on the human factor in the development of a nation. Many underdeveloped countries have large populations but face an acute shortage of trained and skilled manpower. What is needed is not only acquisition of knowledge but also its dissemination, and what is even more important is its translation into effective and purposeful action. In a word, persons at all levels need the best available training to bring out the best performance they are capable of. Thus the Foundation's emphasis for many years has been on education, research, and training. The Foundation has sought to promote these objectives by supporting projects in higher education, food production, and public health.

Higher education involving advanced study and research has been encouraged by giving fellowships to Indian scholars for study at American universities in a wide variety of related fields. The Foundation has also provided books, special apparatus, and other equipment to some universities. On occasion, the services of an American specialist have been provided for short periods at certain institutions of higher learning.

The subject of increasing food production has of late received some attention from the Foundation. Grants for agricultural improvement are second only to grants for research in the medical and natural sciences. Since 1956, the Foundation has cooperated with the government of India on the Indian Agricultural Program. The two phases of the program, crop improvement and agricultural education, are planned in close interrelationship. The Foundation has been working on the improvement of maize and sorghum; on the educational side it has contributed to the development of the postgraduate school of the Indian Agricultural Research Institute at New Delhi. Some foundation staff members have served as consultants to the Institute; a few well-known American agricultural scientists have also served the Institute as visiting professors. Travel and study fellowships for faculty members as well as library and building grants have been provided by the Foundation for the Institute.

The Rockefeller Foundation has also provided some support to a few other institutions and projects in the general field of agriculture and food production. The Central Potato Research Institute at Simla, which coordinates long-range research work on potatoes, received a three-year grant for the expansion of its research work.

It is, however, in the field of public health and medical education in India that the Rockefeller Foundation has taken the greatest interest and has supported pioneering work. The largest allocation of Rockefeller funds goes each year for study and research in the medical and natural sciences. Throughout its long association with India in this field, the Foundation has supported a variety of projects in public health, environmental sanitation, nutrition, and medical education and research. In recent years it has aided the Virus Research Centre in Poona, a laboratory administered by the Indian Council of Medical Research and the All-India Institute of Medical Sciences at New Delhi, with both funds and professional personnel. The Foundation has also made long-term grants for medical education in Indian universities. Its generous contribution toward the establishment and support of the All-India Institute of Hygiene and Public Health at Calcutta are well known. Since 1947, the Foundation has contributed to the growth of such medical and research institutions as the King George Medical College in Lucknow, the G. S. Medical College in Bombay, the Christian Medical College in Vellore, the Andhra Medical College in Vishakapatnam, the M. P. Shah Medical College in Jamnagar, the National Chemical Laboratory in Poona, the Nutrition Research Laboratory in Hyderabad, the Indian Cancer Research Centre in Bombay, and so forth.

Besides aid to these three major categories, several colleges and research institutes, scholars and scientists, and literary and linguistic ventures have received grants of one kind or another.

These ventures range all the way from studies of international law, linguistic research, and Tibetan studies to the establishment of the India International Centre at New Delhi. Since independence the Foundation's grants to India total more than $15 million.

Asia Foundation. The Asia Foundation is a private, nonpolitical, nonprofit organization incorporated in California with representatives in a number of Asian countries including India. The Foundation was organized in March, 1951, by a group of prominent San Francisco citizens as the Committee for Free Asia. In October, 1954, its articles of incorporation were revised and its name was changed to the Asia Foundation. This Foundation is not the typical foundation, with an individual or family using its own funds, but consists of a group of people who believe in the need to cooperate with and help Asia and who depend on contributions and grants from individuals, civic organizations, foundations, trusts, and corporations.

The objectives of the Asia Foundation are to make private American support available to individuals and groups in Asia who are working for the attainment of peace, independence, personal liberty, and social progress; to encourage and strengthen active cooperation founded on mutual respect and understanding among voluntary organizations—Asian, American, and international—with similar aims and ideals; and to work with other American individuals and organizations for a better understanding in the United States of the peoples of Asia, their histories, cultures, and values.

The Asia Foundation believes that Asian countries not only need political freedom and stability but also material advancement:

> They need, as we did almost two hundred years ago, the time within a framework of peace to grapple successfully with the massive problems that challenge their ability and test their determination at every level of existence.
>
> They also need assistance. They recognize that no country in today's narrowing world can solve its problems in isolation. They want and welcome assistance given with understanding and respect. But they, as we, resent outside interference in their internal affairs. They oppose the encroachment of totalitarian ideologies and movements, and they resist any attempts to reimpose colonialism.[6]

[6] *The Asia Foundation: A Statement of the Foundation's Purposes and Activities* (San Francisco, 1960), p. 2.

The Foundation offers help to those groups and individuals who are promoting artistic, civic, economic, educational, and social aspects of the renaissance in Asian countries. "Its aid is private. It seeks to encourage voluntary activity, believing that action by individuals working as private citizens is a fundamental requisite of democratic societies."[7]

In education, the Foundation awards scholarships and fellowships and establishes and encourages teacher-training institutions. Other projects are designed to aid the diffusion of modern educational theory and practice, with necessary adaptations to suit local conditions. The Foundation extends grants and fellowships for social and economic research projects, supports the publishing and distribution of educational materials in regional languages, and provides consultants in various fields for both governments and institutions.

Besides, these, the Foundation supports some American organizations interested in Asia. This activity includes grants for fellowships or travel to enable Indian experts to visit the United States or other Asian countries to exchange information with their American or Asian counterparts.

And last, the Foundation has its own program of distributing books for students, schools, and colleges in India. The Foundation collects books from American publishers and college students and faculty and distributes them to needy institutions in India. In the United States, the Foundation sponsors the weekly paper *The Asian Student,* which is written and edited by Asians and circulated widely among Asian students in the United States. It serves as a useful forum for Asian students' opinion on contemporary issues and promotes both intra-Asian and Asian-American understanding. The Foundation also supports programs that encourage the writing, publication, and distribution of Asian books in the United States. The Asia Foundation's office in India began functioning in 1962.

The Watumull Foundation. The Watumull Foundation, a private, nonprofit, American philanthropic organization, was founded in 1942 in Honolulu by Gobindram J. Watumull, a successful Indian (Sindhi) businessman who had become an American citizen. The major objectives of the Foundation are to promote Indo-

[7] *Ibid.*

American good will and understanding and to promote India's over-all development.

Besides contributing to various charitable, educational and cultural activities in Hawaii, the Foundation provides scholarships and grants-in-aid to qualified Sindhis in Indian educational institutions and fellowships to Indian scholars for higher studies in the United States. The Foundation also assists American professors to lecture at Indian universities.

The second part of the Watumull program involves the purchase and distribution of worthwhile books on India, written by Indians or Americans, to American college, university, and public libraries. It also distributes American publications on India to Indian libraries and awards annually prizes to the best book published on any Indian subject in the United States. The Foundation has been interested in promoting family-planning work in India. It has made grants to enable Indian organizations to convene international conferences on the subject. It has also given grants to promote research work on the physiology of reproduction, to make contraceptives acceptable to Indian mothers, and to study general demographic problems.

Other Foundations. Besides these foundations with major interests in India, a few other American foundations assist India in various *ad hoc* ways. It is difficult to list these foundations for reasons explained earlier. The trustees of all the foundations periodically review their grants and their results and constantly look for worthwhile causes deserving their attention. Various causes and projects in India occasionally arouse their interest. These foundations do not have regular programs in India and as such do not have representatives or offices in India. The Duke Foundation, the Carnegie Corporation of New York, the Danforth Foundation, the Hazen Foundation, the Hopkins Fund, and the Cowles Foundations are among those foundations that have given occasional grants to India. It is possible that there are other American foundations interested in India, but their activities are not known to the present writer.

American Universities

There were 2,100 institutions of higher learning in the United States in 1962.[8] Of these institutions, 628 were junior colleges. Of

[8] *Education Directory 1962–1963* (Washington, D.C.: U.S. Department of Health, Education and Welfare, 1963), p. 10.

the remaining 1,372 institutions, 766 were undergraduate colleges that offer bachelor degrees in arts or science. The rest can be roughly classified as colleges that provide graduate instruction and universities granting the Ph.D. degree in various disciplines. In other words, there were 606 colleges and universities where graduate instruction is provided and which are recognized by national and regional accrediting agencies. Of these 606 institutions, 228 bear the name "university," but perhaps a third of these are universities in name only and should more appropriately be called "colleges."[9] That is, there are roughly about 75 to 100 universities within the scope of the internationally accepted definition of a university.

On the campus of these universities, the student from India was a rarity before World War II, when there were only a few Indian students scattered across the country. American university degrees were not recognized by the British Government in India and therefore the few students who went to U.S. universities were usually independent nationalists who did not care for government jobs on their return to India. The majority of Indian students who could go abroad flooded the British universities. For the British government in India, having Indian students at British universities was a favorable economic proposition. The students traveled on British steamers, spent money in England on British college fees, books, and so forth, and, more important, imbibed consciously or unconsciously the British way of life. But all this changed after 1947 when India achieved her political freedom.

Today there are Indian students at almost all the large universities in the United States, for many American universities offer scholarships and fellowships to able foreign students. Indian students on their own can write to the universities, obtain some financial assistance, and proceed to the United States for advanced studies. When they arrive in the States, they find they have many opportunities to advance themselves. They can obtain a variety of jobs, and ability is easily recognized and is usually rewarded without prejudice.

There are also a number of American foundations that offer fellowships to Indian students. There are today countless auspices under which an able Indian student can obtain financial assistance to pursue higher studies in the United States. At the outbreak of World War II, there were fewer than 50 Indian stu-

[9] *Encyclopædia Britannica* (London, 1961), Vol. XXII, p. 876.

dents in the U.S., but today there are more than 4,000. Apart from facilities for study and research, several American universities today have Indian scholars and scientists as lecturers and professors, both on visiting and permanent tenures. This is true of several research institutes and industrial plants as well. All this is a private arrangement between the Indian student and scholar and the American college or university.

About fifty American universities, both private and state, assist Indian educational institutions or the government of India. These affiliations range from AID contracts that provide American professors as consultants to Indian institutions as well as training in the United States for Indians working on AID projects in India. Some of these programs in which American universities have contracted to help Indian projects are sponsored by American foundations working in India.

An "exchange program" exists between certain American colleges and universities and certain Indian colleges, whereby students and faculty members from Indian colleges travel to the college of their American counterparts, who, in turn, visit India to study or teach. These arrangements are usually made between Christian colleges.

Of late, several American universities and even colleges have instituted Asian-studies programs. India figures prominently in these programs. Indian experts in various fields are invited to lecture and participate in seminars and conferences. A few American universities send student groups to India to pursue their studies on the spot, as it were (for example, the India Project of the University of California). While this is an expensive program, even for American students, it has led to new experience and awareness for the visiting students as well as for the receiving Indian students. And last, a few American colleges permit their undergraduates to spend a year in an Indian college or university. The students are given full academic credit for the year.

A variety of arrangements are being explored by American universities to bring their knowledge and experience to the benefit of Indian colleges, universities, and other institutions of higher learning. All these efforts can be summed up in one meaningful word—"exchange."

American Church Organizations

In general discussions of foreign aid and the economic development of underdeveloped areas, the role of the Church is seldom mentioned. And if it is mentioned, it is usually as a liability and not as an asset, for the historic role of the Church in non-Christian countries is invariably identified as an evangelical and proselytizing one. The material aid offered by the Church is usually considered only an incentive to conversion and nothing more. Although this was true of many Christian missions and missionaries at the beginning of the nineteenth century, it was not the complete picture, for dedicated examples of service to the people of the underdeveloped countries were not wanting. At the turn of the century, missionary attitudes began to change and today the role of the American missions in India is a beneficent one.

American church missions have long been committed to voluntary technical assistance as a supplemental service to the people of the underdeveloped countries, especially during and since the latter half of the nineteenth century. It is impossible to elaborate here on the valuable contribution of these missionary societies to India's development. Only a few examples of the kind of voluntary and dedicated work undertaken can be given. Besides establishing churches and distributing evangelical literature (which many non-Christians may not consider to be fulfilling any felt need), the American Christian missions, both Catholic and Protestant, have founded schools and colleges, orphanages and homes for the destitute, clinics, hospitals and medical colleges, and social service centers. They have established centers for leprosy patients and homes for unwed mothers and unwanted children. They have trained nurses and doctors, teachers, farmers, and mechanics; they have carried on emergency-relief, refugee-resettlement, and public-health programs in rural areas. They have brought medical aid to remote villages, education to many generations of children and young people, and have provided an opportunity to thousands of Indian workers to learn a trade.

More than seventy American church organizations carry on missionary work in India. These organizations, which belong to diverse denominations, range from coordinating boards and councils, such as the National Council of the Churches of Christ in the United States, to single churches and small committees that raise funds to support mission work in India, primarily in the field of evangelism, education, health, and social work.

The work of the numerous Christian high schools, colleges, medical colleges, and hospitals founded under the auspices of American missionary bodies is too well known and distinguished to need any detailed discussion. The Christian Medical College and Hospital at Vellore, Madras State, the Agricultural Institute at Allahabad, and numerous Christian men's and women's colleges are famous for their long and dedicated service to the communities in which they are located.

Special mention, however, should be made of the work of the American Friends' Service Committee. The American Friends (the Quakers) have rendered disinterested service out of all proportion to their numbers and resources. They usually are the first to arrive in times of crisis—be it famine, flood, or war. Apart from regular relief work, the Friends have undertaken extensive community-development projects in Orissa. They have worked to improve agricultural methods and have introduced new types of pumps, wells, and building materials. They have been training mechanics, teachers, village health workers, and artisans for small industries.

This very brief summary by no means covers all the American missionary activity in India that has been conducive to over-all economic development. The American mission contribution to Indian education, health, and even technical advancement for nearly a century and a half has been a significant one.

Private Organizations

Innumerable private organizations in the United States are interested in India in one way or another. The interest of these organizations in India has its origin in diverse circumstances. An American visitor to India returns to his homeland impressed with the need for some help for a worthy Indian cause he has come to know about and sympathize with in India. Occasionally, some prominent Indian visitor may persuade an American organization to "adopt" India. Often, international-minded Americans who are conscious of their affluence just want to share with people in need in other parts of the world. Whatever the origin and motivation, these small private organizations do dedicated and silent work, helping in innumerable small ways. Often the assistance is unknown to the public at large.

These groups vary in activity and size. They range all the way from a committee that exists expressly to raise some financial support for an Indian institution, to a committee that supplies equipment unavailable in India, or a fund that enables an Indian to visit the United States to further some mutually desirable objective. Sometimes these associations are formed to meet specific needs and are dissolved after the needs are fulfilled, such as the

Bengal Famine Relief Committee in New York in 1943, or the numerous Defend India Funds that were formed on many American campuses and in cities after the Chinese attack on India in 1962. Often, the sole objective of these private American organizations is to provide relief to victims involved in some natural disaster or crisis in India. The number of such private American organizations doing relief and social work is considerable. While a discussion of their useful activities is not within the scope of this book,[10] a brief reference must be made to the work of CARE.

CARE (Cooperatives for American Relief Everywhere) is a nonprofit American organization of twenty-six voluntary service agencies established in New York in 1945. CARE assembles medical supplies, food commodities, and textiles given by American individuals, groups, and organizations and distributes them abroad. Most CARE purchases are made directly from the U.S. Government (agricultural surplus commodities), manufacturers, processors, publishers, and so on, to ensure the lowest possible cost. CARE supplies are admitted tax- and duty-free into foreign countries by contracts with each government.

For the first ten years of CARE in India (1950–60), its activities came under three different agreements: a CARE-India agreement signed in 1950; the general Indo-U.S. agreement of 1951; and a contract signed with the U.S. Information Service in 1954.

The first agreement enabled CARE to ship gifts of food and other supplies through several American voluntary agencies operating in India. The second agreement came in the wake of the India Emergency Food Act (or Food Aid Act) of 1951, which provided a loan of $190 million to India to purchase American wheat. This Act also offered assistance to American voluntary agencies engaged in relief activities. Distribution of CARE supplies was facilitated under the general Indo-U.S. agreement, signed in the same year, which permitted CARE (and other voluntary organizations approved by the Economic Cooperation Administration) to send duty-free goods through the Indian Regional Director of Food to Calcutta, Bombay, Madras, or designated airports. The government of India paid transportation costs in India, port costs, storage, and handling. The third agreement was signed with the United States Information Service in 1954 and made CARE responsible for purchasing, packing, shipping, and

[10] For a detailed coverage of this topic, see *American Institutions and Organizations Interested in Asia: A Reference Directory* (2d ed.; New York: Taplinger Publishing Company, 1961).

distributing books and scientific equipment sent to India under the India Wheat-Loan Educational Exchange Program (see Chapter 7).

Since 1951, CARE has shipped more than 50 million pounds of food to India. This includes milk powder, butter, egg powder, beans, butter oil, cheese, and rice. The milk powder is distributed to school children, refugees, tuberculosis and leprosy patients, old people, and expectant mothers through various Indian social-service organizations.

CARE has also purchased and distributed medical supplies and books to nearly a hundred medical institutions and mobile medical units. Another part of the program provides funds for the purchase of tools and equipment for self-help projects, particularly those connected with India's community-development program. These items include sewing machines and knitting wool, village-classroom kits, plows and other agricultural tools for farmers, and equipment purchased in India for school construction.

CARE food packages have reached people in India in times of distress and disaster. During the 1953 famine in West Bengal, 3,000 villages received milk powder and wheat-barley mixture for making *chappatis*. Similar aid reached victims of the Kashmir flood in 1951 and refugees from Pakistan and Tibet during the early 1960's. Since 1950, CARE has supplied India with about $15 million worth of food and supplies.

Since 1961, the major project of the CARE program became the supply of food for the school-lunch program in the southern states. The food is purchased by CARE in the United States and shipped to India, where the various state governments arrange for its distribution. The cost of administering the program in India is borne by the state governments. Today, as a result, more than 4 million children are receiving free lunches. During the nine- or ten-month academic year, they consume about 44,000 tons of American food commodities—rice, wheat, milk, and oatmeal. This free midday-meal project arranged by CARE is the largest in the world and is a meaningful gift from the American people. The school-lunch program now operates in schools in Andhra Pradesh, Madras, Kerala, and Punjab states, and plans are being made to extend it to children in other states in India.

11. *THE IMPACT OF AMERICAN AID ON THE INDIAN ECONOMY*

WHAT IS THE total impact of American aid on India's progress? What are the effects of American assistance on India's political stability, economic development, and cultural and social progress? There are, of course, short- and long-range, as well as visible and invisible effects. Certain effects in terms of human and international relations cannot be measured in any quantitative or statistical terms, and, in certain other sectors, effects may not be visible for a considerable period, since projects take time to start a chain reaction of beneficent results.

The task of evaluating the impact of foreign aid on India's overall development is complicated by the fact that no objective studies on the basis of each project or on the basis of the amount of aid provided by individual countries have been undertaken. When such a study is made, the character and amount of aid, its form, purpose, range, and role will have to be taken into consideration. The fact that American aid has taken many forms—grants, loans, commodity help, technical assistance—makes its impact difficult to evaluate. What is more, American aid is a continuing phenomenon and has had no time to "simmer" down into the economy, as it were. However, an effort is made here to outline certain obvious and indisputable effects of American aid on overall Indian progress.

To begin with, a preliminary and pertinent point relating to aid must be raised and dismissed as far as India is concerned. An underdeveloped country may receive large-scale foreign economic aid and yet evidence no perceptible economic progress. The country may have a poor administrative machinery, no concerted development plan, or, what is worse, corrupt, inefficient, self-seeking leaders. In such countries, external assistance, more often than not, tends to end up in the private bank accounts of unscrupulous politicians.

In such countries, gift dry milk, instead of being given free to needy children and nursing mothers, may find its way into the black market, and costly machinery may lie rusting in the harbors due to general administrative inefficiency and transportation bottlenecks. Even food grains and other relatively perishable commodities may rot in railway yards for lack of means to transport them. In other words, external aid may be too large, in more than one sense of the term, for the assimilation capacity of the recipient country. There are many countries where foreign aid is a relative if not a total waste.

Fortunately these problems, by and large, do not exist in India. There may be an occasional instance of petty corruption or the incompetence of a lower official, but, on the whole, American and other foreign aid has found its way to its appointed and destined places, thanks to the integrity of the leaders and the administrative service, the vigilance of the parliament, and the existence of an articulate and free press.

As we have noted earlier, American aid has covered a wide variety of projects embracing practically every sector of the Indian economy. Any objective attempt to assess and evaluate the impact of these projects on the Indian economy will pose many questions. What has this aid accomplished for India, for her total economic development and the standard of living of her people? Does the experience of Indo-American aid relations yield any suggestions for the future?

The major objective of the government of India and the Planning Commission during the years since the advent of political freedom has been to transform the economy from a nearly stagnant one into a dynamic and vital one. Has this objective been realized even partially? It is not easy to demarcate particular results as the products of a particular country's assistance. As India receives aid from some fifteen major countries, it is difficult to be precise and definitive on what country's particular aid has led to certain specific results. But, of the total aid given by all the foreign countries since 1947, the aid of the United States alone constitutes more than 50 per cent. India has received from the West, excluding the Soviet Bloc, $8.5 billion in grants and loans, of which the United States has contributed nearly $6 billion. As such, foreign aid means largely American aid.

That American aid (as well as aid from other foreign countries and the United Nations and its specialized agencies) has contributed to the over-all productive capacity of the economy is undeniable, though attempts at quantification may not be successful because of the fact that foreign aid resources cannot be separated from nonaid, internal, and national resources.

For any evaluation of the total impact of American aid on the Indian economy one must take only the utilized aid and not the committed aid. In the transfer of aid, several stages are involved: Aid is promised, then authorized, and then utilized. All the authorized aid may not be utilized because of the limited absorptive capacity of the recipient country.

The over-all progress of the Indian economy since 1947 has been largely due to the foreign aid received by India. There is no doubt that the continuation and acceleration of this progress will continue to depend on substantial contributions of aid in various forms from the more advanced countries, the Aid India Club in particular. (The Aid India Club has committed itself to raising $1,000 million for the completion of the Third Plan.)

Impact of American Aid on Indian Economic and Political Stability

American aid to India has contributed significantly to Indian economic stability. The validity of this statement can be realized if one can imagine the economic position of India today had she not received this aid. The popularity and stability of the government can well be imagined if it had had to extract this huge amount, badly needed and quickly spent on development, from the poor Indian taxpayer!

The United States, by providing India with this unfettered, large-scale aid, has given the country sufficient economic independence to enable her to pursue an independent foreign policy—that of nonalignment. By maintaining a policy of nonalignment it has been easy for India to accept aid from all political camps, including the Communist countries, which can aid only the public sector. If America has thus indirectly supported nonalignment in politics, she has also supported its economic counterpart, a mixed economy. American assistance has been extended both to the public and private sectors, perhaps more to the former than to the latter in India. This need not be considered paradoxical, for America's stake in India's free political and social institutions must be taken for granted. American aid has contributed to India's economic stability and growth and, since a nation's political cohesion and stability are a product of its economic development, it can thus be maintained that American aid has been a contributing factor to India's political stability, a stability that is a rare phenomenon in Asia. The relationship between external aid from America and the recipient country's internal economic development, on the one hand, and its political stability, on the other, seems to be simple and obvious in the case of India.

India's Productive Capacity

American aid since 1951, particularly since 1958, has contributed considerably to the productive capacity of the country, though it is difficult, if not impossible, to gauge the magnitude of this capacity. There is a need here to distinguish between capacity and output. Once the capacity is increased, output will take care of itself.

Contrary to popular belief, there are countless ways in which India's productive capacity can be increased without any proportionate increase of several scarce factors. Apart from mobilizing the substantial surplus of labor, particularly in rural areas, several capital-cheap labor improvements can be effected to increase a worker's output. As John P. Lewis rightly points out,

> To accept the view that, in many consumer goods lines that do not depend heavily on imports or other unmistakably scarce factors, productive capacity is quickly and highly stretchable does not require a retreat from the judgment that Indians by and large are neither afraid of work nor lacking in healthy appetites for material self-improvement. The point rather is that lack of knowledge, fear of change, lack of vigorous, effectively functioning markets and of certain supporting administrative structures—especially in the traditional rural economy—all continue to impede an optimal translation of these healthy appetites into productive capacity. Catalysts are needed to speed the stretching of latent capacities, and one of the most conventional and promising of such catalysts, rather obviously, is additional demand.[1]

American and other foreign aid has been applied at various levels and to various factors to increase the nation's capacity. A particular amount of aid, whether in goods or services, may be applied to a particular project, but the productive capacity created often goes beyond the project in question in a few years, for no project works in a vacuum. The generation of such productive capacity varies from project to project and in different

[1] Lewis, *op. cit.*, p. 64.

sectors of the economy, depending upon the level of development of the sector involved.

As long as foreign aid and indigenous nonaid resources are mutually exchangeable or substitutable, using aid resources for development purposes means that nonaid resources will be available for current consumption. Similarly, if aid resources contribute to current consumption, internal resources can be used for capital formation. India was importing about 2 to 3 million tons of cereals annually before P.L. 480 imports were made available. Now the imports from the United States average 4 million tons annually. These imports have released domestic resources, which in turn have gone toward capital formation. However, the net contribution of foreign aid to the productive capacity of a country depends not only on the economic policies pursued by the recipient country, but also on the over-all total disposable resources at its command.

Disinflationary Effect

In general, it is accepted that foreign economic aid contributes to combating inflation in the receiving country. American aid, particularly the massive P.L. 480 imports of food grains, have had a striking disinflationary effect on the Indian economy.

Inflation, to use its simplest definition, is nothing more than "too much money chasing too few goods." The remedy is obvious. The supply of goods and commodities should be increased without pumping in a proportionate increase of money. Aid can sometimes increase the money in circulation without increasing the availability of goods produced within the country or through increased imports. By importing commodities, such as food grains or cotton, India can, to a considerable extent, fight inflationary trends. However, the total picture is not simple, for the recipient country's fiscal and monetary policies, the demand for and the volume of imports, the wages and price policy, and the general level of living in the country enter into it.

On the whole, the P.L. 480 imports and the funds they create contribute considerably toward a disinflationary trend. India imports American surplus agricultural commodities such as wheat. The government of India sells this wheat to the people at current or lower prices in internal rupee currency. This means, to begin with, that "free"goods are available, and that local purchasing power is siphoned off from the public into government coffers. These rupees are not given back to America but are deposited in the Reserve Bank of India to the credit of the United States treasury. Insofar as these rupees are not spent, we can look upon aid as disinflationary. America grants India loans for development purposes from these rupees of up to 80 per cent of the accumulated amount. And some 5 per cent of these rupees are loaned for "Cooley Amendment" projects, that is, projects involving collaboration between American and Indian joint industrial ventures. These "loans" might eventually become outright grants to India, for these rupees are not convertible into dollars and cannot be paid back unless the United States as the donor country is willing to accept more imports from India. According to one American observer:

> One might speculate whether in procedures laid down for commodity disposal under Public Law 480 the United States is not getting the worst of the two worlds. Although much of the sales proceeds is reloaned for development on the "never-never," as the British aptly call their installment plans, we insist on calling the transactions "sales." As a result, some recipient countries feel they are doing the United States a good turn by taking the surpluses off our hands but in reality these transactions are apt to become permanent investments, or perhaps even grants, unless the United States eventually becomes willing to accept more imports and in this way uses inconvertible currencies.[2]

Elgin Groseclose takes the view that foreign aid is inflationary. He writes:

> According to theory, foreign aid funds should be deflationary in effect in the recipient countries since they increase the supply of goods available within the economy without increase of the money supply (since the goods are provided as U.S. gifts). This theoretical result does not follow in practice. The reasons are simple. The effect is somewhat like that upon a high school boy's allowance from the gift of an automobile. . . . Even though the automobile may save him carfare he becomes involved in the expense of gasoline, tires, and repairs, not to say a whole scale of expenditures which the status of an owner of an automobile seems to impose.[3]

It is of course possible that foreign aid can lead to inflation if the amount, kind, and timing are such that it increases consumption or reduces saving and consequent investment.

[2] Henry G. Aubrey, "Sino-Soviet Aid to South and Southeast Asia," *World Politics*, October, 1959, pp. 65–66.

[3] Elgin Groseclose, in James W. Wiggins and Helmut Schoech (eds.), *Foreign Aid Re-examined* (Washington, D.C.: Public Affairs Press, 1958).

However, as far as American aid and the Indian economy are concerned, there is no doubt that, on the whole, P.L. 480 imports and even the expenditure of counterpart-fund rupees have contributed to a disinflationary effect for two obvious reasons. One is the supply effect. The imported food grains and cotton have increased the total internal supply. This has led to a reduction in the price of food grains and cotton as the demand is always there for a certain amount of supply at certain prices. The other is the demand effect. As observed already, the government sells the food grains to the Indian consumer and thus withdraws a certain amount of purchasing power from the people; this is tantamount to the collection of extra taxes.

Expansion of India's Exports

American aid has proved to be a stimulant to the expansion of India's exports, for it is a vital factor in international trade. While it is true that since the beginning of 1958 (the year of India's foreign-exchange crisis), a growing share of India's imports has been financed by American foreign aid, India's exports have also increased. Indo-American trade has been to India's advantage and has contributed to her economic development. Between 1951 and 1955, India had a surplus in her merchandise trade with the United States (1952 was an exception for during that year American wheat worth $490 million arrived in India). For this five-year period as a whole, India's exports to the United States exceeded the imports from the United States by $118 million.

As a United States Department of Commerce Report points out:

> India's dollar receipts from exports to the United States were augmented by dollar exchange made available under U.S. development loans. Until October 1959, proceeds of these loans could be used by India for purchases from sources of its choice. The extent is not known, but it is apparent that a substantial portion of the proceeds of these global procurement loans was used for purchases from non-U.S. sources. Thus the real spread between India's dollar earnings and its expenditure for U.S. goods was wider than if measured by the trade balance alone. Net payments by India for invisibles, particularly shipping, reduced this spread, but India still earned considerably more dollars than it spent for U.S. goods.[4]

Although this particular role of American aid has been a relief, India has to expand her exports considerably, for otherwise she

[4] Jackson B. Hearn, *India: A Growing Market for U.S. Products and Investment* (Washington D.C.: Department of Commerce, 1963), p. 8.

will be faced with serious difficulties. If India cannot increase her export earnings she will have to depend on foreign aid even more than she does now. In fact, India's current budget and other economic policies are directed toward the goal of stepping up India's exports. The government is giving preferential aid to such industries as have export potential. The import licensing policy also has a definite export bias, for imports will have to be utilized to enable the country to export more. Perhaps export earnings may need a certain income-tax relief. American aid has indeed aided India's exports both directly and indirectly, but the government of India itself is leaving no stone unturned to consistently expand her exports to finance her Third Five-Year Plan as much as possible.

Indian Industrialization

In the realm of Indian industrialization, American aid has been helpful in at least three major areas. The most significant has been developing the country's infrastructure. Both the importance and the expensiveness of the infrastructure are sometimes overlooked in planning the rapid development of an underdeveloped country. The overhead of an industrial society takes the form of roads, railways, docks, harbors, basic technical schools and polytechnics, power installations, and industrial housing, all of which involve heavy investment with no promise of quick returns.

The infrastructure does not contribute directly and immediately to an increase in the national income but rather paves the way for an explosive increase in the national income at the time when productive enterprises—both in the public and private sectors—begin to build on and draw from the infrastructure. This factor indicates to some extent the soundness of Indian planning in making provision, especially during the Third Plan period, for infrastructural development rather than for industries to supply consumer needs when Indian resources at present are not adequate to meet both. That is, there has to be a choice between development facilities for the production of consumers' goods on the one hand and the creation of the infrastructure on the other.

The second significant factor in the general area of Indian industrial development is the help rendered by the United States through the National Productivity Councils. The major objective of these Councils is to make Indian management more efficient in mobilizing and applying the available limited Indian resources to more effective and productive use in both the public and private sectors. The simple rationale behind this objective is that the management of any enterprise controls the bringing together of such resources as raw materials, machinery, capital funds, labor, and land for the production of goods and services in such a manner as to ensure the greatest reward. It is the way in which any management controls the combination of these resources that determines managerial ability and efficiency. Thus, the better and more efficient the management, the more productive will be the particular combination of resources it selects, and the greater the contribution that these resources will make to the total of goods and services available in India.

The third area is the American contribution to enlarging the sources of funds for investment and for operating capital for private-sector enterprises through loans of foreign exchange and rupee capital made available through such institutions as the Industrial Finance Corporation (IFC), the Industrial Credit Investment Corporation of India (ICICI), and the Refinance Corporation for Industry (RFC). The United States has not only provided these institutions with funds to lend to private enterprise but has also to some extent contributed to the organization and policies of these institutions to enable them to serve better the needs of productive enterprises for investment and working capital, which are essentially different in a developing economy as distinguished from an advanced and industrialized one.

In addition to these three major areas of help, American aid has contributed to Indian industrialization by supplying raw materials, machinery, and equipment.

Foreign Exchange

It is interesting to note that during the first half of the Indo-American aid period only 10 per cent of the total U.S. aid was provided; the remaining 90 per cent of the total aid was provided during the second half. American aid in large quantity really dates from 1958 when India was faced with her foreign-exchange difficulties during the Second Five-Year Plan.

The provision of foreign exchange is perhaps the most important component of American aid to Indian development. The amount of this provision, particularly to set up power plants, is quite large. Here it is both possible to separate sector and purpose, and calculate the magnitude of foreign exchange made available to India. The foreign exchange provided by the United States has contributed to the total amount of capital formation, particularly in the public sector, some $4 billion (Rs.2,000 crores), including the P.L. 480 imports.

Food, Clothing, and Prices

Perhaps the most significant contribution that America has made to India is to supply her with food and clothing. America's wheat and cotton have given support to a perennially weak and vulnerable spot in the Indian economy. Man needs these two commodities—food and clothing—more than any others. In fact, by providing these commodities, America has made a large contribution to the stability of the Indian Government.

Second, American supplies of wheat have stabilized the price of wheat and other food grains in India. The price index of food grains as a whole has remained relatively constant from 1958 to 1964 except for a brief period in 1964, nor have the prices of cereals risen. In fact, wheat prices have come down a little while rice prices have risen only slightly. The P.L. 480 imports, which began only in 1956–57, have had a welcome repercussion on India's cost-of-living index, especially since food is by far the largest item in the average Indian family budget.

Thus American food aid has made a certain maneuverability possible for the Ministry of Food with regard to food prices. These food imports have enabled India to maintain not only stability of prices but also a reserve stock and an even food supply without either glut or scarcity. The American food supplies have, in a word, provided an intelligent framework in which India's food problem can be viewed and a workable and predictable attack mounted.

In spite of the major contribution made by American food supplies to Indian economic development, criticism of these imports has not been wanting. Some have complained that the American grant of so much agricultural commodities has robbed the Indian farmer of the incentive to produce more food grains. It is also contended that the fact that P.L. 480 wheat has not only prevented the rise in the price of food grains but has even lowered it in view of the increased supply against the existing demand has been unfair to the Indian wheat grower. But an examination of the present total acreage under cultivation in wheat and other food grains, agricultural investments, farm inputs, and the over-all conditions under which Indian farmers live today show that P.L. 480 food grains have not only not adversely affected Indian agricultural production but have contributed to its stabilization.

Of course, what is really wanted is not stabilization but increased production.

Labor Problems

Although India is not sufficiently industrialized to have a large industrial labor force, the beginnings of large-scale industrialization have brought in their wake certain serious labor problems. American aid to India in the field of labor relations has been concentrated in three areas. The first is that of labor training. The labor-training scheme is really devoted to the training of teachers who in turn will train the workers, thus increasing the opportunity for basic technical training to labor at large. In this connection, America has started the Bombay Craftsmen Training Institute, whose parent body, Dunwoodie Institute in Minneapolis, helped to set it up. The Bombay Institute is devoted to the training of craftsmen in metal, wood, and leather, and of electricians, mechanics, printers, plumbers, and foremen.

The second approach has been to create, if nonexistent, and to augment, if available, certain services that the government of India can give labor in general. For instance, India already had "employment exchanges" in her major cities. These acted as clearinghouses between employers seeking skilled workers and workers seeking jobs. Expert American advice has strengthened these. Another scheme is for the government to pass on, to workers who will benefit by them, the results of the latest research in various skilled occupations. It is not easy to disseminate the latest information on, for example, certain new plumbing techniques to all the plumbers in India. Workers at this level in India are not used to reading professional and trade magazines, for not only are a great proportion of them barely literate, but there are no professional magazines devoted to these crafts in their mother tongues. Nor do these workers have all-India organizations like those of the medical, law, and engineering professions. With American assistance, useful efforts are being made to improve this situation.

The third approach, that of working with labor leaders and labor unions in the general field of improving labor relations, is perhaps the most important. American help in this area has been confined to working with India's two large non-Communist labor-union federations. Some Indian labor leaders have been sent to the United States to travel, study, and meet American labor leaders and to become acquainted with the modern conception of labor-union leadership. Indian labor leaders have much to learn of the role of a labor union in a democratic society and in an economy that is being gradually industrialized. A labor union in a developing country like India has a vitally constructive role to play. Union leaders must be able to organize and demand labor's legitimate dues from the employers and society on the one hand, and to discipline their labor to get better services for the industry in which they are employed, the community, and the country at large on the other.

That there is a need to cultivate a skilled, contented, and well-informed labor force in an economy that is being industrialized can hardly be overemphasized. An articulate and enlightened labor leadership can play a significant liaison role between the workers and the employers and the government.

The government of India has become the biggest single employer in the country. Under these circumstances, India's labor leaders have to face new challenges and responsibilities far beyond their conventional role of seeking higher wages and better conditions of work. The leaders must be educated and informed enough to preside over collective bargaining so that ultimately the interests of the country and not those of a particular group prevail. America's matchless experience in this sphere is proving to be a major guide to the nascent struggles of the Indian labor movement.

India has yet to produce labor leaders like Sidney Hillman, Walter Reuther, George Meany, or John L. Lewis with their tremendous political influence to sway the labor vote in favor of one party or another. When India is industrialized, labor leadership will come to the fore and may come to command considerable political leadership. But such leadership, if it is to be responsible, must be astute, educated, and enlightened. The history of the American labor movement has many lessons for future Indian labor leadership.

Cultural and Educational Effects of American Technical Assistance

Perhaps the most abiding contribution that the United States has made to India, other underdeveloped countries, and the world at large is in the realm of technical assistance. A rich country can give grants and loans, can supply goods and commodities, but only a few countries can impart their technical knowledge and share their special skills. America, which is so full of inventive genius, has been responsible for many a modern marvel. Lesser nations might jealously guard their science and skills, knowledge and technology, but America has been more or less an exception. A few other nations might equal the United States in their scientific advancement, but, unlike America, they are not always eager to share their knowledge with the less-developed world.

American technical assistance to India has been extremely important because it introduces new ideas, novel and improved work techniques, and a new and daring spirit of doing things—a spirit that persists till success is achieved. These characteristics cannot be evaluated in any quantitative sense.

America has sent numerous experts to teach and train Indians participating in American-aided projects and to help build plants and institutions. These experts have been drawn from virtually every discipline, all the way from home science to nuclear physics. No matter how simple or complicated the task, these American technicians have a dedicated attitude toward India's reconstruction—an attitude that cannot be bought. Whether it is teaching hot-lines maintenance or building a huge dam, setting up an agricultural university or an institute of technology, eradicating malaria or organizing traffic in a congested city, demonstrating the latest method in surgery or devising procedures, techniques, and systems to promote efficiency and increase productivity, these Americans have given of themselves unstintingly, despite difficult odds in an alien cultural milieu.

As for the provision of training for Indians in India and the United States, Indians working on the Indo-American projects receive instruction and training on the spot from the American experts. Besides this, nearly 5,000 Indian participants on aid projects have been sent to the United States for further training, and some have been sent to other countries such as the United Kingdom, Canada, Japan, and West Germany, where the training facilities are more appropriate for India's immediate needs. The impact of the returned American-trained students on the Indian economy and culture is referred to in Chapter 7.

U.S. aid for the establishment of new or the development of existing educational and scientific institutions originally occurred in the form of textbooks and laboratory equipment, adviser-consultant services, visiting professors, and grants for building and general equipment. But of late, American help has concentrated on a few strategic and vitally important pace-setting educational centers like the Indian Institute of Technology at Kanpur and the Agricultural University at Rudrapur.

India's greatest need has been and continues to be technical education, a field that was relatively neglected during the last century, one of the factors responsible for India's backwardness and low standards of living. A frontal attack on India's poverty calls for establishing a scientific and technological bias in her education in order to transform her agrarian economy into an industrialized one. In this much neglected sphere America's contribution has been of paramount importance in the reconstruction of the Indian economy. Technical assistance is only one phase of the over-all development of what may be called human capital.

Development of Human Capital

India's vast population constitutes a problem both quantitatively and qualitatively. The qualitative level of the people is low because of their unmanageable quantity in relation to the limited resources. If the quality of the people is raised, the population of a country becomes its greatest asset. A country's population is its human capital, the development of which must be of paramount importance, particularly in a developing country.

Health and education are the major factors contributing to the development of human capital. The various health programs covering malaria eradication, health education, and support to medical and nursing colleges are discussed elsewhere in the book. The variety of educational programs, also referred to elsewhere in this study, includes not only training of Indians associated with the aid projects in India and the United States but also such pioneering and unique institutions as the All-India Institute of Medical Sciences at Delhi, the Indian Institute of Technology at Kanpur, and the Agricultural University at Rudrapur. Apart from training imparted to Indians working on aid projects in India by American technical experts, some 5,000 Indian participants have been sent to the United States during this period under the auspices of TCM (now AID) for some kind of training in the United States.

What effect do these American-trained Indians have on India? The changed attitudes and new ideas as well as new and improved work techniques that they bring with them are bound to have leavening effects on the communities in which they live and work. AID has carefully selected young men and women that have ability and leadership potentialities.

It is true that the total impact of some 5,000 young trainees is too small to change basically Indian cultural attitudes. But nevertheless, these American-trained people do contribute a new and vital element to that segment of enlightened Indian opinion which will, undoubtedly, increase in importance as time goes by.

What effect do the Indian students, scholars, and trainees have on the United States? Indo-American educational, scientific, and cultural exchanges are a real two-way street. Indian exchange personnel have some impact on the United States in the sense that they have helped change the image of India in the United States; this change has to some extent made it easier to maintain and enlarge the American program of assistance to India.

On the other hand, American Fulbright students and professors in India not only take back to the United States some Indian values, but they also leave behind certain American values. That there is benefit in getting acquainted with each other's attitudes and views is undeniable.

American efforts to make Indian education more pragmatic and to contribute more directly to desirable changes in cultural, economic, and political life have been closely allied with the efforts of the government of India. As people become more educated, they are bound to take a great interest in the country's political problems, and the creation of an enlightened public opinion becomes possible. The result will be less emotionalism in political life; national issues are apt to be considered with more light and less heat.

A broad-based educational system in India must accomplish much more than imparting formal instruction to the students. The first aim of such an educational system must be to increase the ability of the individual so that he is productive and is able to contribute his share to the nation's development. The second aim must be to inculcate and increase a sense of civic responsibility and participation—a sense that is sorely lacking today.

At the same time, an educational curriculum and system can be dangerous if it arouses an individual's premature awareness of a higher standard of living and of ways of demanding them through political channels. Until the country is able to create a productive economic system that permits a rather high level of employment, if not full employment, and some equality of opportunities, the revolution of rising expectations is apt to misfire. Although the promise of a socialist pattern of society, made so frequently by political leaders to the vast illiterate electorate, is tantalizing, the slogan should not be taken either literally or too seriously by the people. Their disappointment will be all the greater because not only is there no socialism, but there is a rising cost of living and greater tax burden. In the name of a socialist society of the future, the citizen is treated with scant respect in the present.

A country's educational system can be looked at in two ways, from the point of view of the individual and from that of society. From the individual's point of view, education should make him more productive and a better citizen. It should give him access to a higher standard of living and develop his individual potentialities to the maximum limit. As for society, it has a right to expect from the educational system a stable, prosperous, and progressive community made up of integrated individuals who are anxious to promote societal welfare as a whole.

The impact of American activities on education in a country as large and diverse as India has to be selective rather than general in its approach. American aid authorities have experimented with several approaches and have come to the conclusion that American assistance to education is best concentrated in one particular and limited area.

American aid has, of late, as observed already, been concentrated on certain specific key, standard-setting institutions like the All-India Institute of Medical Sciences in New Delhi, the Indian Institute of Technology in Kanpur, the Agricultural University at Rudrapur, and the National Institute of Education in New Delhi. The idea is that the available limited resources should be concentrated on a few strategic institutions whose value to the country can be tested and can be copied in other parts of the country with suitable modifications in the light of this experience.

International Demonstration Effect

To some critics, the presence of a large number of affluent Americans in India and their comfortable, if not luxurious, ways of living (in terms of Indian conditions) create frustration among Indians who come in contact with them. This acts as a kind of "international demonstration effect" and is a barrier to capital formation in India and other underdeveloped countries. The argument usually runs as follows: The contact with developed economies directly or indirectly through their representatives' ways of living in underdeveloped countries is damaging to underdeveloped countries because it raises the propensity to consume among the indigenous population, thus discouraging saving and preventing investment.

In the words of Professor Ragnar Nurkse, "knowledge of or contact with new consumption patterns opens one's eyes to previously unrecognized possibilities. . . . In the poorer countries such goods are often imported goods, and not produced at home; but that is not the only trouble. The basic trouble is that the presence or the mere knowledge of new goods and new methods of consumption tends to raise the general propensity to consume."[5] While the adverse influence of the "international demonstration effect" on capital formation in an underdeveloped country is not denied, it has certain desirable results. In India, the relatively opulent ways of the rich foreigners, particularly the Americans, create new wants and encourage new methods and, perhaps, better ways of living. When certain sectors of the Indian population come into contact with the American way of life and decide to emulate it, the probable result is an acceleration in economic growth. The desire for better things in life is sometimes matched by an increased effort to obtain them.

In a sense, "international demonstration effect" is not new in India, for the British lived there for a couple of centuries. Also, Indians have always been exposed to the luxurious ways of living of a small section of quite wealthy Indians. But these ways of living have usually been marked more by mere conspicuous consumption than by healthy patterns of living. Their diet, because of ignorance, is often almost as unbalanced as the poor man's diet, and their tastes in other matters are not necessarily refined. We can cite numerous examples from various Indian communities in support of this contention. On the other hand, the ways of living of wealthy Americans may have pointers for Indians who would like to emulate some of the desirable aspects of the American way of life. Unfortunately, all the customs, habits, and manners of the foreigners are not necessarily commendable.

Indo-American Aid Relations: Forecast

What of the future? It is not easy to forecast the future pattern of Indo-American aid relations. Judging from the various factors governing current Indo-American relations, it is realistic to hope

[5] Nurkse, *Problems of Capital Formation in Underdeveloped Countries* (London and New York: Oxford University Press, 1953), pp. 61–62. Professor Bauer writes: "The usual formulation of international demonstration effect omits to note that the new types of consumer goods can be bought only if incomes are first earned to purchase them; consumption can stimulate saving and investment as a means to such consumption." *Economic Analysis and Policy in Underdeveloped Countries,* p. 65.

for a closer, more cordial relationship leading to much greater aid to India from the United States.

Of course, from the Indian point of view, the ultimate end of all foreign aid is that it should cease—that is, the economy of the country should become creative, productive, and self-generating at such a desirable high level that foreign assistance becomes by and large unnecessary.

The *modus operandi* of American aid to India is simple and well known. American aid for any specific project is predicated on the request for such aid by the government of India. The initiative is taken by the government of India since it is known that the United States Government is ready and willing to entertain such requests for aid. The magnitude as well as the conditions of aid for the proposed project are negotiated between the two governments or their designated agencies (such as the Foreign Aid Division of the Ministry of Finance and the United States AID Mission in New Delhi). Once the request for aid for a particular project is submitted, the U.S. aid authorities examine the proposed project from various points of view, call for more details, and, if they are satisfied that it is a worthwhile and rewarding project within the financial and technical competence of the United States, approve of it.

Normally, the United States does not suggest the kind of project the recipient country should have. Once the aid is granted, the implementation of the project rests by and large with the government of India. If differences between the American technical experts and the government of India personnel assigned to execute the project arise, they are settled through negotiations to mutual satisfaction, for both the parties are interested in the quick and efficient implementation of the project on hand.

The United States sets up credits in the United States that are used to pay for equipment or technical personnel for a particular project, and then the American aid to and direct interest in the project ceases. The task of seeing a particular project carried out is left to the Indians. There is no specific machinery at present to watch over the project till it is completed and to evaluate its impact on the economy. To some extent, of course, this is done here and there, particularly when things are not going well.

New Priorities

In all underdeveloped countries, the question of priorities is one of fundamental importance. The new rulers of the emergent countries find it extremely difficult to choose between what is essential and what is showy, between necessity and ornamentation, and between productive projects and status symbols. American and U.N. aid experts who have worked in underdeveloped countries know, to their exasperation, that the new leaders in the poor countries want jet planes and television sets before underground sewers and night soil-refuse-disposal plants. They prefer steel plants to schools and automobiles to clinics. Indian political leaders, though not totally enlightened on this difficult question, have been on the whole reasonable.

As the Indian economy is one of shortages, the question of priorities assumes paramount importance. To some, priorities are a matter of opinion; to others, certain priorities are basic and obvious, for instance, the mobilization of the countryside. That is, India should get an agricultural revolution going in the villages, and until this revolution has gathered momentum no serious attention should be paid to heavy industrialization.

The second major task is one of administration and organization. An administrative machinery designed by the British during the nineteenth century can hardly cope with economic, sociological, and anthropological problems inherent in implementing aid programs on a vast scale. What is needed is an entirely different mental equipment, knowledge, and training. This will involve many reforms, both major and minor, but none too difficult to implement.

The decision-making apparatus has to be overhauled and radically changed, and the bureaucracy needs to be retrained. The trouble with Indian bureaucracy is that it does not trust its own lower echelons, much less the citizens of the country it administers. (How else can one explain the enormous number of petty, tiresome, and meaningless rules? The British framed these rules because, as ruling foreigners, they could not trust the colonial Indians, but the government of free India has made even more rules!)

The third major task before the country is that of rapid and large-scale industrialization. Here much is being done and even the worst sceptic must concede that India has made more advancement in this area in the last decade and a half than in the last half-century. There is no need to discuss again the question of the merits of the public sector as against those of the private sector. However, one suggestion may be made. It would perhaps be wiser to let more outsiders come in, start industries, set up plants, train Indians, and help raise the total wealth of the country, even if this means, as it must, that the foreigner makes and takes some profits. Today, the government appears to take almost sadistic pleasure in putting obstacles in the path of foreign investors and collaborators in India. No country, as observed earlier in the book, has pulled itself up by its own bootstraps. Therefore, it would be profitable in the long run for the Indian government not to put too many obstacles and objections in the path of the American and other foreign industrialists who are willing to share their capital and know-how with Indians for mutual benefit. It must be remembered that, today, the foreigner, no matter who he is, can neither exploit the local people nor carry away his plant and industry from India. The days of nineteenth-century imperialism and exploitation are definitely over.

To give just one random example, India wants to attract foreign tourists, particularly Americans, not only because India has many ancient and beautiful things to show, but also because India needs precious foreign exchange, particularly American dollars. And yet, the government of India with its endless red tape and blight-breeding bureaucracy does just about everything possible, from the granting of the visa through the hotel accommodation to the giving of the exit permit, to discourage foreign tourists. There are few hotels adequate for the needs of foreign tourists, or even for Indians for that matter. The country's old hotels have never seen real cleanliness or efficiency. New mausoleums, like the Ashoka Hotel in New Delhi, have more protocol-conscious servants than paying patrons. It is true that the Ashoka has made some profit of late, but one Ashoka is not enough. Why not let the Americans come in and build a network of clean, efficient, modern hotels on the lines of the Hiltons? This American hotel organization has built first-class hotels in many foreign countries that have apparently not lost their sovereignty on this account. An Indo-American joint venture in hotel-building might be a welcome idea. Private enterprise in India is not up to this task as yet because it is used to such shoddy, second-rate accommodation that it cannot think in first-class terms. Once India has a chain of comfortable and functional hotels the tourist business will boom.

Tied Aid

The question of "tied aid" is also important. Tied aid is, of course, the American insistence on the recipient country's buying, with American aid funds, food and services of United States origin only. This policy, which applies to all American development loans, officially came into being in early 1960.

From the American point of view the motive behind tied aid is to prevent her from suffering from an adverse balance-of-payments situation that is brought about when India, for example, buys various commodities and services with U.S. dollars from Germany because German goods are cheaper than those of U.S. origin. This situation could be prevented if all the advanced countries participated in programs of foreign aid to less-developed countries in proportion to their resources and national income. But since they do not, America has to bear an unduly large burden. Therefore, she has to insist on tied loans to safeguard her economic position. It is true that the United States prefers untied aid just as much as India desires it, and it is hoped that such untied loans will become the rule once the burden of assisting underdeveloped countries is shared by all the rich countries.

Scatter versus Concentration

American aid has been scattered over various spheres of Indian economic development. Although the total U.S. aid, as already pointed out, is more than half of all the aid received by India from nearly a score of countries, American aid appears to be spread rather thinly.

Soviet aid, for instance, produces such tangible results as the Bhilai steel plant and its products, but American aid has been diffuse and rather intangible, directed as it is toward communication, community development, and the general infrastructure. While the importance of these in the nation's total economic development is unquestionable, years have to elapse before their beneficent effects can be felt. It is but natural that a foreign country willing to help India would like to impress the recipient country with some kind of dazzling gift. Although such a desire may appear juvenile and superficial, something must be said in its favor. It is desirable, on the whole, for a donor country to concentrate its aid resources on a particularly important sector of the recipient country where it can demonstrate the possibilities of impressive development within a reasonable period of time. Once what can be achieved under certain circumstances can be shown, the recipient country may do likewise in other areas capable of development.

The reason why the United States scattered her aid in diverse areas of development in earlier years is because she did not know exactly what was needed (and every sector appeared to be crying for help) or what the core of the Indian economic problem was. Now America has realized that she must concentrate her aid in particularly critical areas of the Indian economy and in fields where she has special and unrivaled competence. Through such concentrated assistance, India and the United States are likely to obtain larger results for a given unit of effort toward Indian economic development.

In a sense, America recently has struck the golden mean in her approach to problems of Indian development by concentrating certain portions of her aid on more and more specifically defined projects, but at the same time increasing and broadening the general goods and services supplied to support the development effort on the whole.

Pattern of New Loans

As is well known there are two kinds of American loans: project loans and nonproject loans. The former are for development imports whereas the latter are for maintenance imports used by the government of India to import industrial raw materials (like nonferrous metals, iron and steel, sulphur, synthetic rubber, lubricants, chemicals, accessories, etc.) to help her in the balance of payments.

In discussing the evolution of American aid two things must be remembered: the mode and agency through which a grant or loan is distributed, and whether the loan is to be repaid in dollars or rupees.

The pattern of American aid to India through the various development-aid agencies is constantly under review as to both criterion and policy. One recent innovation is that loans repayable in local currency, rupees, with a fairly high interest rate and shorter terms have been superceded by loans for longer terms with only a nominal service charge but repayable in dollars.

The conditions under which American loans are granted to India have been changed recently for the better. She now charges low rates of interest, as low as .75, and the amount is repayable in 40 years. But India has to repay this type of loan in dollars, not in rupees. However, it is hoped that India will have developed sufficiently in 40 years to be able to repay the loans in dollars without any strain. In the meantime, there is a minimum of strain on India's current balance-of-payments position. There is a 10-

year grace period before repayment need start. Loans to the private sector are payable in rupees (not in dollars) to the Indian Government, which in turn repays the United States Government in 40 years with a .75 per cent service charge. The basic question in matters of aid is the recipient country's capacity to repay.

Reform of Administrative Machinery

In the art of public administration India can learn a lesson or two from the United States, if only a lesson in how to increase the over-all efficiency of the Indian administration. It is true that India inherited from the British a relatively efficient civil service. But this Indian (half of it was British) civil service, with its particular pro-British (if not anti-Indian) bias and training, which unfortunately knew nothing beyond British ways, has almost disappeared since 1947. The number of Indian Civil Service men left today in the Indian administration is very few.

The Indian Administrative Service has succeeded the Indian Civil Service. The chief defect of the IAS is that it reflects the general fall in standards that the country has witnessed during the last decade. (This is not the place to explore the reasons behind the decline in standards.) Unlike the ICS, the IAS young men and women have neither seen nor experienced anything better organized and more efficient than their own slow, delaying, bureaucracy. They are being trained by senior and retired ICS people, as well as a few visiting scholars, in the traditional chores of the nineteenth-century British administration of a backward country. They have unfortunately not yet learned that they are being trained in rules and regulations that are the very antithesis of the needs of a rapidly developing economy of a free nation. The days when a man with a chemistry degree who passed a competitive examination at the age of twenty-three or twenty-four was put in charge of the finances of a state after a few years of training are gone, one hopes, forever.

What is needed today is a civil servant who is extremely well informed (this means that the present Indian university education must be overhauled and the English language must be retained for contact with the external world and all-India communication) and who is trained to examine issues competently and quickly and take serious, responsible decisions. Today, the Indian administration is top-heavy with a platoon of secretaries accompanied by an army of parasitic *chaprasis* (servants) who seem to grow in numbers with the increase of the country's total population; and they are all lost in a maze of countless strangulating rules and procedures. Parkinson's Law par excellence!

These men are victims of an invidious system of rules. Many of these basic rules were framed three-quarters of a century ago by an alien government that did not believe in the integrity of the average colonial citizen. It is amazing that the administration of free India has increased these pettifogging rules a hundredfold. This can only be explained on the assumption that the government considers the average citizen of free India a criminal till proved otherwise. Try and obtain ten rupees sanctioned by the government through what is called a contingent bill at a government pay-and-accounts office. If a man can obtain this paltry sum after ten visits and signing countless receipts and vouchers, he is a lucky man indeed!

In the rapid industrialization of an underdeveloped country, the efficiency of the administrative procedures plays a vital role. Authority to make decisions has been denied at almost all levels till one reaches the top. Even at the top it is not always one man's decision but a group decision. On the other hand, even when individuals have power they often refuse to exercise it for fear of going wrong. One must be able to make an honest mistake and have his boss be able to back him up. The concept of the collective responsibility of the cabinet (whether this is followed in the government of India or not) is certainly not in evidence at the lower levels.

It is a pity that the United States has not offered any help in streamlining the Indian administration beyond Appleby's reports, which were not really part of the formal U.S. aid-to-India program and which were shelved anyway. But U.S. aid is given only on India's request. And India has not asked for any aid in this direction. How can the civil servants who constitute the administration ask for aid that will reform them!

The Population Problem

American aid has at least touched, if not completely covered, just about every major sector of the Indian economy. In the earlier and experimental years, American aid was extended to all kinds of projects, because no one, including the Indian authorities, knew for certain which were the most vulnerable spots in the economy. American aid to the stability and even vitality of the Indian economy has already been commented upon. However, it cannot be denied that American aid could have been even more effective and could have had a more lasting impact had she given some solid support to India in two difficult and vulnerable areas that have been crying for help for some time. One is her population problem, and the other the problem of public health, hygiene, and sanitation.

India's population problem, which arises from a relatively high fertility and a declining mortality, is simply the net annual addition of more than 9 million people to the existing base of about 460 million; this annual increase by and large nullifies much of the national effort toward a higher level of living. Fortunately, the AID authorities in Washington, are very much aware of the pressing population problem in India and other underdeveloped countries. The Third Interim Report of the President's Committee to Study the United States Military Assistance Program warned in 1959 that:

> No realistic discussion of economic development can fail to note that development efforts in many areas of the world are being offset by increasingly rapid population growth. . . .
>
> Basically, the problems of rapid population growth and of adequate economic progress must be faced and solved by the individual countries. The United States and the other more advanced countries can and should be prepared to respond to requests for information and technical assistance in connection with population growth. Such information will help to point up the seriousness of the problem, and to encourage action in countries where population pressures exist. Such information is also useful in defining the areas in which initial efforts will be most effective. Recognizing an immediate problem created by the rapid growth, the United States should also increase its assistance to local programs relative to maternal and child welfare.
>
> We recommend: That, in order to meet more effectively the problems of economic development, the United States (1) assist those countries with which it is cooperating in economic aid programs, on request, in the formulation of their plans designed to deal with the problem of rapid population growth, (2) increase its assistance to local programs relating to maternal and child welfare in recognition of the immediate problem created by rapid population growth, and (3) strongly support studies and appropriate research as a part of its own Mutual Security Program, within the United Nations and elsewhere, leading to the availability of relevant information in a form most useful to individual countries in the formulation of practical

programs to meet the serious challenge posed by rapidly expanding populations.[6]

The second problem is India's filth. Indian communities, whether they are large cities, small towns, or villages, do not as yet have modern sanitation and environmental hygiene. They have yet to obtain a modern potable water supply, sanitary conservancy systems, underground sewage collection and disposal, and even proper garbage-disposal systems. This filthy situation, apart from its disgusting, physical ugliness, leads to a catalogue of diseases that have been controlled and conquered in the advanced countries of the West. The deplorable lack of sanitation and lack of health consciousness leads to a high incidence of morbidity of a primitive kind. It is shocking to record that during the year 1963 hundreds of Indians died of smallpox and cholera in India's major cities. To say the least, all this profoundly affects Indian economic and social development through high infant, maternal, and general mortality rates and through the loss of millions of man hours every year in the field, factory, and office.

American aid could make a splendid contribution in both of these areas. American communication and educational techniques could be pressed into service to bring home the importance of family planning for economic, health, and social reasons. The government of India, unlike the governments of some underdeveloped and even developed countries, has taken a progressive attitude on the question of her population growth. The various attitude surveys conducted in different parts of the country have revealed that Indian parents are in favor of family limitation. Family planning has been given an important place in all the three Five-Year Plans. American aid could easily give a push and a fillip to the existing Indian family-planning programs.

America could set up with her latest technical know-how large plants for the manufacture of contraceptives. These contraceptive factories could operate under the public sector with little or no profit; and, with the tremendous sale that could be expected, they could sell contraceptives at extremely low prices. Today, the imported contraceptives are too costly for the average Indian villager. American supply of raw material (rubber) and technical

[6] *President's Commission to Study the United States Military Assistance Program. Third Interim Report: Economic Assistance Program and Administration* (Washington, D.C., 1959).

assistance in the manufacture of contraceptives could make a tremendous contribution to lowering the Indian birth rate. Once the Indian birth rate is lowered and the net annual addition to the existing population numbers becomes manageable, American aid in other sectors would then be able to effect a real rise in the Indian level of living.

But, unfortunately, population problems are often bedeviled with matters of politics and theology. Contrary to what the American Roman Catholics believe, there is a large body of public opinion in America—Protestant, Jewish, and even Catholic—that contends that America should give birth-control aid to underdeveloped countries that request it. It is to be hoped that India will ask for such aid and that America will provide it.

Public Health, Hygiene, and Sanitation

As for public hygiene and environmental sanitation, all the problems involved in these can be solved easily. They are merely matters of education and expense. The average Indian's "sanitary" habits are far from desirable. He needs to be educated. If his behavior as far as the rules of health are concerned is atrocious, it is often because there is no alternative. Even the lowly do not love dirt, filth, and poverty.

On the question of expense, most municipalities cannot afford modern hygiene and sanitation. This expenditure must be considered an important part of the infrastructure that will yield rewarding gains in the long run. If in the next decade India could be rescued from her dirt and filth and converted into a clean and healthy country, the effect of such a transformation on her economic and social development would be beyond any calculation.

Counterpart Funds

The question of counterpart funds is a rather controversial and vexing one, and those who are familiar with the problem have not yet come up with a satisfactory solution. The counterpart funds involve the vast amount of local currency (Indian rupees) that has accumulated to the credit of the United States Government in India.

How did these funds accumulate? An example: American aid to India includes several million tons of wheat. Technically, this wheat is not a gift or a "give away;" the government of India pays for it, not in U.S. dollars, which she has in limited supply, but in Indian rupees. The government of India sells the wheat to the Indian consumer and deposits the sales proceeds to the credit of the United States Government in India. These funds are utilized to meet the expenses of the large American Embassy, the consulates, the various United States Information Services in India, and some American cultural and exchange programs. However, these expenses use up a very small part of the existing counterpart funds.

Today, the total amount of the counterpart funds in India exceeds $400 million (about 2 billion rupees), and they increase each year by about $70 million.

The government of India is reluctant to raise the question of how these funds are to be used, since the money belongs to the United States. The State Department is apparently unwilling to raise the question for fear the U.S. Congress might want to reduce American aid to India in the coming years to the amount of the available counterpart funds. Obviously, such action would not be helpful to India. For example, if India were to buy American steel, she would require dollars and not rupees.

Since the State Department has hesitated so far to ask Congress to permit the utilization of these funds for constructive purposes, the AID authorities in India are now examining the question of setting up a binational foundation in New Delhi with the counterpart funds as capital. Such a foundation could support projects which would contribute to India's advancement as well as promote Indo-American goodwill.

This writer feels that the funds can best be used to promote family planning, as the nation's alarming population growth is at the heart of the problem of Indian poverty. It has been found that under present Indian conditions, sterilization, particularly vasectomy for fathers who want to permanently limit the number of children in their families, is the best answer. Today various state governments offer a 50-rupee bonus (about $10) to each father who undergoes vasectomy. So far, about 2 million sterilizations have been performed. If the bonus could be raised to 100 rupees, the number of sterilizations might increase significantly. (In India, sterilization is voluntary, requires the consent of both husband and wife, and is only performed after the couple sign papers stating that they understand the permanency of the operation.) The sterilization program, apart from cash bonuses, would involve the administrative expenses necessary to carry this vital program to India's half a million villages.[7]

Intangible Effects of American Aid to India

And last, there are some intangible benefits flowing from American aid to India. There is, for instance, a considerable improvement in the understanding between the two countries because of an enlarged exchange of people and information through articles, books, and films about each other in both the countries. Before World War II, the average American's knowledge of India was practically nil. Apart from a handful of India specialists, the man in the street equated India with fabulous Maharajas, tiger hunting, sadhus on beds of nails, sacred cows, snake charmers, the caste system and untouchables, and Gandhi in his loin cloth. Today, twenty years later, the picture has almost completely changed, and for the better, thanks to India-returned Americans, America-returned Indians, exchange students and professors, the publication of an increasing number of books on India by both Indians and Americans, and, to a limited extent, the role of the diplomatic establishments and the information services in both the countries. In fact, today there is more serious and scholarly interest about India in the United States than about the United States in India.

There is a deep, abiding, and invisible psychological effect arising from a greater knowledge and consequent better appreciation of mutual merits, difficulties, and problems. The fact that a powerful and affluent nation is sympathetic and helpful to India and will stand behind her materially and morally in case of serious difficulties is very reassuring to India. The psychological effect on the nation that things are really moving and that the country is gradually but definitely becoming developed and industrialized is bound to be tremendous. The years 1965 and 1966 will show a considerable upturn in India's industrial output, after all the machinery that has been ordered from the United States is fully in action. In a word, nothing succeeds like success. By the end of the Fourth Five-Year Plan and the beginning of the Fifth Five-Year Plan, India will really be a going concern.

[7] See my speech on this subject in the Indian Parliament, December 15, 1964. *Indian Republic. Parliament, Rajya Sabha. Debates* (New Delhi, 1965). See also S. Chandrasekhar, "A Billion Indians by 2000 A.D.?," *The New York Times Magazine,* April 4, 1965; John Fischer, "How to Save a Few Million Lives—and Save Money at the Same Time," *Harper's Magazine,* October, 1964.

APPENDIXES

Appendix 1. American-Aided Projects in India (TCM)

Aid to Agriculture

Acquisition and distribution of fertilizers
Acquisition and distribution of iron and steel for agriculture
Agricultural economics research
Agricultural and home-science extension and training
Agricultural information, production and training
Augmenting fertilizer supply
Calcutta milk scheme
Cooperative membership education
Crop production and development
Dairy development
Determination of soil fertility and fertilizer use
Development of forest research and desert afforestation
Expansion and modernization of marine and inland fisheries
Farmers' organization
Fertilizers imports
Flood control
Forest research and desert afforestation
Ground-water exploration
Ground-water irrigation
Hybrid maize and other improved seeds
Jungle-reclamation machinery
Livestock improvement
Marine and inland fisheries
Milk schemes
Modern storage of food grains
Plant protection and locust control
Provision of engineering services to Damodar Valley Corporation
Provision of technical advisory services to Central Water Power Commission
River-valley development
Soil laboratories

Soil and water conservation
Steel for agricultural implements
Survey of Sindri expansion
Technical services in water resources and power development
Technical assistance to irrigation-research institute
Training in agricultural machinery utilization
Uttar Pradesh Agricultural University
Water-resources survey and minor irrigation works

Aid to Industry

Assistance to coal industry
Assistance to industrial research and technical organization
Augmenting steel supply
Bombay Central Training Institute for Craftsmen and Instructors
Building-materials development
Cement
Delhi Thermal Plant
Electric distribution systems maintenance training centers
Exploratory lignite excavation and development
Foremen training
Foundry training
Geological survey of India
Indian Institute of Technology, Kanpur
Indian Institute of Technology, Kharagpur
Improvement of Rajasthan power facilities
Industrial Credit and Investment Corporation of India (P.L. 480 rupees; no dollar aid)
Industrial Finance Corporation (P.L. 480 rupees; no dollar aid)
Industrial technical services
Mineral development
National Productivity Council
Orissa iron ore
Refinance Corporation for Industry, Ltd. (P.L. 480 rupees; no dollar aid)
Rihand Valley development
Rural electrification
Safety measures in factories
Sharavathi Hydro-Electric Project (P.L. 480 rupees; no dollar aid)
Small-industries development
Steel-casting foundry
Steel engineers' training
Telecommunication development
Training construction-equipment operators and mechanics
Tube-well casing
University of Roorkee (technical education)

Aid to Health

All India Institute of Medical Sciences Hospital (P.L. 480 rupees; no dollar aid)
Assistance to health agencies
Assistance to medical colleges and allied institutions
Control of filaria
General nursing
Health education
Health Instruction Training Centres
Insect-borne disease control
Malaria eradication
National Water Supply and Sanitation Programme
Medical education
Medical College, Baroda
Medical College, Trivandrum
Osmania Medical College, Hyderabad
Technical education
Bengal Engineering College, Howrah
College of Engineering, Guindy, Madras
College of Engineering, Poona

Aid to Transport

Expansion of aviation ground facilities
Indian airlines
Jet liners for Air India International
Radar and other equipment for airports
Railway rehabilitation and expansion of national highways
Telecommunication development

Aid to Education

Adult education
Assistance to Central Institute of Education
Assistance to Educational Administration
Agricultural education and research
Assistance to extension program for secondary-school teachers
Assistance to home-science education and research
Assistance to National Institute of Basic Education
Assistance to National Professional Education Centre
Assistance to teacher training in audio-visual education
Assistance to technical-education institutions
Assistance to training in adult education
Audio-visual education
Foundry training
Indian Institute of Technology, Kanpur

National program for professional education
Rural institutes
School-building improvement
Social-welfare education

Aid to Miscellaneous Projects

Assistance to Indian Statistical Institute
Assistance to nuclear research
Bombay Central Training Institute for Craftsmen and Instructors
Building-materials development
Community Development Program
Demonstration of improved methods of low-cost housing construction
Establishment of Central Labour Institute
Housing construction
Improved operating statistics and reports
Industrial safety
Investment promotion and tax study
Organization and management techniques
Social welfare
Study of effects of thermal environment conditions
Trades training
Training in public administration

Appendix 2. Selected Indo-American Projects: A Geographical Listing

Andhra Pradesh

Hyderabad	(Agriculture) agricultural-university development
	(Health) medical education
	(Health) general nursing
	(Health) public-health education
Nagarjunasagar	(Industry) Heavy Equipment Training Centre
	(Water resources) river-valley development
Vijayawada	(Agriculture) irrigation and drainage
	(Agriculture) extension
	(Agriculture) farm management

Assam

Barapani	(Power) hydroelectric station
Gauhati	(Agriculture) agricultural-university development
Jorhat	(Agriculture) agricultural-university development

Bihar

Barauni	(Power) thermal plant
Chandrapura	(Power) thermal plant
Damodar Valley	(Water resources) river-valley development
Kosi	(Water resources) river-valley development
Ramgarh	(Industry) coal-mine development
Ranchi	(Industry) steel-training (Hindustan Steel)

Delhi

New Delhi	(Health) medical-educator training
	(Health) public-health education
	(Health) hospital administration
	(Education) National Institute of Education
	(Industry) National Productivity Council
	(Industry) Indian Investment Centre
	(Power) thermal plant
	(Agriculture) poultry husbandry
	(Agriculture) agriculture information
	(Agriculture) soil testing
	(Agriculture) seed testing
	(Agriculture) fertilizer promotion

Gujarat

Ahmedabad	(Power) thermal plant
Cambay	(Power) thermal plant
Mahi	(Water resources) river-valley development
Rajkot	(Industry) small-industries development (Product Development and Training Centre)

Kerala

Ettamanur	(Industry) Production and Training Centre (foundry training)
Pamba-Kakki	(Power) hydro-electric project
Trivandrum	(Agriculture) soil conservation
	(Health) medical-educator training

Madhya Pradesh

Bhopal	(Education) multipurpose higher secondary education
Birsinghpur	(Power) thermal plant
Indore	(Health) general nursing
Morena	(Agriculture) irrigation and water use
Raipur	(Agriculture) soils and fertilizer
	(Agriculture) farm management

Madras

Coimbatore	(Agriculture) agricultural-university development
Kundha	(Power) hydro-electric project
Guindy (Madras City)	(Education) Technical Education Institution
	(Industry) National Productivity Council
Tanjore	(Agriculture) irrigation and drainage

Maharashtra

Bombay	(Industry) Trombay Fertilizer Plant
	(Industry) nuclear engineering and research
	(Industry) Refinance Corporation
	(Industry) Industrial Credit and Investment Corporation of India (ICICI)
	(Industry) National Productivity Council
	(Labor) Central Training Institute for Craftsmen and Instructors
Kakrapur	(Water resources) river-valley development
Koyna	(Power) hydro-electric project
Nagpur	(Agriculture) soil testing
Poona	(Agriculture) soil conservation
	(Agriculture) agriculture information
	(Education) Technical Education Institution

Mysore

Bangalore	(Agriculture) irrigation extension
	(Industry) "hot lines" maintenance training
Bhadra	(Water resources) river-valley development
Hebbal	(Agriculture) agricultural-university development
Mysore City	(Education) multipurpose secondary education
Sharavathi	(Power) hydro-electric project
Tungabhadra	(Water resources) river-valley development

Orissa

Bhubaneswar	(Agriculture) agricultural-university development
	(Education) multipurpose secondary education
Hirakud	(Water resources) river-valley development
Talcher	(Power) thermal plant

Punjab

Beas Dam	(Water resources) river-valley development
	(Power) hydro-electric project

Chandigarh	(Agriculture) soil-conservation engineering
	(Agriculture) hybrid maize production
Ludhiana	(Agriculture) agricultural-university development
Rajasthan	
Ajmeer	(Education) multipurpose secondary education
Chambal	(Water resources) river-valley development
Jaipur	(Health) nursing-college development
Kotah	(Industry) Heavy Equipment Training Centre
Pali	(Agriculture) agriculture extension (agronomy)
Udaipur	(Agriculture) agricultural-university development
Uttar Pradesh	
Aligarh	(Agriculture) agricultural engineering
	(Agriculture) irrigation and drainage
	(Agriculture) farm management
Kanpur	(Agriculture) agricultural-university development
	(Education) Technical Education Institute (IIT)
	(Power) thermal plant
Pant Nagar	(Agriculture) agricultural-university development
Rihand	(Water resources) river-valley development
	(Power) hydro-electric project
Roorkee	(Education) Technical Education Institution
Singrauli	(Industry) coal-mine development
Terai	(Agriculture) hybrid maize production
Varanasi	(Agriculture) agricultural-university development
West Bengal	
Bandel	(Power) thermal plant
Calcutta	(Agriculture) milk plant and cattle farm
	(Industry) National Productivity Council
Durgapur	(Power) thermal plant
	(Industry) steel training
Howrah	(Education) Technical Education Institution
Kharagpur	(Education) Technical Education Institution

Appendix 3. American Christian (Catholic and Protestant) Missions Doing Agricultural, Educational, Evangelical, and Medical Work in India

The large-scale economic, technical, and military aid offered by the advanced countries to certain underdeveloped countries is technically a postwar phenomenon, although capital assistance from one country to another is quite old. In all discussions of American economic and technical assistance to the underdeveloped countries, the role of American Christian (both Catholic and Protestant) missions is never mentioned, particularly since certain non-Christian underdeveloped countries view with suspicion the proselytizing activities of the American missionaries, and since the amount involved is not substantial.

However, I feel that the American Christian missions' work in India must be treated as a part of American aid to India's development. From the beginning of the nineteenth century, American missionaries have come to India and opened with their own resources educational, medical, philanthropic, and evangelistic missions. Since the American missionary work constitutes private, unilateral transfers of funds from the United States to India, it must be considered a part of American economic aid to India.

A detailed discussion of the funds and technical personnel made available and the nature and magnitude of the over-all services provided by the missionaries could easily fill a book. Therefore, this appendix merely lists the better known American Christian missions working in India.

Advent Christian Church, American Advent Mission Society, Brookline, Massachusetts
American Baptist Convention, New York; in Madras
American Council of Christian Churches, New York
American Council of the Ramabai Mukti Mission, Philadelphia, Pennsylvania; in Kedgaon, Poona District
American Friends Service Committee, Philadelphia, Pennsylvania; in Orissa
American Jesuits in India, Chicago and Detroit provinces of the Society of Jesus; in Bihar
American Leprosy Missions, Inc.
American Lutheran Church, Division of World Missions, Minneapolis, Minnesota; in Andhra Pradesh and Madras states
American Ministerial Association, York, Pennsylvania
Assemblies of God, General Council, Springfield, Missouri
Association of Baptists for World Evangelism, Inc., Philadelphia, Pennsylvania

Augustana Lutheran Church, Minneapolis, Minnesota; in South India
Baptist Bible Fellowship, Springfield, Missouri
Baptist General Conference, Chicago, Illinois
Baptist Mid-Missions, Cleveland, Ohio; in Makunda and Alipur
Bible Presbyterian Synod, Inc., Washington, Illinois
Brethren in Christ Church, Harrisburg, Pennsylvania; in Saharsa and Madhipura, Bihar
Brothers of the Holy Cross, Foreign Mission Society, Washington, D.C.
Catholic Medical Mission Board, Inc., New York
Ceylon and India, General Mission and Pakistan Christian Fellowship, Wheaton, Illinois
Christian and Missionary Alliance, New York; in Maharashtra and Gujarat
Christian Missionary Fellowship, Aurora, Illinois; in Mussorie, Uttar Pradesh
Christian Missions in Many Lands, New York
Church of the Brethren, General Brotherhood Board, Elgin, Illinois
Church of Christ, Scientist, Boston, Massachusetts
Church of God, Cleveland, Tennessee
Churches of God in North America, Board of Missions, Inc., Brackenridge, Pennsylvania
Congregation of the Religious Sisters of Mercy, Merion, Pennsylvania; in Bihar
Congregational Christian Churches of the United States, General Council, Boston, Massachusetts
Conservative Baptist Foreign Mission Society, Wheaton, Illinois; in Kothara
Disciples of Christ, the United Christian Missionary Society, Indianapolis, Indiana
Divine Word Missionaries, Techny, Illinois
Evangelical Alliance Mission, Chicago, Illinois
"Evangelize China" Fellowships, Inc., Los Angeles, California
Franciscan Missionaries of Mary, New York
Franciscan T.O.R. Mission of India, Loretto, Pennsylvania; in Gokhla, Baramasia, Harimohra, Godda, Poreya Hat
Free Methodist Church of North America, Winona Lake, Indiana
General Conference Mennonite Church, Board of Missions, Newton, Kansas; in Madhya Pradesh, Raipur, Yeotmal Vellore
Holy Spirit Missionary Sisters, Techny, Illinois; in Indore, Madhya Bharat
Independent Board for Presbyterian Foreign Missions, Philadelphia, Pennsylvania; in North India
International Catholic Auxiliaries, Evanston, Illinois; in Madras State
International Child Evangelism Fellowships, Grand Rapids, Michigan
International Christian Leprosy Missions, Inc., Portland, Oregon; in Bihar

International Missions, Inc., Jersey City, N.J.; in Andhra Pradesh
International Pentacostal Assemblies, Atlanta, Georgia; in Uttar Pradesh
Jesuit Mission Bureau, Maryland Province of the Society of Jesus, Baltimore, Maryland
The Lutheran Church (Missouri Synod), St. Louis, Missouri
Medical Mission Sisters, Philadelphia, Pennsylvania; in Kerala, Bihar, Bombay, New Delhi
Mennonite Brethren Church of North America, Board of Foreign Missions, Kansas; in Andhra Pradesh
Mennonite Church, Board of Missions and Charities, Elkhart, Indiana; in Dhamtari, Bagtari, Balodgahan, and Shantipur
The Methodist Church, New York
The Metropolitan Church Association, Dundee, Illinois; in Suvait (near Allahabad) and in Gundala
National Association of Free Will Baptists, Nashville, Tennessee
National Council of Churches of Christ in the USA, New York
National Lutheran Council, New York
North East India General Mission, Inc., Philadelphia, Pennsylvania; in Manipur State
Ohio Yearly Meeting, Friends Foreign Missionary Society, Damascus, Ohio; in Madhya Pradesh and New Delhi
Oriental Missionary Society, Los Angeles, California
Protestant Episcopal Church in the USA, National Council, New York
Reformed Church in America, New York; in Ranipet, Katpadi, and Vellore (Madras State)
Regions Beyond Missionary Union, Philadelphia, Pennsylvania
The Santal Mission of the Northern Churches, American Board, Minneapolis, Minnesota
Schwenkfelder Church, Philadelphia, Pennsylvania
Seventh-Day Adventist Church, General Conferences, Washington, D.C.
Sisters of Charity of Nazareth, Kentucky; in Mokameh, Bukhtiarpur, and Gaya
Sisters of Notre Dame, Chardon, Ohio; in Bihar
United Lutheran Church in America, Board of Foreign Missions, New York; in Andhra Pradesh
United Missionary Society, Elkhart, Indiana
United Presbyterian Church in the United States of America, Commission on Ecumenical Mission and Relations, New York
Wesleyan Methodist Church, Department of World Missions, Marion, Indiana; in Surat and Thana districts (Maharashtra) and in Raj Nandgaon
Woman's Union Missionary Society of America, New York; in Allahabad, Fatehpur, Jhansi, and Kanpur
World Gospel Mission, Marion, Indiana

World Missions to Children, San Jose, California
World Mission Prayer League, Inc., Minneapolis, Minnesota
Worldwide Evangelization Crusade, Fort Washington, Pennsylvania
Young Men's Christian Association of the USA and Canada, International Committee, New York; all over India
Young Women's Christian Association of the United States of America, New York; all over India

Appendix 4. A Statistical Comparison of India and the United States, 1960–62: Some Indexes of Affluence and Poverty

Item	*India*	*United States*
Demographic indexes		
Area	1,178,995 sq. miles (1961)	3,615,213 sq. miles (1960)
Population	439,235,082 (1961)	179,323,000 (1960)
Density per square mile	373 persons (1961)	49 persons (1960)
Annual population growth rate	19.7 per 1,000 (1951–61)	14.1 per 1,000 (1959)
Number of rural communities	564,258 (1961)	13,749 (1960)
Number of cities with a population of 100,000 or more	113 (1961)	203 (1960)
Number of cities with a population of 1,000,000 or more	7 (1961)	14 (1960)
Birth rate	24.6 per 1,000 (1961)	23.6 per 1,000 (1960)
Death rate	10.4 per 1,000 (1961)	9.5 per 1,000 (1960)
Infant mortality rate	92 infant deaths per 1,000 live births (1960)	26 infant deaths per 1,000 live births (1960)
Expectation of life at birth	42 years (1955–61)	69 years (1958)
Expectation of life at birth for males	33.45 (1951–61)	66.5 (1959)
Expectation of life at birth for females	31.66 (1951–61)	73.0 (1959)
Sex composition	940 females per 1,000 males (1961)	1,029 females per 1,000 males (1960)
Cultural and social indexes		
Literacy	237 literates per 1,000 (1961)	980 literates per 1,000 (1960)
Number of elementary and high schools	8 per 10,000 (1959)	18 per 10,000 (1958)

Number of colleges and other institutions of higher education	5 per 1 million (1961)	11 per 1 million (1960)
Number of teachers	33 per 10,000 (1960)	89 per 10,000 (1960)
Number of children in schools	41 per 100 in age group 5–14 (1959)	96 per 100 in age group 5–14 (1960)
Number of students in colleges	1.8 per 100 in age group 17–23 (1959)	33 per 100 in age group 19–25 (1960)
Number of doctors	2 per 10,000 (1960)	13 per 10,000 (1960)
Number of dentists	1 per 10,000 (1960)	5 per 10,000 (1960)
Number of nurses	1 per 10,000 (1960)	27 per 10,000 (1960)
Number of hospital beds	4 per 10,000 (1960)	91 per 10,000 (1959)
Number of newspapers	1 per 1 million (1960)	545 per 1 million (1958)
Number of newspaper copies in circulation	9 per 1,000 persons per issue (1959)	327 per 1,000 persons per issue (1959)
Number of periodicals	12 per 1 million (1959)	26 per 1 million (1959)
Number of periodical copies in circulation	42 per 1,000 persons per issue (1959)	2,252 per 1,000 persons per issue (1959)
Number of books published per year	11,979 (1959)	14,876 (1959)
Economic indexes		
Per capita income	$65 per capita (1961)	$2,214 per capita (1960)
Food consumption in calories	2,100 per person per day (1961)	3,200 per person per day (1960)
Consumption of milk	11 lbs. per capita per year (1956)	807 lbs. per capita per year (1959)
Consumption of cotton textiles	16 yards per capita per year (1961)	45 yards per capita per year (1959)
Consumption of electricity	30 kilowatt-hours per capita per year (1961)	4,489 kilowatt-hours per capita per year (1959)
Consumption of steel	18 lbs. per capita per year (1959)	1,082 lbs. per capita per year (1960)
Consumption of fertilizers	0.5 ton per 1,000 per year (1961)	142 tons per 1,000 per year (1959)
Number of telephones in use	11 per 10,000 (1961)	4,081 per 10,000 (1960)
Number of radio sets in use	57 per 10,000 (1961)	9,655 per 10,000 (1960)
Number of television sets in use	Negligible	2,988 per 10,000 (1960)
Total amount insured	$10.60 per capita per year (1960)	$3,108 per capita per year (1960)

Number of motor vehicles in use	1 per 1,000 (1960)	397 per 1,000 (1960)
Railroad-route mileage	8 per 100,000 (1960)	123 per 100,000 (1960)
Number of locomotives	2 per 100,000 (1960)	18 per 100,000 (1960)

SOURCES: Compiled from various sources, but primarily from *India, 1963* (New Delhi: Ministry of Information and Broadcasting, 1963), and *Statistical Abstract of the United States* (Washington, D.C.: U.S. Bureau of the Census, 1961).

APPENDIX 5. A STATISTICAL COMPARISON OF INDIA IN 1947 AND 1961: PROGRESS OF A DEVELOPING ECONOMY

Item	*1947*	*1961*
Demographic indexes		
Population	338,727,000	439,235,082
Density per square mile	289 persons	373 persons
Birth rate	26.6 per 1,000	23.0 per 1,000 (1959)
Death rate	19.7 per 1,000	9.9 per 1,000 (1959)
Infant mortality	146 per 1,000	92 per 1,000
Annual population growth rate	12.6 per 1,000 (1941–51)	19.7 per 1,000 (1951–61)
Expectation of life at birth	32 years (1941–51)	45 years
Social and cultural indexes		
Literacy	166 per 1,000 (1951)	240 per 1,000
Number of primary schools	4 per 10,000	7 per 10,000 (1959)
Number of secondary schools	3 per 100,000	12 per 10,000 (1959)
Number of colleges	2 per 1 million	5 per 1 million (1959)
Number of students in primary schools	29 per 1,000	69 per 1,000 (1959)
Number of students in secondary schools	8 per 1,000	19 per 1,000 (1959)
Number of students in colleges	6 per 10,000	18 per 10,000 (1960)
Number of teachers	15 per 10,000	33 per 10,000 (1960)
Number of hospital beds	2 per 10,000	4 per 10,000 (1960)
Number of doctors	16 per 100,000	18 per 100,000 (1960)
Number of nurses	4 per 100,000	7 per 100,000 (1960)
Economic indexes		
Per capita income	Rs.228	Rs.327

Consumption of food grains	273 lbs. per capita	398 lbs. per capita
Consumption of electric energy	12 kilowatt-hours per capita	39 kilowatt-hours per capita
Consumption of steel	9 lbs. per capita	18 lbs. per capita (1959)
Consumption of cloth	11 yards per capita	16 yards per capita
Railroad-route mileage	10 miles per 100,000	8 miles per 100,000 (1960)
Goods carried, net ton miles	59 ton miles per capita	116 ton miles per capita (1960)
Surfaced roads	45 miles per 100,000	49 miles per 100,000 (1960)
Number of telephones in use	3 per 10,000	11 per 10,000
Number of radio sets in use	n.a.	57 per 10,000
Number of motor vehicles in use	4 per 10,000	5 per 10,000 (1959)
Number of bicycles sold to the public	7 per 10,000 per annum	24 per 10,000 per annum
Number of persons whose annual income is greater than Rs.50,000	7,078	10,073 (1960)
Number of post office savings accounts	12 per 10,000 (1950)	19 per 10,000
Number of life insurance policies in force	1 per 1,000	18 per 1,000 (1960)
Total amount of life insurance business in force	Rs.3 per capita	Rs.53 per capita (1960)

SOURCES: *Statistical Abstract of India, 1947* (New Delhi: Government of India, 1949).
Statistical Abstract of India, 1950 (New Delhi: Government of India, 1952).
Statistical Abstract of India, 1961 (New Delhi: Government of India, 1962).
India, 1962: A Reference Annual (New Delhi: Ministry of Information and Broadcasting, Government of India, 1962).
Census of India, Paper No. 1 of 1962 Final Population Totals (New Delhi: Government of India, 1962).

n.a. not available

Appendix O. Sources of External Assistance to India

(in the order of the magnitude of their help)

Free World

United States
West Germany
United Kingdom
Canada
Japan
Yugoslavia
Australia
Switzerland
France
Norway
Netherlands

Soviet Bloc

Soviet Union
Czechoslovakia
Poland
Romania

International Institutions

International Development Association
United Nations and its specialized agencies

Appendix 7.

Summary of U.S. Economic and Technical Assistance Programs in India by Type of Program

(In Millions of Dollars)

	1951–56	*1957*	*1958*	*1959*	*1960*	*1961*	*1962*	*1963*	*1964*	*Total*
Development grant	47.5	6.2	6.3	7.4	8.7	8.0	8.6	4.9	7.1	104.7
Malaria control and eradication	21.1	6.5	12.0	10.2	15.6	13.5	11.0	0.1	0.1	90.1
Development financing										
Prior to June 30, 1957	259.1	47.5	—	—	—	—	—	—	—	306.6
DLF Loans	—	—	64.9	100.0	98.7	159.1	320.6	—	—	743.3
AID Loans	—	—	—	—	—	—	156.1	321.3	399.4	876.8
Beas Dam Project	—	—	—	—	—	—	33.0	—	—	33.0
Orissa Iron Ore Project	—	—	18.4	—	—	—	—	—	—	18.4
Export-Import Bank Loans	—	—	151.9	—	13.6	79.5	25.7	40.3	32.2	343.2
Food for Peace										
1951 Wheat Loan	189.7	—	—	—	—	—	—	—	—	189.7
P.L. 480 Sales Agreements, Title I	—	354.5	55.3	259.8	1,667.7	—	39.3	103.1	5.1	2,484.8
P.L. 480 Title II	3.5	1.4	—	—	—	0.3	3.3	—	—	8.5
P.L. 480 Title III	60.4	17.8	17.6	19.4	10.0	18.4	22.8	13.6	8.7	188.7
Miscellaneous relief grants	5.5	—	—	—	—	—	—	—	—	5.5
Triangular trade	—	—	—	4.0	1.8	—	—	—	—	5.8
Total	586.8	433.9	326.4	400.8	1,816.1	278.8	620.4	483.3	452.6	5,399.1

Source: *Fact Sheet on U.S. Economic Assistance to India* (New Delhi: USIS, 1965).

GLOSSARY

Agency for International Development (*AID*). American aid is now administered by the Agency for International Development, which represents the incorporation in November, 1961, of the Technical Cooperation Mission (until then administered by the ICA), the Development Loan Fund, and the Food for Peace Program under one administration. AID makes both developmental grants and loans; the latter are repayable only in dollars, but they carry the low interest of .75 per cent. AID also provides technical assistance and training abroad for project participants, as did TCM. The range of AID projects covers agriculture, industry, health, education, and labor.

Development enterprises in India received a total of $359.3 million (Rs.171.1 crores) in grants and a total of $468.7 million (Rs.223.2 crores) in loans from AID, as of December 17, 1962.

Agricultural Trade Development and Assistance Act of 1954 (*Public Law 480*). This Act was passed in July, 1954, as the 480th Public Law by the 83rd Congress of the United States and is known as P.L. 480. Its main objectives are to promote the economic stability of American agriculture, to expand international trade in agricultural commodities, to encourage the economic development of friendly countries, and to promote the collective strength of the Free World.

The Act has three titles: Under Title I, the President is authorized to sell agricultural commodities for foreign currencies (not necessarily surplus, for the foreign purchasers may buy from the most advantageous source). Title II permits the donation by the President of supplies to foreign countries to meet famine or other urgent relief requirements. Title III permits two very different uses of American agricultural commodities: for bartering in exchange for strategic or other materials, and for donation to nonprofit voluntary agencies that assist needy persons both in and outside the United States.

Thus, although this Act is essentially a device to dispose of agricultural surpluses in the United States by authorizing the government to make supplies available to underdeveloped countries on generous terms, it has made significant contributions to development by combating hunger and controlling inflation in certain low-income countries and by using payments for the products as loans or gifts toward development projects in those countries.

The Cooley Amendment to P.L. 480 sets aside 25 per cent of the sales proceeds under Title I for loans to private industry. Under Title I, eight agreements with India were concluded, as of December 17, 1962, for importing agricultural commodities worth approximately $2,428.3 million (Rs.1,156.3 crores).

Aid India Club. The club is a ten-nation aid consortium sponsored by the World Bank to coordinate free-world assistance to India. The ten nations participating are the United States, Austria, Belgium, Canada, France, West Germany, Italy, Japan, the Netherlands, and the United Kingdom.

For the third year (1963–64) of India's Third Five-Year Plan, the consortium pledged a total of $1,052 million, of which the United States contributed $435 million, or 41 per cent of the total.

American National Red Cross. The American National Red Cross was founded in 1881 and operates under the authority of a Congressional charter. It is affiliated with the League of Red Cross Societies and is supported by voluntary contributions.

In Asia, the Red Cross has contributed experts as consultants on medicine, first aid, etc., and on the organization of Red Cross services. The Red Cross also assists Asian Red Cross societies with equipment for disaster relief.

Through November, 1959, American Red Cross contributions in India came to $800,000 for earthquake relief in August, 1950; famine relief in 1951–52; flood relief in 1953, 1955, and 1956; Salk vaccine in 1958 and 1959; and relief for Tibetan refugees in 1959. The American Red Cross also carries on a youth program that includes the exchange of albums containing letters, reports, and drawings between American and Asian students.

Asian Economic Development Fund. Special funds were set aside by Congress in 1955 for development projects that will help to strengthen economic ties between free Asian countries. India received a loan of $20 million (Rs.9.5 crores) from the Fund in 1958 to be used for acquiring equipment and improving port facilities to make possible the annual export of 2 million tons of iron ore to Japan from the Kiriburu iron ore mines in the Rourkela area of Orissa.

Asia Foundation. The Asia Foundation is a private American philanthropic organization founded in 1951. It supports projects usually administered by Asian organizations in education, scientific research, community development, and cultural activities. Some American institutions interested in arranging joint programs with Asians to increase U.S. understanding of Asian civilization also receive Foundation support.

The Foundation provides Asian universities and libraries with books and journals contributed by American university students, publishers, and civic organizations.

CARE. See Cooperatives for American Relief Everywhere.

Carnegie Endowment for International Peace. The Carnegie Endowment for International Peace was founded in 1910 to encourage research on the nature and purpose of international organizations, education on world affairs in American educational institutions, and the study of war and ways to avoid it. The Indian Council of World Affairs has assisted in a study, sponsored by the Endowment, of national attitudes toward the United Nations.

China Area Aid Act of 1950. Due to the rapid advance of the Communists into China in 1949–50, $89 million for economic aid to China was still unobligated by June, 1950. This Act made these funds available through fiscal year 1951 for the "general area of China" as well as for China proper. Under authority of this Act, India received her first economic assistance from the United States: a grant of $4.5 million to purchase U.S. agricultural commodities to ease a food shortage in August, 1950.

Cooley Amendment. This amendment to P.L. 480 sets aside up to 25 per cent of the local currency proceeds from the sales of American agricultural commodities for loans to the private sector. Companies eligible for Cooley loans include American firms or their subsidiaries operating in the host countries or indigenous firms having an affiliation with an American firm, and indigenous firms of the host countries that have no American affiliation but that are facilitating the disposal of American agricultural products, e.g., local private warehouses storing grain, or flour mills processing the grain. Sixteen private firms in India have received Cooley Loans with a total value of Rs.14.25 crores.

Cooperatives for American Relief Everywhere (CARE). CARE is an organization of twenty-four American private relief agencies. It was founded in 1945. CARE organizes the delivery of gifts from American institutions and individuals (food, clothing, farm tools, medical equipment, books, etc.) to individuals and institutions in other countries, and it also helps the U.S. Government to distribute P.L. 480 agricultural commodities.

In India, CARE has helped in the distribution of agricultural and household implements, playground equipment, and children's books. CARE also participates in emergency relief and rehabilitation measures in Asia and all over the world.

Development Assistance. Until 1957 and the establishment of the Development Loan Fund, funds allocated by the U.S. Government for the purchase of certain capital goods and related services for basic developmental projects in foreign countries were considered under the heading of development assistance. Beginning with fiscal year 1954, allocations for development assistance were separated from those for technical assistance. In fiscal year 1955, the U.S. Congress amended P.L. 665 so that a portion of U.S. development assistance had to be in the form of agricultural commodities. In the same year it was ruled that at least 30 per cent of development assistance must be in loans. (Previously, development assistance in India had been entirely in grants.) Development assistance in India came to a total of $307.8 million as of June 30, 1957.

Development Financing. Development financing makes possible the purchase and importation of certain capital goods and equipment, and related services, for planned basic developmental projects and programs. Such assistance, both loans and grants, has been provided in different forms by several U.S. agencies, including the Development Loan Fund and TCM (now AID).

Development Loan Fund (DLF). The DLF was established in 1957 by an Act of Congress and remained an autonomous U.S. Government corporation until November 3, 1961, when it was incorporated into the Technical Cooperation Mission under the U.S. Agency for International Development. The DLF provides long-term loans to both the public and private sector in friendly countries to finance development projects; loans are repayable in local currency. The DLF made 28 loans, totaling $513.4 million, to Indian private firms and government projects.

Economic Cooperation Administration (ECA). The ECA administered the European Recovery Program from 1948 to 1951 as well as aid authorized under the China Area Aid Act of 1950. It was succeeded by the Mutual Security Agency authorized by the Mutual Security Act of 1951.

European Recovery Program (ERP). This program was initiated in 1948 under the Economic Cooperation Act. Through fiscal year 1951, a total of $10.9 million was allocated for the program, which aimed at increasing investment and production in Europe in order to lower imports, raise exports, and thus balance Western Europe's dollar accounts.

Export-Import Bank. The Export-Import Bank was created in 1934 and operates now under the Export-Import Bank Act of 1945, as amended. The Bank assists in financing export-import trade between the United States and other countries. Loans are made to both the private and public sectors, and the proceeds are used for purchase, in the United States, of capital equipment and related services. Loans are repayable in dollars, and interest rates are determined according to the maturity of the loan, the credit risk, and prevailing U.S. commercial and government rates.

Between November, 1957, and December, 1962, the Bank made 10 loans, totaling $271,927,000, to India, including 3 to the government.

Food for Peace. This is a title used by the U.S. State Department to cover foreign aid involving American surplus agricultural commodities. In India, the Food for Peace Program includes the Wheat Loan of 1951, transactions under Section 402 of P.L. 665, and five P.L. 480 agreements.

Ford Foundation. The Ford Foundation is a private American philanthropic organization founded in 1936 by Henry and Edsel Ford. Since 1951, the Foundation has worked on Indian development projects in cooperation with the government of India, the U.S. Government, and international agencies. The Foundation has been especially interested in rural development, community development, and social-welfare projects. The total of Ford Foundation grants to government, private, and semiofficial bodies in India came to $45,692,627 through July 15, 1961.

The Fulbright Act. On August 1, 1946, President Harry S. Truman signed the Fulbright Act (Public Law 584) amending the Surplus Property Act of 1944 so that some of the credits and currencies of other countries acquired by the United States through the sale of surplus property abroad might be used for educational exchanges.

Senator J. W. Fulbright of Arkansas launched this legislation in answer to two compelling needs: the need for broader international understanding, and the shortage of dollars. Nations wishing to buy the millions of dollars' worth of surplus property that the United States shipped abroad during the war could not obtain enough American dollars to do so. The Fulbright Act authorizes the Secretary of State to negotiate executive agreements so that foreign currencies and credits realized through surplus-property sales may be used for financing studies, research, instruction, and other educational activities of, or for, American citizens in schools and institutions of higher learning located outside the continental United States, including payment for transportation, tuition, maintenance, and other expenses incidental to scholastic pursuits; or for furnishing transportation to the U.S. for citizens of foreign countries who desire to attend schools and institutions of higher learning in the continental United States.

The Act stipulates that no more than $20 million or its equivalent be spent on educational exchanges in any one country. It specifies that sums thus allocated be spent at a rate of not more than the equivalent of $1 million annually.

Fund B. This fund derives from the sales proceeds of Mutual Security dollar aid generated by commercial sales of commodities granted to India. Also accruing to Fund B are reimbursements to the U.S. by the government of India after it has turned over AID-financed equipment to revenue-earning public enterprises such as railways. Repayments of loans by the various Indian states to the central government for AID-financed equipment given to the states are deposited in Fund B, which is a source of revenue to finance development projects in India.

ICA. See International Cooperation Administration.

India Emergency Food Act of 1951 (Wheat Loan). A loan of $189.7 million was granted to the Indian Government to purchase 2 million tons of U.S. agricultural commodities to tide over a food crisis caused by floods and drought in 1950. Funds accruing to the government of India from the sale of these commodities were used for financing central government development schemes and for loans to the state governments. It was also stipulated that the first $5 million paid by India as interest on the loan was to be set aside for the improvement of Indian institutions of higher learning. This gave rise to the India Wheat Loan Educational Program in 1954. When repayment was due to begin (June 30, 1957), India was in the midst of foreign-exchange difficulties, so the U.S. Government postponed the eighteen semiannual installments. They will start to fall due in December, 1986, and will continue through June, 1995. The interest is 2.5 per cent, and the loan is repayable in dollars.

Indo-U.S. Technical Cooperation Agreement. Under this agreement, the government of India initiates projects in support of its Five-Year Plans for economic development and can then request technical aid from the U.S. Government, which must approve the project. U.S. technical aid includes American experts who tour and/or work in India on specific projects, training of Indian participants in the projects, either abroad or in the U.S., and a limited amount of supplies and equipment.

The government of India contributes toward rupee expenditures (i.e., local construction, project sites, domestic transport, part of the salaries of U.S. technicians, salaries of Indian personnel, and salaries and other rupee costs of Indians training abroad). The ultimate aim of the government is to develop India's human resources by helping her technicians and specialists to acquire the skills and know-how necessary for working with modern equipment and for carrying out the program of economic development.

India Wheat Loan. See India Emergency Food Act of 1951.

India Wheat Loan Educational Program. The funds for this program were designated in the India Emergency Act of 1957, which provided that the first $5 million in interest to be paid by the government of India on the U.S. loan of $189.7 million was to be set aside for grants for the improvement of Indian institutions of higher learning. The Educational Exchange Program began in fiscal year 1954 under the administration of the United States Information Service. The money has been allocated as follows: $1,824,275 for scientific equipment to Indian institutions of higher learning; $1,376,513 for books for their libraries; $1,005,614 for an exchange-of-persons program; $75,000 for purchase from the central and state governments of books for the U.S. Congressional Library; and $652,000 for administration.

International Bank for Reconstruction and Development (World Bank). The IBRD was founded in 1945 as an autonomous body affiliated with the United Nations. The fund of $10 billion is provided by the U.N. member countries to be used for loans to member nations to facilitate productive investment, encourage foreign trade, and pay international debts.

As for June 30, 1960, the IBRD had agreed to make 22 loans, totaling $620,610,000, to the Indian Government and Indian private industry. Seven of the loans were for railways development, three for power, and one for a multipurpose project. The other loans went to the iron and steel industry, the ICICI, the power industry, Air-India International, and the Calcutta and Madras port authorities.

International Cooperation Administration (ICA). The U.S. Agency for International Development (AID) was created on November 3, 1961, to bring American economic assistance under a unified administration. The assistance programs were previously administered by the International Cooperation Administration represented in India in turn by the Development Loan Fund (DLF), the Technical Cooperation Mission (TCM), and the Food for Peace Program (P.L. 480).

The ICA makes grants and loans for defense support, technical assistance, and economic development. Its funds are appropriated by Congress each year under the Mutual Security Foreign Aid Program. Repayment of ICA loans and advances are usually in foreign currency with an option to repay in dollars. The ICA also operates an investment-guarantee division, under which it guarantees U.S. private investments overseas against currency inconvertibility, expropriation, and war risk.

International Development Association (IDA). The IDA, founded on September 24, 1960, and administered by the World Bank, makes loans to developing countries on terms that are more flexible and less hard on the balance-of-payments position of the recipient countries than the terms of ordinary loans. The President of the World Bank is *ex officio* President of IDA, which supplements the activities of the Bank. As of February 15, 1962, IDA had agreed to 19 loans totaling $199.3 million to 10 countries.

International Finance Corporation (IFC). The IFC was established in July, 1956, and became affiliated with the United Nations World Bank in 1957 (with $94 million capital), but it remains a separate legal entity with separate funds obtained from the subscribed capital of its member countries. Its purpose is to encourage the growth of private enterprise, when sufficient private capital is not available, by coordinating investment opportunities, private capital (foreign and domestic), and experienced management. The Board of Governors consists of representatives to the World Bank from countries that are members of the IFC.

International Monetary Fund. The Fund was founded in 1947 as an autonomous body affiliated with the United Nations. Its $8 billion is used by member nations to buy foreign currencies in order to pay international debts.

Lend Lease. The Lend-Lease Act was passed in 1941 to enable the U.S. President to sell, transfer, lend, or lease war supplies to nations of vital interest to the U.S. in World War II. Most of the members of the United Nations were declared eligible by the end of the war. When the end of Lend Lease was declared on August 31, 1945, the total value of aid given came to more than $50.5 billion.

Marshall Plan. A program for recovery from the effects of World War II, primarily in Europe. It was not aimed at economic development but at economic redevelopment—an entirely different process.

Mutual Defense Assistance Act, 1949 and 1950. The Act was approved in October, 1949, and was meant to authorize extension of new military assistance to friendly countries and to coordinate military aid programs already under way. When the Korean War broke out in 1951, MDA appropriations were supplemented by an allocation of $4 billion, an increase of 400 per cent over the original program, for fiscal year 1951.

Mutual Security Act, 1951. The MSA brought under one administration economic and military aid that had previously been authorized separately under the Foreign Economic Assistance Act of 1950 (which included the ERP and China Area Aid, both administered by ECA, TCM, and the Mutual Defense Assistance Act of 1949 and 1950, administered by the Defense Department).

Mutual Security Aid. This provides defense funds, a part of which contribute to economic development, the Development Loan Fund, and funds for technical cooperation and other programs. Since mid-1961, programs formerly directed by the International Cooperation Administration, and including the Development Loan Fund, were placed under the direction of a new coordinating body, the Agency for International Development. Mutual Security Aid served as the legislative model for U.S. foreign aid, as amended every year, until 1955; its intention was to strengthen the military aspect of aid.

Mutual Security Act, 1954, as Amended, P.L. 665, Section 402. In 1955, P.L. 665 was amended to provide that a large portion of development assistance be supplied by American surplus agricultural commodities. The sales proceeds are set aside for development projects agreed upon by the government concerned and the U.S. Government. As of January, 1962, India received under Section 402 agricultural commodities valued at $67.8 million (Rs.32.3 crores).

Point Four. The fourth point in President Truman's inaugural address in January, 1949, stated that economic aid to developing countries was an integral part of America's program for peace. The point was eventually embodied in the Act for International Development of the Foreign Economic Assistance Act, in June, 1950. The Point Four Program emphasized technical rather than capital assistance, and in India it was under the direction of the TCM.

P.L. 480. See the Agricultural Trade Development and Assistance Act.

P.L. 665. See Mutual Security Act of 1951.

Rockefeller Foundation. The Rockefeller Foundation, a private American philanthropic organization, was founded in 1913. It has been active in India since 1920. At first, the emphasis of the Foundation's projects was on public-health services, field studies, and personnel training, but gradually it has shifted to medical research and education, while continuing to emphasize training of personnel. Rockefeller grants to the government and private institutions and individuals of India totaled $12,572,963 (Rs.5.987 crores) through June, 1961.

Smith-Mundt Act. In January, 1948, the President signed the Smith-Mundt Act (Public Law 402), which includes in its provisions an extension of the Department of State's authority to carry on various kinds of educational, scientific, and cultural exchanges with countries the world over that may be prepared to reciprocate. The extent of this program will depend on the funds that Congress allocates annually for such purposes. In India, the Smith-Mundt funds cover the travel costs of scholars proceeding to the United States for educational purposes.

Technical Cooperation Mission (TCM). The TCM in India carried out development projects in cooperation with the Government of India as agreed upon under the terms of the Indo-U.S. Technical Cooperation Agreement, 1952. In November, 1961, the TCM was incorporated with the Development Loan Fund into the Agency for International Development, which now administers TCM projects in India. TCM aid included American experts, training abroad for project participants, and some commodity contributions. (See Indo-U.S. Technical Cooperation Agreement, January 5, 1952.)

"Triangular Trade" (*Third-Country Trade*). Under Section (d) of P.L. 480, local-currency sales proceeds may be used to purchase equipment and services for other friendly countries. For example, the U.S. Government has purchased fertilizer for India with Japanese yen generated by the sale of U.S. agricultural commodities to Japan. The fertilizer sales proceeds are in turn set aside for U.S. Government operations in India.

Truman Doctrine. The Truman Doctrine was enunciated on March 12, 1947. It declared that a program of military and economic aid was necessary to counter Soviet expansion. The immediate result was the approval by Congress of a $400 million program for economic and military aid to Greece and Turkey.

Watumull Foundation. The Watumull Foundation, a private American philanthropic organization, was founded in 1942 by Gobindram J. Watumull. Its major objectives are to promote Indo-American good will and understanding, and to promote India's over-all development. It gives scholarships to Indian scholars for higher studies in the United States, enables American professors to visit Indian universities, and distributes worthwhile books to libraries in both countries.

BIBLIOGRAPHY

Aid in Action: How U.S. Aid Lends a Helping Hand Around the World. Washington, D.C.: Department of State, 1961.

ALPERT, PAUL. *Economic Development: Objectives and Methods.* New York: The Free Press of Glencoe, 1963.

American Cooperation With Higher Education Abroad. Washington, D.C.: Department of Health, Education and Welfare, 1957.

American Educational Exchange Programs in India. New Delhi: USIS, 1961.

American Embassy Newsletter (New Delhi), February 14, 1962.

APPLEBY, PAUL H. *Re-examination of India's Administrative System.* New Delhi: Government of India, 1956.

ASHER, ROBERT E. *Grants, Loans, and Local Currencies: Their Role in Foreign Aid.* Washington, D.C.: The Brookings Institution, 1961.

BALASSA, BELA. *Trade Prospects for Developing Countries.* Homewood, Ill.: Richard Irwin, 1964.

BAUER, P. T. *Economic Analysis and Policy in Underdeveloped Countries.* Durham, N.C.: Duke University Press, 1957.

———. *Indian Economic Policy and Development.* London: Allen & Unwin, 1961.

BENHAM, FREDERICK. *Economic Aid to Underdeveloped Countries.* London and New York: Oxford University Press, 1961.

BLACK, EUGENE R. *The Diplomacy of Economic Development.* Cambridge, Mass.: Harvard University Press, 1961.

BLAIR, WALTER S. "Indo-U.S. Cooperation in the Cause of Higher Education." New Delhi: USIS, 1960. Mimeographed.

BOWLES, CHESTER. *Ambassador's Report.* New York: Harper & Bros., 1954.

———. *The New Dimensions of Peace.* New York: Harper & Bros., 1955.

———. *Why Foreign Aid?* New Delhi: USIS, 1963.

BROWN, WILLIAM ADAMS, JR., and OPIE, REDVERS. *American Foreign Assistance.* Washington, D.C.: The Brookings Institution, 1953.

BUCHANAN, NORMAN S., and ELLIS, HOWARD S. *Approaches to Economic Development.* New York: The Twentieth Century Fund, 1955.

BUNKER, ELLSWORTH. "India and the U.S.A.," *United Asia* (Bombay), September, 1957.

BURKE, JAMES W. *TCM Participant Training Program*. New Delhi: American Embassy, 1961.

CAINCROSS, A. K. *Factors in Economic Development*. New York: Frederick A. Praeger; London: Allen & Unwin, 1962.

CHANDRASEKHAR, S. *Hungry People and Empty Lands*. 3d. ed. London: Allen & Unwin, 1953.

———. *Population and Planned Parenthood in India*. 2d ed. London: Allen & Unwin, 1961.

———. "Population Growth and Food Supply in India," *Population Review* (Madras), January, 1959.

———. *Infant Mortality in India*. London: Allen & Unwin, 1959.

———. "Population Growth and Economic Development," *Population Review* (Madras), January 1961.

———. "Population Growth and Economic Development in India—1951–61," *Population Review*, July, 1961.

———. "Population Growth, Socio-economic Development and Living Standards," *International Labour Review*, June, 1954.

———. "Impact of U.S. Aid on the Indian Economy: An Evaluation of Results," *Capital* (Calcutta), Seventy-fifth Anniversary issue, December, 1963.

———. "Agricultural University in Uttar Pradesh," *The Hindu Weekly Magazine* (Madras), December 22, 1963.

———. "American Aid to Indian Agriculture," *Commerce* (Bombay), Part 1, February 8, 1964; Part 2, February 15, 1964; Part 3, February 29, 1964.

———. "India's Public Health Problems: U.S. Aid Acts as an Eye-opener," *The Mail* (Madras), March 20, 1964.

CHENERY, HOLLIS B. "Objectives and Criteria of Foreign Assistance," in ROBERT A. GOLDWIN (ed.), *Why Foreign Aid?* Chicago: Rand McNally, 1963.

CLEVELAND, H. *The Theory and Practice of Foreign Aid*. Syracuse, N.Y.: Syracuse University Press, 1956.

COLLADO, E. "Economic Development Through Private Enterprise," *Foreign Affairs*, July, 1963.

Composite Report of the President's Committee to Study the United States Military Assistance Program. Washington, D.C., 1959. Vol. I.

CONNELLY, R. G. "America's Contribution to Dairy Development in India." New Delhi: U.S. Technical Cooperation Mission, 1961. Mimeographed.

COWAN, C. D. (ed.). *The Economic Development of Southeast Asia*. New York: Frederick A. Praeger, 1964.

DAWES, NORMAN. *A Two-way Street: The Indo-American Fulbright Program 1950–1960*. Bombay: Asia Publishing House, 1962.

Development of the Emerging Countries: An Agenda for Research. Washington, D.C.: The Brookings Institution, 1962.

The Development Loan Fund. New Delhi: USIS, 1960.

Economic Development Assistance. New York: Committee for Economic Development, 1957.

The Economy of the American People: Progress, Problems and Prospects. Washington, D.C.: National Planning Association, 1958.

Eisenhower in India. New Delhi: USIS, 1959.

Enke, Stephen. *Economics for Development.* Englewood Cliffs, N.J.: Prentice-Hall, 1963.

Export-Import Bank of Washington Report to the Congress. June 30, 1959.

FEIS, H. *Foreign Aid and Foreign Policy.* New York: St. Martin's Press, 1964.

Food for Peace. United States Pavilion, Madras Agricultural Fair. January, 1962.

Food for Peace. New Delhi: USIS, February, 1962.

The Ford Foundation and Foundation Supported Activities in India. New Delhi: Office of the Ford Foundation Representative in India, 1955.

The Ford Foundation Annual Report. New York: The Ford Foundation, 1959 and subsequent years.

FRANKEL, HERBERT S. *The Economic Impact on Underdeveloped Societies.* Cambridge, Mass.: Harvard University Press, 1955.

FRIEDMAN, MILTON. "Foreign Economic Aid: Means and Objectives," *The Yale Review,* Summer, 1958.

———. "Economic Aid Reconsidered: A Reply," *The Yale Review,* Summer, 1961.

GALBRAITH, JOHN KENNETH. *American Capitalism.* New York: Houghton Mifflin, 1952.

———. "Rival Economic Theories In India," *Foreign Affairs,* July, 1958.

———. *The Affluent Society.* Boston: Houghton, Mifflin, 1958.

———. "A Positive Approach to Economic Aid," *Foreign Affairs,* April, 1961.

———. *Economic Development in Perspective.* New Delhi: USIS, 1963.

———. *Economic Development.* Cambridge, Mass.: Harvard University Press, 1964.

HAGEN, EVERETT, E. *On The Theory of Social Change: How Economic Growth Begins.* Homewood, Ill.: Dorsey Press, 1962.

HAMBRIDGE, GOVE (ed.). *Dynamics of Development.* New York: Frederick A. Praeger, 1964.

HANSEN, ALVIN. *Economic Issues of the 1960s.* New York: McGraw-Hill, 1960.

Harbison, Frederick. *The Strategy of Human Resource Development in Modernizing Economics.* Princeton, N.J.: Princeton University Press, 1962.

———, and Meyers, C. A. *Education, Manpower and Economic Growth: Strategies of Human Resource Development.* New York: McGraw-Hill, 1964.

Hearn, Jackson B. *India: A Growing Market for U.S. Products and Investment.* Washington, D.C.: Department of Commerce, 1963.

Herman, Celia L. *Investment in India: Basic Information for United States Businessmen.* Washington, D.C.: Department of Commerce, 1961.

Higgins, Benjamin. *Economic Development: Principles, Problems and Policies.* New York: W. W. Norton, 1959.

Highlights of President Kennedy's New Act for International Development. Washington, D.C.: Department of State, 1961.

Hirschman, A. O. *The Strategy of Economic Development.* New Haven, Conn.: Yale University Press, 1958.

Hoffman, Paul G. "The Challenge of Economic Development," *The Hyphen* (Bombay), March-April, 1960.

———. *One Hundred Countries and One Quarter Billion People.* Washington, D.C.: Albert D. and Mary Lasker Foundation, 1960.

———. "Bread upon the Waters: The Problems and Promises of Development," *1962 Britannica Book of the Year.* New York, 1962.

Hoselitz, B. F. "Non-Economic Factors in Economic Development," *American Economic Review,* May, 1957.

———. *Sociological Aspects of Economic Growth.* Glencoe, Ill.: The Free Press, 1960.

Hultman, Charles W. "Agricultural Disposal as Foreign Aid: An Appraisal," *Journal of Inter-American Studies,* October, 1961.

Hunck, J. M. *India's Silent Revolution: A Survey of Indo-German Cooperation.* Düsseldorf: Verlag Handelsblatt, 1958.

India Wheat Loan Educational Exchange Program. New Delhi: USIS, 1955.

India's Food Crisis and Steps to Meet It: A Report of the Ford Foundation's Visiting Agricultural Production Team. New Delhi: Ministry of Food and Agriculture, 1959.

India's New Horizons. New Delhi: USIS, 1959.

Indo-American Technical Cooperation 1952–1956. New Delhi: USIS, 1957.

Indo-U.S. Technical Cooperation Programme. New Delhi: Ministry of Finance, 1959.

Indo-U.S. Technical Cooperation Programme. Report 1960. New Delhi: Ministry of Finance, 1961.

Indo-U.S. Technical Cooperation Programme. Report 1961. New Delhi: Department of Economic Affairs, 1961.

Investing in India. New Delhi: Indian Investment Centre, 1961.

Jordan, Amos A., Jr. *Foreign Aid and the Defense of Southeast Asia.* New York: Frederick A. Praeger, 1962.

Knauth, Oliver D. *U.S. Foreign Policy in a Changing World.* Washington, D.C.: National Planning Association, 1960.

Krause, Walter. *Economic Development—The Underdeveloped World and the American Interest.* San Francisco: Wadsworth Publishing Company, 1961.

———. *International Economy.* New York: Houghton, Mifflin, 1955.

Kurihara, Kenneth K. *The Keynesian Theory of Economic Development.* New York: Columbia University Press; London: Allen & Unwin, 1959.

Lee, Douglas H. K. *Climate and Economic Development in the Tropics.* New York: Harper & Brothers, 1957.

Leibenstein, Harvey. *Economic Backwardness and Economic Growth.* New York: John Wiley, 1963.

Lewis, John P. *Quiet Crisis in India.* Washington, D.C.: The Brookings Institution, 1962.

Lewis, W. A. "The Capital Needs of Underdeveloped Countries," in *Financing of Economic Development of Underdeveloped Countries.* London: United Nations Association, 1955.

Lippmann, Walter. "American Foreign Aid Policy," *The Hindu* (Madras), June 6, 1961.

Lockwood, W. W. "The Socialistic Society: India and Japan," *Foreign Affairs,* October, 1958.

McGovern, George. "The United States Food for Peace Program." New Delhi: USIS, 1962. Mimeographed.

Malenbaum, Wilfred. *East and West in India's Economic Development.* Washington, D.C.: National Planning Association, 1959.

———. *Prospects for Indian Development.* New York: Macmillan, 1962.

Manual of the Malaria Eradication Operation. New Delhi: Malaria Institute of India, 1958.

Measures for the Economic Development of Underdeveloped Countries. New York: United Nations, 1951.

Meier, G. M. *International Trade and Development.* New York: Harper & Row, 1963.

———. *Leading Issues in Development Economics.* London and New York: Oxford University Press, 1964.

Meyer, Karl E. "Foreign Aid: U.S. Government's Headache," *The Hindu* (Madras).

Millikan, M. F., and Blackmer, D. L. M. (eds.), *The Emerging Nations: Their Growth and the U.S. Policy.* Boston: Little, Brown, 1961.

Millikan, M. F., and Rostow, W. W. *A Proposal.* New York: Harper & Bros., 1957.

Morehouse, Ward (ed.). *American Institutions and Organizations Interested in India.* New York: Taplinger Publishing Co., 1961.

Mutual Security Program, 1961 A Summary Presentation, 1960. Washington, D.C.: U.S. Government Printing Office, 1960.

MYRDAL, GUNNAR. *An International Economy: Problems and Prospects.* New York: Harper & Bros.; London: Routledge and Kegan Paul, 1956.

———. *Economic Theory and Underdeveloped Regions.* London: Routledge and Kegan Paul, 1957.

———. "Indian Economic Planning," *Population Review,* January, 1959.

NEHMER, STANLEY. *U.S. Foreign Aid in 1959: Programs and Administration.* Washington, D.C.: International Bank for Reconstruction and Development, 1960.

The New India. Prepared by the Planning Commission of the Republic of India. New York: Macmillan, 1958.

PEACE CORPS. *1st Annual Report to Congress for the Fiscal Year Ended June 30, 1962.* Washington, D.C.: Government Printing Office, 1962.

Peace Corps Fact Book. Washington, D.C.: Government Printing Office, 1961.

Peace Corps Handbook. Washington, D.C.: Government Printing Office, 1962.

PHELPS, EDMUND S. *The Goal of Economic Growth: Sources, Costs, Benefits.* New York: W. W. Norton, 1963.

THE PRESIDENT'S MATERIALS POLICY COMMISSION [Paley Commission]. *Foundation for Growth and Security: Reasons for Freedom.* Washington, D.C.: Government Printing Office, 1957.

THE PRESIDENT'S COMMITTEE TO STUDY THE MILITARY ASSISTANCE PROGRAM [Draper Committee]. *Composite Report* (Vol. I) and *Supplement to the Committee Report* (Vol. II). Washington, D.C.: Government Printing Office, 1959.

RANIS, GUSTAV (ed.). *The United States and the Developing Economies.* New York: W. W. Norton, 1964.

The Rockefeller Foundation Annual Report. New York: The Rockefeller Foundation, 1959 and subsequent years.

RODAN, ROSENSTEIN P. N. "International Aid for Underdeveloped Countries," *Review of Economics and Statistics,* May, 1961.

ROSEN, GEORGE. *Industrial Change in India.* Glencoe, Ill.: The Free Press, 1958.

ROSINGER, L. *India and the United States: Political and Economic Relations.* New York: Macmillan, 1950.

ROSTOW, W. W. *The Stages of Economic Growth.* New York and Cambridge: Cambridge University Press, 1961.

SHANNON, L. W. (ed.). *Underdeveloped Areas.* New York: Harper & Bros., 1957.

SHENOY, B. R. "The Right Road to Indian Progress," *Fortune*, April, 1960.

SINGER, HANS W. *International Development: Growth and Change*. New York: McGraw-Hill, 1964.

SPENGLER, J. J. "Economic Development: Political Preconditions and Political Consequences," *The Journal of Politics*, August, 1960.

STALEY, EUGENE. *The Future of Underdeveloped Countries*. New York: Harper & Bros., 1954.

SUPPLE, BARRY (ed.). *The Experience of Economic Growth*. New York: Random House, 1963.

Supplement to the Composite Report of the President's Committee to Study the United States Military Assistance Program. Washington, D.C.: Government Printing Office, 1959. Vol. II.

"The United States Contribution to Indian Development." New Delhi: TCM Program, 1961. Mimeographed.

"United States Economic Programs in India." (Status as of June, 1959.) New Delhi: U.S. Technical Cooperation Mission, 1959. Mimeographed.

United States Government Assistance to India. New Delhi: USIS, March, 1962.

Uses of Agricultural Surpluses to Finance Economic Development in Underdeveloped Areas—A Pilot Study in India. Rome: Food and Agriculture Organisation, 1955.

VILLARD, HENRY H. *Economic Development*. New York: Holt, Rinehart & Winston, 1964.

WARD, BARBARA. *India and the West*. New York: W. W. Norton, 1961.

———. *Five Ideas that Change the World*. New York: W. W. Norton, 1959.

WIGGINS, JAMES W., and SCHOECK, HELMUT. *Foreign Aid Re-examined*. Washington, D.C.: Public Affairs Press, 1958.

WIGGINS, J. R. "Re-examination of U.S. Aid Programmes," *The Mail* (Madras), March 10, 1961.

WINGENBACH, CHARLES E. *The Peace Corps—Who, How and Where*. New York: John Doy, 1961.

WOLF, CHARLES, JR. "Economic Aid Reconsidered," *The Yale Review*, Summer, 1958.

WOOD, C. TYLER. "U.S. Assistance to the Development of India's Power Resources." New Delhi: United States Embassy, 1961. Mimeographed.

———. *American Aid to Indian Industry*. New Delhi: United States Embassy, 1960.

———. "Indo-American Economic Cooperation Leads to Prosperity." New Delhi: United States Embassy, 1960. Mimeographed.

———. "The Role and Character of Foreign Aid: Problems of Foreign

Aid Viewed from the Inside," *The American Economic Review*, May, 1959.

———. *Foreign Aid: Theory and Practice in Southern Asia*. Princeton, N.J.: Princeton University Press, 1960.

ZINKIN, MAURICE. *Development for Free Asia*. Rev. ed. London and New York: Oxford University Press, 1963.

INDEX